THEY RULE

THEY RULE

The 1% vs. Democracy

PAUL STREET

Paradigm Publishers
Boulder • London

Published in the United States by Paradigm Publishers, 5589 Arapahoe Avenue, Boulder, CO 80303 USA.

Paradigm Publishers is the trade name of Birkenkamp & Company, LLC, Dean Birkenkamp, President and Publisher.

Library of Congress Cataloging-in-Publication Data

Street, Paul Louis.
  They rule : the 1% vs. democracy / Paul Street.
    pages cm
  Includes bibliographical references and index.
  ISBN 978-1-61205-327-1 (pbk. : alk. paper)
  ISBN 978-1-61205-608-1 (consumer ebook)
  1. Elite (Social sciences)—United States—History. 2. Democracy—United States—History. 3. Protest movements—United States—History. 4. Wealth—United States—History. I. Title.
  HN90.E4S77 2014
  305.5'20973—dc23
                                                            2013043046

Printed and bound in the United States of America on acid-free paper that meets the standards of the American National Standard for Permanence of Paper for Printed Library Materials.

18 17 16 15 14   1 2 3 4 5

We must make our choice. We may have democracy in this country, or we may have wealth concentrated in the hands of a few, but we cannot have both.
—*Louis Brandeis, US Supreme Court Justice, 1941*[1]

Today, for the one-tenth of 1 percent of the population who benefited most from these decades of greed and deceit, everything is fine, while for most of the population, real income has stagnated or declined for thirty years. . . . So we have the plutonomy and the precariat: the 1 percent and the 99 percent, in the imagery of the Occupy Movement—not literal numbers, but the right picture.
—*Noam Chomsky, talk at the Occupy Boston encampment, October 22, 2011*

The rich are destroying the earth. . . . We cannot understand the concomitance of the ecological and social crises if we don't analyze them as two sides of the same disaster.
—*Herve Kempf,* Le Monde *environmental editor, 2007*[2]

Contents

Acknowledgments

This book was inspired by the many thousands of Americans who participated in the Occupy Movement in the late summer, fall, and early winter of 2011. Those citizens and activists rekindled my faith in the possibilities for democratic transformation beneath and beyond the rule of the wealthy few—"the 1%." I am indebted to numerous left scholars and writers cited and quoted in this volume (none more than Noam Chomsky), on whose shoulders I feel privileged to stand while trying to understand who rules America, how they rule, with what consequences, and what we can and must do about that rule. I am grateful to Michael Albert and Eric Sargent of *ZNet*, Lydia Sargent of *Z Magazine*, Glen Ford of *Black Agenda Report*, Jeffrey St. Clair of *Counterpunch*, Robert Hughes of the Open University of the Left, Henry Giroux and his associates at *Truthout*, professors Joseph Wegwert and Wayne Ross of the Rouge Forum, and Vincent Kelley of Grinnell College for providing me welcome outlets for the development of my written and spoken reflections on these and related matters. Special thanks are due also to Jennifer Knerr and Dean Birkenkamp at Paradigm Publishers for opening their press to another provocative (I hope) project, and to Terry Thomas, historian and wordsmith, for his thoughtful edit of an earlier draft of this book. My greatest debt is as always to my remarkable partner Janet Razbadouski, whose love, encouragement, example, and advice make my own writing efforts—and much more—possible.

John Carpenter's Magic Sunglasses and the Real Choice

Who could have imagined Occupy Wall Street (OWS), its urgent and fierce opposition to the US financial, corporate, and economic elite, and its rapid spread across US cities large, medium, and small in the late summer and early fall of 2011? Several prominent left commentators seemed prescient in their pre-Occupy writings and ruminations, including no less than Noam Chomsky as well as Charles Derber, Yale Magrass,[1] Sheldon Wolin, and several others we will mention as we explore this territory. Perhaps no one, however, presaged the themes of OWS as early or as vividly as the filmmaker John Carpenter.

They Live

John Carpenter (*Halloween*, *The Thing*, *Escape from New York*, etc.) deserves special credit for partly envisioning the Occupy Movement as early as 1987. All the way back then, he penned and directed what the prolific left social critic and historian Mike Davis calls Carpenter's "subversive tour de force"—*They Live*, a "depicti[on of] the Age of Reagan as a catastrophic alien invasion." In Carpenter's brilliant, outwardly campy spoof, America is ruled by aliens disguised as members of the business and professional elite. The extraterrestrials colonize America and the Earth, dismantling the nation in the name of "the free market." They speak in hushed tones to one another through small radios installed in Rolex watches that symbolize their elevated status while providing a safe conduit for intra-alien communication. In a vast underground complex whose existence is kept secret from the hated human herd, they communicate in outwardly idealistic terms of their real objectives—ruthless economic exploitation for the galactic Few sold as "growth" and "development" for the earthly Many—to a large audience of fellow aliens and a minority of well-off and co-opted human collaborators. Hyper-mobile across the galaxy in their shiny business suits, they send resources off-planet and manipulate

1

the citizenry through subtle, subliminal forms of thought control encoded in advertisements and other corporate mass media content.

"They're free enterprisers," a leading human resister of the alien presence explains: "The Earth is just another developing planet—*their Third World.*"

"We are like a natural resource to them," a different resister elaborates. "Deplete the planet and move on to another. They want benign indifference. They want us drugged."

Some humans are cultivated for co-optation, rewarded for their collaboration with fancy jobs, money, and consumer goods. They are invited to sumptuous banquets where aliens dressed as business chiefs regale them with the latest data on the robust "per capita income growth" enjoyed by earthlings who cooperate with the extraterrestrials' "quest for multi-dimensional expansion.... The gains have been substantial," one such alien explains, "both for us and for *you, the human power elite.*"

Resistance is futile and there is no alternative, so you might as well play ball with the invaders and enjoy the rewards. So the collaborationist story goes, encouraged by bribery and media messages selling personal consumption, keeping up with fashion, and narcissistic self-display as the meaning of "the good life." As one turncoat explains to *They Live*'s resister heroes near the movie's end,

> It's business, that's all it is. There ain't no countries anymore. They're running the whole show. They own everything, the whole goddamned planet. They can do whatever they want. What's wrong with having it good for a change? And they're gonna let us have it good if we just help them. They're gonna leave us alone. Let us make some money. You could have a taste of that good life too.... We all sell out every day. Might as well be on the winning team.

Those who cannot be co-opted or numbed by dominant media and consumer gratifications and who dare to question and challenge alien and state-capitalist authority are designated as "terrorists" and "communists who want to bring down the government." They are subjected to violent repression by a heavily armed high-tech police state, whose tools of surveillance and repression include airborne spy cameras that prefigure low-flying military police and border patrol drones currently being prepared for use inside the United States.

To make matters worse for the mostly working-class American human subjects, they struggle with strong internal divisions of race and ethnicity that are richly cultivated and enjoyed by the wealthy few in their Machiavellian quest to divide and conquer. "Maybe they love it," *They Live*'s leading black protagonist muses, "seeing us hate each other, watching us kill each other off, feeding off our cold fucking hearts."

Along the way, the aliens' economic system generates unprecedented levels of carbon dioxide and methane, heating the environment in ways that fit their own home climate but threaten life on Earth.

The aliens are opposed by a revolutionary human cadre that has developed special sunglasses and contact lenses that decode the deadening messages of the alien-run corporate mass media and reveal the repulsive nonhuman identity of many of the privileged. When the glasses are donned, billboards, magazines, newspapers, and television programs are shown to express their real intended meaning, telling humans to "OBEY," "CONSUME," "WATCH TV," "SLEEP," "CONFORM," "SUBMIT," "BUY," "HONOR APATHY," "MARRY AND REPRO-DUCE," and "WORK EIGHT HOURS." Bills of money are shown to say "THIS IS YOUR GOD" while billboards are seen to proclaim "NO THOUGHT," "DO NOT QUESTION AUTHORITY," and "NO IMAGINATION."

The cadre oversees a makeshift campsite of mostly poor and unemployed working-class Americans. Sitting behind a threadbare church in the shadow of Los Angeles's downtown financial district, the multiracial and multiethnic camp captures the rising poverty and joblessness of the reckless get-rich-quick Reagan years and harkens back to previous episodes of mass homelessness in American history.

The campsite is brutally cleared by a militarized Los Angeles Police Department early in *They Live*, a key moment in protagonist Nada's (played by professional wrestler Roddy Piper) political evolution. Reviewing this scene as I prepared this manuscript for publication, I was struck by how closely it presaged the police-state clearances of Occupy Movement encampments in the fall of 2011.

The cadre struggles to escape detection and repression as it seeks to break into the all-powerful media to tell ordinary Americans what they have discovered about who is really running and ruining the country. The movie ends when Nada and his black construction worker comrade Frank Armitage (played by Keith David) succeed in penetrating the aliens' corporate media headquarters to disable the aliens' great satellite cloaking mechanism, thereby exposing the alien identity of the privileged on television and in daily life. The uncovering portends the coming of a great popular rebellion.

Beneath the science-fiction and horror-film surface, of course, Carpenter was portraying the subordination of late twentieth-century America to its own unelected dictatorship of corporate and financial wealth—what would become known twenty-three years later as "the 1%." "Who," Davis wrote in the wake of Occupy's emergence,

> can ever forget the brilliant early scenes [in *They Live*] of the huge third world shantytown reflected across the Hollywood Freeway by the sinister mirror glass of Bunker Hill's corporate skyscrapers? Or Carpenter's portrayal of the billionaire bankers and evil mediacrats ruling over a pulverized

American working class living in tents on a rubble-strewn hillside and begging for casual jobs?... From this negative equality of homelessness and despair, and thanks to the magic sunglasses, the proletariat finally achieves interracial unity, sees through the subliminal deceptions of capitalism, and gets angry. Very angry.[2]

The Occupy Movement was dismantled before it achieved anything like interracial proletarian unity, the disablement of modern mass media and advertising, or a popular rebellion that removed corporate exploiters from their privileged perches. Still, with some real if short-lived help from the mass media itself,[3] Occupy Wall Street and the hundreds of copycat populist encampments it inspired across the country donned and passed out something of a version of Carpenter's magic sunglasses in a way that not only held the news cycle for a few weeks in 2011 but altered the political discourse and consciousness of the nation ever since. It brought the language of class and the inseparably linked problems of economic inequality and plutocracy (the latter term refers to government by and for the wealthy) to the front and center of the national political culture like no time since the 1930s.[4] And that is no small part of why it was taken apart by coordinated state repression within and beyond New York City, where a brutal police-state eviction was ordered by Michael Bloomberg, a leading financial titan and media mogul who also happened to be the mayor of the world's leading capitalist city—something John Carpenter would certainly have appreciated.

This volume is not, however, primarily about the Occupy Movement, possibly better described as "the Occupy Moment." The primary focus here is on key questions posed by Occupy, questions that have also been raised by previous generations of labor, farmer, socialist, anarchist, and populist protestors and critics, including Carpenter (whose *They Live* heroes are heirs to the antiplutocratic rebels and revolutionaries portrayed in such past American novels as Upton Sinclair's *The Jungle*, Jack Conroy's *The Disinherited*, John Steinbeck's *In Dubious Battle*, Ray Bradbury's *Fahrenheit 451*, Jack London's *The Iron Heel*, Kurt Vonnegut's *Player Piano*, and John Brunner's *The Sheep Look Up*): Who owns and rules America beneath and beyond the claims and indeed the pretence of democratic popular governance? Why and how does it matter that the nation's economy, society, culture, and politics are torn and shaped and deformed by stark class disparities and a steep concentration of wealth and power in the hands of a privileged few, a "ruling class"? What is the price—or more precisely what are the prices—of that savage inequality? How did and do the privileged few gain their remarkable wealth and power, and how do they keep it? How does the ruling class rule, over and against the desire of most Americans for a more roughly equal and genuinely democratic, not plutocratic and savagely unequal, society? What can "we the people" do to resist and end that rule in defense of democracy, the common good, a livable natural environment, and a decent future?

In tackling these and related questions, I have been struck at the significant extent to which the answers resonate with key themes in Carpenter's film. To be sure, the real Earth-specific story of US ruling-class power is far more complicated and detailed than what can be conveyed in a short and often deliberately comic, cartoon-like sci-fi horror film like *They Live*. Disentangling that story has involved consulting a vast nonfiction literature and the reflections of numerous scholars and critics, including leading "power elite" analysts like George William Domhoff and Thomas R. Dye—none more deeply and recurrently insightful than Noam Chomsky (who will be quoted and cited more than a few times in the present volume). Still, having returned from that nonfiction journey and conducted my own empirical and primary source research, I am struck by the haunting relevance of *They Live*'s nightmarish vision—a nation ruled by amoral, sociopathic, hyper-mobile, highly organized, and *socially (if not literally) alien* capitalists who operate within and beyond national boundaries as they cultivate human divisions and exploit mass media and culture along with the high-tech repressive apparatus of the state to propagate mass consumerism, individualism, narcissism, and an ideology of endless growth and to demobilize, depress, delude, diminish, demoralize, degrade, and drug the citizenry and the democratic ideal. Along the way, "they" advance a savagely soulless and unequal political-economic order that warms the planet to a dangerous degree while dismantling the nation in service to endless selfish wealth accumulation—the common good be damned.

"Neither Is It a Democracy in Any Recognizable Form"

As the Occupy Movement was being dismantled by armed state forces for having committed the sin of rendering visible the nation's real rulers and some of the hidden injuries of America's class hierarchy, I was contacted by a television reporter from Iran. "How," the reporter wanted to know, "can America credibly claim to advance democracy in the Middle East and across the world when it crushes freedom of expression and protest in its own city streets?" "Why," another reporter at the same network asked me, "do American people tolerate the control of their government and politics by a small and wealthy elite, what Occupy Wall Street calls 'the 1 percent'?"

This book is my belated answer to tackle these difficult and unpleasant questions. The contemporary United States, I find in the volume, is neither a dictatorship nor a democracy. It is something in between or perhaps different altogether: a corporate-managed state-capitalist pseudo-democracy that sells the narrow interests of the wealthy business and financial elite as the public interest, closes off critical and independent thought, and subjects culture, politics, policy, institutions, the environment, daily life, and individual minds to the often hidden and unseen authoritarian dictates of money and profit. It is a corporate and financial plutocracy whose managers generally prefer to rule through outwardly democratic and noncoercive means since leading American corporations and their servants have worked effectively at draining and disabling democracy's radical and progressive potential by propagandizing, dulling, pacifying, deadening, overextending, overstressing, atomizing, and demobilizing the citizenry. At the same time, American state and capitalist elites remain ready, willing, and able to maintain their power with the help from ever more sinister and sophisticated methods and tools of repression, brutality, and coercive control.

The contemporary United States may not be a fascist state. But this hardly means it deserves to be considered anything like a genuine democracy. As the brilliant Australian filmmaker, author, and commentator John Pilger (long a close and knowledgeable follower of US politics) noted in January 2012, as the presidential election spectacle took center stage in American mass media,

> America is now a land of epidemic poverty and barbaric prisons: the consequence of a "market" extremism which, under Obama, has prompted the transfer of $14 trillion in public money to criminal enterprises in Wall Street. The victims are mostly young jobless, homeless, incarcerated African-Americans, betrayed by the first black president. The historic corollary of a perpetual war state, *this is not fascism, not yet, but neither is it democracy in any recognisable form*, regardless of the placebo politics that will consume the news until November. The presidential campaign, says the *Washington Post*, will "feature a clash of philosophies rooted in distinctly different views of the economy." This is patently false. The circumscribed task of journalism on both sides of the Atlantic is to create the pretense of political choice where there is none.[5]

As veteran political scientist Sheldon Wolin argued in 2008, the United States may have "morphed into a new and strange kind of political hybrid, one where economic and state powers are conjoined and virtually unbridled." Wolin's chilling book *Democracy Incorporated* describes a mass-incarcerationist and hyper-militarized nation "where citizens are politically uninterested and submissive—and where elites are eager to keep them that way. At best," Wolin argued, "the nation has become a 'managed democracy' where *the public is shepherded, not sovereign*. At worst it is a place where corporate power no longer answers to state controls" and where "unchecked economic power risks verging on total power and has its own unnerving pathologies" (emphasis added). In Wolin's view, America has the potential to become modern history's third great totalitarian formation, succeeding the brown fascism of Hitler's Germany and the red fascism of Stalin's Russia.[6]

Particularly "unnerving" is the possibility that this formation could be the most sophisticated and powerful species of authoritarian rule yet developed. As the brilliant Australian propaganda critic Alex Carey noted back in the pivotal Ronald Reagan–Margaret Thatcher era, the greatest and most potent long-term menace to "the liberal-democratic freedoms we are all supposed to enjoy" has not come from the 1984 "left" but rather in the deceptively "un-coercive" form of "a widespread social and political indoctrination" in the ostensibly liberal West—"an indoctrination which promotes business interests as everyone's interests and in the process fragments the community and closes off individual and critical thought." The critical homeland and headquarters of this indoctrination and the oxymoronic "corporate-managed democracy" it breeds is the outwardly freedom-loving United States, where the art and science of *"taking the risk out of democracy"* (something different and arguably even more dangerous than twentieth-century fascism's and Stalinism's open and explicit bludgeoning of democracy) have, for various historical reasons, been carried to new levels.[7]

Clearly, however, the American ruling class is not so confident of its success in softly de-fanging democracy as to forego extremely dangerous forms of hard authoritarian coercion and control. Deadly tools of brute repression remain a highly relevant and increasingly significant part of the contemporary power elite's privilege-preserving toolbox when a significant number of Americans throw off the habit of submission. At the same time, the US elite continues to rely also on its ability to exploit numerous divisions within the nation's demoted citizenry or ex-citizenry—divisions that must be overcome by activists who want to have any chance of saving America from the depredations of the rich and powerful.

But authoritarianism is not the worst threat posed by the super-rich and their profits system. The single greatest and most imminent peril is environmental collapse, the death of livable ecology and hence of the prospects for a livable future—a topic that will be addressed repeatedly in this book. It's "socialism *or barbarism if we're lucky,*" the Hungarian Marxist philosopher Istvan Meszaros wrote in 2001, adding a critical environmental caveat to Rosa Luxemburg's famous slogan ("socialism or barbarism") on capitalism's long-run tendency to breed authoritarianism, repression, and war.[8]

The chief beneficiaries of the "new and strange kind of political hybrid" are found among the richest slice of Americans, those for whom the Occupy Movement gave the instantly famous shorthand designation "the 1%." Alongside the ever more imminent specter of ecological destruction—itself the single greatest current risk and inextricably bound up with the intimately related problems of capitalism and inequality (so I will argue)—and the ever-present danger of nuclear war, this great authoritarian threat (potentially "totalitarian" by Wolin's account) underlines the desperately "fierce urgency of now" (to quote Dr. Martin Luther King Jr.) when it comes to growing and multiplying the nascent American democracy upsurge that emerged in 2011. The stakes—the fate of the democratic ideal and a livable Earth, the very prospects for a decent and desirable future—could hardly be higher. Tying it all together, I shall argue, are the amoral institutional imperatives of the state-capitalist profits system, absurdly described as the "free market" in reigning US political discourse.

"The Choice"

Captive to and controlled by corporate, financial, and professional elites, the 2012 highly personalized and quadrennial US presidential "electoral extravaganza" (Chomsky's evocative phrase) swallowed up the lion's share of official American domestic news and commentary for the year that followed Occupy's dismantlement. One month before the spectacle's culmination, the Public Broadcasting System's investigative journalism show *Frontline* broadcast a show purporting to "present the definitive portraits of Barack Obama and Mitt Romney." The show, titled "The Choice,"[9] provided sensitive, deeply researched, and highly personal biographies of the two official contenders, Barack Obama and Mitt Romney. "The Choice" was as remarkable for what it left out as it was for what it included, however. It was loaded with details about the candidates' family histories and marriages and past careers and campaigns. At the same time, it was conspicuously silent about the different and yet—from the perspective of many observers—all too similar policy agendas of the two business-backed candidates and about the massive amounts of elite money that paid for both of the campaigns in what had already become far and away the most expensive US election of all time.

Americans need to look through John Carpenter's magical shades and pick from options that go deeper than recurrent once-every-1,460-days contests between two elite-sponsored state-capitalist politicians. "We must make our choice. We may have democracy in this country," US Supreme Court Justice Louis Brandeis noted more than six decades ago, "or we may have wealth concentrated in the hands of a few, but we cannot have both."[10] That is the *real choice* for serious citizens beneath and beyond the much ballyhooed choice offered by two candidates selected for us in advance by the powers that be. It was the choice that Occupy Wall Street and its many hundreds of offshoots across the country tried to place before the American people in the late summer and fall of 2011.

Acting on that choice in a seriously democratic fashion, however, is not a simple or easy matter. It involves difficult and detailed movement-building work each and every day, not just once very four years. As the great radical American historian Howard Zinn explained in an essay on the *"election madness"* he saw "engulfing the entire society, including the left" with special intensity in early 2008,

> The election frenzy seizes the country every four years because we have all been brought up to believe that voting is crucial in determining our destiny, that the most important act a citizen can engage in is to go to the polls and choose one of the two mediocrities who have already been chosen for us.... Would I support one [presidential] candidate against another? Yes, for two minutes—the amount of time it takes to pull the lever down in the voting booth.... But before and after those two minutes, our time, our energy, should be spent in educating, agitating, organizing our fellow citizens in the workplace, in the neighborhood, in the schools. Our objective should be to build, painstakingly, patiently but energetically, a movement that, when it reaches a certain critical mass, would shake *whoever is in the White House*, in Congress, into changing national policy on matters of war and social justice.[11]

By the time I completed this book (started in the summer of 2012, months before the election that returned Barack Obama to the White House), the latest and current "election frenzy" had begun to recede like a bad hangover. It always does. As the dull crush of persistent plutocratic rule beneath and beyond quadrennial election spectacles sinks back into popular consciousness, the time is ripe again for serious and sustained popular mobilization, dedicated to a serious, at least partly Occupy-informed version of radically democratic politics. It is my hope that this book will aid that project by sharpening the subversive egalitarian vision one can garner from donning a good pair of *They Live*'s demystifying sunglasses. And that it will suggest at least some of what might be done to save democracy and a livable future after we see through the powerful myths and propaganda that do much to sustain the contemporary de facto dictatorship of the rich.

CHAPTER 1

"They Own the Place"

Scenes from America's Unelected Dictatorship, 2009–2013

I witnessed the raid on the Occupation Oakland camp ... and it was terrifying to see. *It harkened back to old footage I had seen of Nazi Germany....* It had that tenor.
          —*Witness to the police raid on Occupy Oakland, October 26, 2011*[1]

You're going to have to do something to lower peoples' expectations of what they're going to get, the entitlements and all people think they're going to get, because you're not going to get it.
          —*Lloyd Blankfein, CEO of Goldman Sachs, November 19, 2012*[2]

Fall and Early Winter 2011: Repressing Dissent

"To Fight for the America We Believe In" (Bay Area, October 2011)

Two and a half days in the American West in the fall of 2011 speak volumes about money and power in the United States, the self-declared homeland and headquarters of democracy. For US president Barack Obama, Tuesday, October 25, 2011, started in Los Angeles with an interview with television talk show host Jay Leno, broadcast later that night on *The Tonight Show.* After taping at NBC's studios, Obama and his entourage flew on Air Force One to San Francisco for a $1 million luncheon fundraiser with a gathering of millionaires at the posh W Hotel. Singer Jack Johnson performed at the event, in keeping with the Obama reelection campaign's tactic of "turning on star power for top donors." The president had spoken at two fundraisers in Los Angeles on Monday evening, including a Latino-oriented event at the Hollywood mansion of actors Antonio Banderas and Melanie Griffith.

At the W, Obama made a poignant appeal to 200 contributors who paid a minimum of $5,000 to attend. "Whether you are an old grizzled veteran or new to the scene, I need your help," he said. The coming election, Obama said, was "more consequential, more important" than the last one. He said that a jobs bill he was advancing would "give the economy the jolt it needs right now" and likened the nation's current difficulties to prior challenges: the Great Depression, the Civil Rights Movement, and landing on the moon. "If we don't work even harder than we did in 2008, then we're going to have a government that tells the American people, 'You're on your own,'" he said. "That's not the America I believe in; it's not the America you believe in. We're going to have to fight for the America that we believe in."[3]

It was Obama's "third visit to the Bay Area—always a lucrative fundraising location for him—in a little more than six months and his seventh since taking office," the *San Jose Mercury News* reported. The previous month he had collected nearly $6 million at lucrative fundraisers in the affluent Bay Area communities of Woodside and Atherton. After two and a half hours on the ground in the Bay Area, Obama left for Denver, Colorado, where he had two more fundraisers scheduled as part of a three-state western fundraising sweep.[4] It was all part of a major push focused largely on wealthy donors, an epic quest for campaign cash that helped Obama gather $90 million by the end of November 2011. He was averaging one big fundraiser every five days in 2011.[5] In early March of the following year, *USA Today* found that the president had already attended 191 elite fundraisers—a new first-term presidential record with ten months still to go. The previous standard of 173 had been set by the notoriously plutocratic George W. Bush,[6] who once referred (at a black tie New York campaign event in 2000) to the nation's super-rich as "my base."[7]

Early the following morning, long after *The Tonight Show* had been broadcast and the president had settled into a comfortable suite in Denver, something unpleasant happened across the San Francisco Bay. Dozens of activists were camped out in Oakland to "fight for the America that we believe in" in ways that had little to do with electoral politics. "Occupy Oakland" had staked out a park in the depressed city's downtown earlier in the month. It was one of hundreds of local Occupy movements that had sprung up under the inspiration of and in solidarity with Occupy Wall Street, the remarkable New York City protest that began on September 17, 2011, against economic inequality and the control of US society and politics by "the 1%"—against the very wealthy few whose money Obama was soliciting in person once every five days.

The Oakland Occupation had never sat well with the city's "progressive" Democratic mayor Jean Quam. She had decided to move against it in a predawn raid. In the still-dark hours of the very early morning, heavily armored and visor-wearing riot police from no less than ten Bay Area jurisdictions assaulted the protestors with a barrage of rubber bullets, chemical agents, and concussion grenades. They fired a "sonic canon" designed to attack protestors' ear drums.[8] The attack was described by a downtown security guard who beheld a massive, Nazi-like police rush on one hundred or so peaceful occupiers:

> I witnessed the raid on the Occupation Oakland camp, at a little bit after 4:30 in the morning, and it was terrifying to see.... There were just so many policemen ... the numbers were incredible.... They lined up almost like in a phalanx, on the street, and then they moved in.... There were helicopters flying about and with high beams on the camps ... the beams were moving across every which way.... There were young people in these camps and children, infants in a lot of the tents.... They shot ... tear gas into the middle of the camp ... and then they moved to the next stage of taking the barricades and kicking them down. And then they moved in and the first thing they hit was the information tent, and they just started just tearing everything down.... This was a military type operation, the way they moved in. It harkened back to old footage I had seen of Nazi Germany.... It had that tenor.... The helicopters, and the lights, and the loudspeaker, all those were all intended to create panic and terror for the people inside.... It was something like out of a *Star Wars* movie except instead of being in white they were all in black ... they were all in riot gear ... with the visors, they looked like automatons, they just moved in, in a line.... They had these vehicles that looked like armored boxes, black, special riot vehicles.... The thing that stays in my mind's eye is in the middle ground with the lights from the helicopters, the police moving in and just stomping on these tents, and moving in one layer, after another, moving in deeper and deeper.[9]

This chilling militarized police action put a US military veteran (Scott Olson) in intensive care with a fractured skull and inflicted numerous other injuries.

The White House had nothing to say about the repression unleashed on homeless Americans and populist protestors by a big city mayor from the president's own party—sixteen and a half hours after he had just raised a million dollars from the rich and powerful in the same metropolitan area. The silence was telling. When the Occupy Movement broke into the national and global spotlight from its original base in New York City's financial district earlier that month, top Democrats had smelled opportunity—popular anger they could yoke to their electoral strategy against the Republicans. "For a Democratic Party dispirited by its president's sliding approval ratings," the *Wall Street Journal* explained, "the new energy has been greeted as a tonic comparable to what Republican congressional leaders tapped in the Tea Party movement—and are now finding it difficult to harness.... Democrats see an avenue to bring the anger back to their side."[10] Still, Obama offered no words of encouragement or recognition of the movement—no praise for its determination to act in accord with a notion that he had invoked more than once on the campaign trail in 2007 and 2008: that progressive "change doesn't happen from the top down. Change happens from the bottom up." There were no words of White House concern over the violation of peaceful protestors' human and civil rights.

"Measures More Reminiscent of a Dictatorship" (New York City and Other US Cities, November 2011)

The president was silent weeks later when a slew of mostly Democratic big city mayors across the country cracked down on the Occupy Movement in mid- and late November. Especially chilling was the eviction conducted against the original Occupy Wall Street site in New York City's Zuccotti Park in the early morning of November 15 on the orders of Wall Street titan turned New York mayor Michael Bloomberg—himself a true 1%-er (the twelfth richest person in the United States, in fact). By one eyewitness account,

> The area around Zuccotti Park was subject last night to a 9/11-level lock-down over peaceful, lawful protests by a small number of people.... Martial law level restrictions were in place. Subways were shut down. Local residents were not allowed to leave their buildings. People were allowed into the area only if they showed ID with an address in the 'hood. Media access was limited to those with official press credentials, which is almost certainly a small minority of those who wanted to cover the crackdown.... They were kept well away from the actual confrontation (for instance, the tear gassing of the Occupiers in what had been the [OWS] kitchen, as well as the use of pepper spray and batons). News helicopters were forced to land. As of 10 a.m.... police helicopters were out in force buzzing lower Manhattan.[11]

A former New York Supreme Court justice served as an independent legal observer of the police action. When she witnessed a New York Police Department (NYPD) officer force a protestor to the ground and beat her on the head, the observer asked the officer why he had done it. The officer, *Harper's Magazine* columnist Jeff Madrick notes, "pushed her up against the wall and asked if she wanted to be arrested. A New York City councilman," Madrick adds, "was pushed to the ground and arrested. The use of batons and pepper spray and the dragging of protestors was well-documented.... Examples of violence against reporters were also plentiful." Such abuses received scant attention thanks in part to Bloomberg's imposition of a "media blackout" (as the *New York Times* "Decoder blog" accurately reported) on the eviction raid—a technical violation of international human rights law. The local CBS television affiliate (WCBS) reported that the NYPD blocked its news helicopter from filming the police, though only the Federal Aviation Administration has the legal authority to restrict airspace access. It all followed weeks of police abuse against Occupy Wall Street. A report published in the summer of 2012 documented 130 incidents of excessive force by the NYPD—actions that violated protestors' civil and human rights—during the occupation and over subsequent months.[12]

The human rights advocate Dr. Marsha Coleman-Adebayo was reminded of past visits to South Africa, where she heard anti-apartheid activists recall "the dark days of repression and how police would conduct raids during the early morning hours knowing that their victims would be groggy and fearful in the dark." "It seems," a friend of Coleman-Adebayo's wrote her from England after the NYPD raid, "like US police are resorting to measures more reminiscent of a dictatorship." As president, Coleman-Adebayo argued, Obama "should be the primary defender of the Constitution, yet he *remains silent*, apart from hypo-critically pontificating on global platforms while at home the economy crashes and violent police actions against peaceful protestors take place."[13]

Over the previous ten days, violent police raids and clearances of the Occupy Movement had been carried out in the name of "public health and safety" against protestors in a number of other cities, including St. Louis (Friday, November 12), Denver (Saturday, November 13), Portland, Oregon (Sunday, November 14), Salt Lake City (Saturday, November 12), Albany (Saturday, November 13), and Dallas (Thursday, November 17). A police action against Occupy Seattle included the pepper-spraying of an eighty-four-year-old woman. Student Occupiers were beaten by Alameda County sheriffs in the full light of day on the campus of the great liberal bastion the University of California at Berkeley. None of this repression elicited the slightest bit of commentary from Obama. He was touring Asia and Australia to promote "free trade" and an expanded US military presence in the Far East while much of the repression unfolded in the "homeland."

Eight days after the martial law action in lower Manhattan, the president flew up to New York City to speak at three big donor fundraising events there. On November 30, Wall Street protestors tried to greet Obama outside a $10,000-a-plate fundraiser at the Sheraton New York. Police officers there kept demonstrators penned in what the NYPD called "frozen zones." At 9 p.m., police barricaded fifty protestors into a small space at Seventh Avenue and 53rd Street. At first blush, this seemed to be nothing new. Officially designated "free speech zones" had long been routine outside high-level political events in the United States. "But here's the twist," *Mother Jones* reporter Josh Harkinson noted, "Protestors in the NYPD's free speech zone were trapped.... Not only could nobody enter after a certain point, but for about an hour and a half, nobody could leave.... When I arrived outside the event, I found that the police had cordoned off the sidewalk a block in all directions and were not admitting the press. Deeper inside this 'frozen zone,' as the police called it, were the kettled protestors, who occupied a sort of Faberge egg of dissent that was completely inaccessible to anyone not already there.... I couldn't even read their signs."[14]

Two months later, the NYPD was on hand in large numbers along with the US Secret Service and other federal officers to safeguard another big money presidential fundraiser in Manhattan. Obama raised $1.6 million at the Upper East Side home of filmmaker Spike Lee, where sixty guests paid $71,600 per couple. Stars such as Mariah Carey and Nick Cannon attended the event, which started at 6:00 p.m., right after another chic gathering in which wealthy Jewish New Yorkers paid $25,000 to meet and get a picture taken with Obama.[15] The evening contradicted Obama campaign manager Jim Messina's claim at the time that rumors of a $1 billion Obama reelection campaign were "bullshit" since "we fund this campaign in contributions of three dollars or five dollars or whatever you can do to help us." As progressive commentator Alex Marin noted, such fundraisers "expose ... the double standard of an administration that has supposedly taken a populist stance by publicly demonizing the rich but cuddling with them in private.... The business-as-usual fundraising events also fly in the face of Obama's claim that he had embraced the Occupy Wall Street movement's message of economic inequality."[16]

State Capitalism: Public Repression in Service to Private Wall Street Power

Around the same time, Obama delivered a speech at a high school in Manchester, New Hampshire. Using their patented "human microphone" method, Occupy activists interrupted the president minutes into his oration, decrying the repression across the country. An Occupier got close enough to Obama to pass him a note that read as follows: "Mr. President: Over 4,000 peaceful protestors have been arrested while bankers continue to destroy the American economy. You must stop the assault.... Your silence sends a message that police brutality is acceptable. Banks got bailed out. We got sold out."[17]

American Intelligence as a Private Intelligence Arm for Wall Street

But the administration was *far more than merely silent* in the crackdown on the Occupy Movement. The multiple metropolitan repressions and evictions were partly coordinated with assistance and advice from the executive branch's Federal Bureau of Investigation (FBI) Department of Homeland Security (DHS), which recommended that city mayors and police chiefs cite concerns for public health and public safety in justifying attacks on and evictions of the Occupy Movement.[18] Formerly secret documents obtained after long federal delay by the civil libertarian group Partnership for Civil Justice Fund (PCJF) in December 2012 revealed that from its inception the Occupy Movement was treated by the FBI as a criminal and terrorist threat—this even as the FBI acknowledged that Occupy organizers explicitly advocated peaceful, nonviolent protest. FBI agents intensively monitored and infiltrated what would become the Occupy Movement as early as August 2011, a month before OWS took over Zuccotti Park. The documents show the FBI and DHS "functioning as a de facto intelligence arm of Wall Street and corporate America." As the movement spread across the nation, FBI agents exchanged information and repressive practices with local and state police, the global US Naval Criminal Intelligence Services (NCIS), the Federal Reserve, and numerous leading private banks and corporations. The monitoring of the movement was coordinated with the private corporate sector and what domestic intelligence officials called "the corporate security community." The PCJF learned that the FBI in New York met with the New York Stock Exchange "to discuss Occupy Wall Street protests that wouldn't start for another month. By September, prior to the start of the OWS, the FBI was notifying businesses that they might be the focus of an OWS protest."

This corporate and state collaboration in repression was coordinated through the federal Domestic Security Alliance Council (DSAC), described by the federal government as "a strategic partnership between the FBI, the Department of Homeland Security, and the private sector." A DSAC report garnered by the PCJF shows covert collaboration between US intelligence and corporate clients. The document included a "handling notice" that the information it contained was "for use primarily within the corporate security community" and was not to be released to the public or media.

The DSAC offered advice to corporations on how to respond to "civil unrest," ranging from "small, organized rallies to large-scale demonstrations and rioting." It told business personnel to avoid political discussions and "all large gatherings related to civil issues," warning that "even seemingly peaceful rallies can spur violent activity or be met with resistance by security forces. Bystanders may be arrested or harmed by security forces using water cannons, tear gas or other measures to control crowds."[19]

As PCJF executive director Mara Verheyden-Hilliard told the progressive broadcaster Amy Goodman, "there is repeated evidence of ... American intelligence agencies really working as a private intelligence arm for corporations, for Wall Street, for the banks, for the very entities that people were rising up to protest against."[20] The liberal commentator Naomi Wolf went further: "The documents ... show a nationwide meta-plot unfolding in city after city in an Orwellian world: six American universities are sites where campus police funneled information about students involved with OWS to the FBI, with the administrations' knowledge; banks sat down with FBI officials to pool information about OWS protestors harvested by private security; plans to crush Occupy events, planned for a month down the road, were made by the FBI—and offered to the representatives of the ... organizations that the protests would target."[21]

The timing of the FBI's long-delayed release of the heavily redacted documents just before Christmas was hardly accidental. It reflected the agency's calculation that the public would be too distracted by the holiday season to pay attention.

Indemnified by the Taxpayer, Hired by Wall Street

A similar state-capitalist dynamic of repression was evident at the metropolitan level in New York City at the height of OWS. Had the president chosen to denounce the repression of Occupy activists in New York (he did not), he might have been intrigued to learn that some of the NYPD officers pepper-spraying, clubbing, and otherwise brutalizing peaceful protestors in and around Wall Street were hired by the financial sector. Wearing white shirts instead of the standard NYPD blue, they were members of the city police force's Paid Detail Unit (PDU). As the veteran left Wall Street activist and financial critic Pam Martens noted in early October 2011, the PDU "allows the New York Stock Exchange and Wall Street corporations, including those repeatedly charged with crimes, to order up a flank of New York City's finest with the ease of dialing the deli for a pastrami on rye." Further:

> The corporations pay an average of $37 an hour (no medical, no pension benefit, no overtime pay) for a member of the NYPD, with gun, handcuffs and the ability to arrest. The officer is indemnified by the taxpayer, not the corporation.
>
> New York City gets a 10 percent administrative fee on top of the $37 per hour paid to the police. The City's 2011 budget called for $1,184,000 in Paid Detail fees, meaning private corporations were paying wages of $11.8 million to police participating in the Paid Detail Unit. The program has more than doubled in revenue to the city since 2002.
>
> The taxpayer has paid for the training of the rent-a-cop, his uniform and gun, and will pick up the legal tab for lawsuits stemming from the police personnel following illegal instructions from its corporate master.
>
> When the program was first rolled out, one insightful member of the NYPD posted the following on a forum: "regarding the officer working for, and being paid by, some of the richest people and organizations in the City, if not the world, enforcing the mandates of the private employer, and in effect, allowing the officer to become the Praetorian Guard of the elite of the City."[22]

Public Health and Safety

The "public health and safety" pretext for the repression reeked of bad faith and rich irony. The Occupy encampments were generally sanitary and safe, reflecting activists' determination to prefigure their vision of a positive and cooperative future (beyond the rule of the rich) and their knowledge that city officials were eager to find reasons to justify closing down the encampments. Given the extreme poverty of a significant and rising share of the nation's urban population and the refusal of many young Occupiers to shun the long-demonized urban "underclass,"[23] it was inevitable perhaps that (somewhat on the model of the doomed Los Angeles campsite depicted in *They Live*) the camps would attract a number of city residents plagued by homelessness, addiction, criminal records, mental instability, and chronic joblessness. Still, the Occupy Movement had for the most part dealt well and sensitively with the problems of these forgotten and oppressed people, problems Occupiers hardly created and that they sought to alleviate. By contrast, the assaults on the movement were monuments to *public un-safety*: violent, injury-causing, and armed state-terrorist raids on nonviolent protest and free speech.

Meanwhile, a genuine threat to public health and safety stalked the land: economic misery for a growing mass of Americans alongside stupendous opulence at the top, in the newly notorious "1%"—a topic we shall examine at some length in Chapter 2. The Brookings Institution reported in a study released eleven days before the NYPD raid on Zuccotti Park that between 2000 and 2010, "the country saw the poor population grow by 12.3 million, driving the total number of Americans in poverty to a historic high."[24] By Brookings' estimation, the number of Americans living in "extreme poverty neighborhoods"—neighborhoods and census tracts where at least 40 percent of the residents lived below the poverty line—had risen by one-third between 2000 and 2009. Brookings determined that 11 percent of America's officially poor people lived in such neighborhoods, up from 9 percent in 2000.[25] New York City, where the financial titan-turned-mayor recently *spent $7 million repressing and evicting Occupy from the city's financial district*, was home to 1,575,032 officially poor people and to 174 "extreme poverty census tracts" (EPCTs) that housed 697,375 people, including 375,876 poor. Chicago, where corporate mayor Rahm Emmanuel had denied Occupiers a campsite, was home to 593,000 poor and 124 EPCTs. Los Angeles, where Antonio Villaraigosa would evict his city's Occupy Movement over public protest in early December, was home to 844,712 poor people and to 65 EPCTs. Philadelphia, where Occupy was evicted with the standard civic justification around the same time, was home to 352,265 poor people and 58 EPCTS.[26] Brookings' study bore a revealing title: *The Re-Emergence of Concentrated Poverty*.

Government officials who were serious about advancing and protecting public health and safety would have diverted resources from the repression of their downtown Occupy Movements to meeting the needs of the rising mass of poor US citizens, especially those stuck in the many ghetto neighborhoods and barrios that wallowed in the shadows of urban America's shining financial districts. By 2010, black unemployment had risen to between 30 and 35 percent in thirty-five of the largest US cities—"levels equal to the worst days of the Great Depression."[27]

"The Authorities Decided We Would Never Have Another Zuccotti"

In New York City, run by the nominally Republican mogul Bloomberg, the repression of Occupy continued into the following year, reflecting authorities' determination that no such populist uprising would raise its head again in the city. An original OWS sparkplug, the radical anthropologist David Graeber opens his book *The Democracy Project* with a chilling account of what happened to activists attempting in the spring of 2012 to replace the camp they'd been evicted from the previous fall:

> For more than a month, we had been attempting to reestablish a foothold in lower Manhattan.... Even if we weren't able to establish a new camp, we were hoping to at least find some place where we could hold regular assemblies, and set up our library and kitchen.... The city authorities, however, had decided that we would never have another Zuccotti. Wherever we found a spot we could legally set up shop, they simply changed the laws and drove us off. When we tried to establish ourselves in Union Square, city authorities changed park regulations. When a band of occupiers started sleeping on the sidewalk on Wall Street itself, relying on a judicial decision that explicitly said citizens had a right to sleep on the street in New York as a form of political protest, the city deemed that part of lower Manhattan "a special security zone" in which the law did not apply.

Graeber's recollection ends when he and his comrades gathered on the marble steps of Federal Hall, where the Bill of Rights—a great monument to civil liberties including the First Amendment rights of free speech and public assembly—had been signed in 1789. There US Park Police let the NYPD build two large steel cages around the activists. Further:

> A SWAT team was positioned by the entrance, and a white-shirted police commander carefully monitored everyone who tried to enter, informing them that for safety reasons no more than twenty people were allowed in either cage at any time.... Soon large signs were banned. Then anything made of cardboard. Then came the random arrests.... The officer in charge seemed to be making a point: even at the very birthplace of the First Amendment, he still had the power to arrest us just for engaging in political speech.[28]

Consistent with this account, the left author and activist Chris Hedges learned something interesting from members of the antiwar veterans' group Veterans for Peace on why a large number of them were arrested for holding a peaceful demonstration at the Vietnam Veterans Memorial in New York City in October 2012. "Look, we're vets, we don't want to arrest you," NYPD officers told the protestors, "but the Occupy movement messed it up for you because we can't allow another one."

"Let's remember that whatever the internal faults of the Occupy movement—and they were there—the Occupy movement was destroyed," Hedges told a television interviewer last July. "The state was quite rattled by the Occupy movement and is determined not to allow a movement, a mass movement like that to rise up again."[29]

Super-Rich Irony, 2009–2012

The Political 1 Percent of 1 Percent

Mass joblessness and destitution aside, President Obama was schmoozing with the super-rich in the fall and winter of 2011 for a very obvious reason. As the *Bloomberg News* reported with no evident dismay twelve days after OWS set up camp, the 2012 elections were "shaping up to be the most expensive ever." Between the congressional and presidential contests, *Bloomberg* reported, the elections were on track to cost an all-time record of more than $6 billion.[30] And in the 2012 election cycle as across the past three decades, Obama's strategists knew that a tiny and disproportionately wealthy slice of the populace (significantly smaller than just "the 1%") would account for the dollars required to feed the nation's burgeoning "money and media election complex" that was "now more definitional than any candidate or party"[31] and "effectively the foundation of electoral politics in the United States."[32]

In mid-December 2011, the liberal Sunlight Foundation released a major campaign finance study titled *The Political One Percent of One Percent*. The report found that fewer than 27,000 Americans each gave at least $10,000 to federal political campaigns in 2010. Their combined expenditure of $774 million accounted for nearly a quarter of all donations to candidates, political action committees, political parties, and independent expenditure groups in the 2010 midterm elections. "It's the 1 percent of the 1 percent who account for almost a quarter of all individual campaign contributions," Sunlight reported. "There are very few Americans who can afford to write the kind of big checks that candidates depend on."

The problem was getting worse over time. "Over the past 20 years," Sunlight reported, "the $10,000-plus donors have accounted for an ever bigger share of political contributions.... Everybody—not just candidates—leans harder on the wealthy as campaign spending escalates. Parties want to be able to tap into donor networks of people who can give $10,000, $20,000 to the party." Within "the 1 percent of the 1 percent," Sunlight found, the most elite donors, those with corporate ties, gave on average $29,000 per election cycle—more than what half of Americans earn in a single year.[33]

"He Is of Their World"

Also making attendance at elite fundraisers mandatory for President Obama, the opulent Wall Street interests that had funded him with record-setting contributions in 2008 appeared to be jumping ship for the super-wealthy Mitt Romney. "After a fling with Obama—the charismatic Democrat embraced four years ago during the severe credit crisis that erupted under President George W. Bush—Wall Street is backing Romney in a return to its largely Republican inclinations. As they line up behind Romney," Reuters reported, "banks and investment firms are being joined by a new generation of hedge fund and private equity managers with deep pockets. They are backing the candidate who comes from their ranks—Romney, a former private equity executive." The financial sector had "preferred Romney from the beginning," one campaign finance expert told Reuters, adding that "he is of their world."[34]

"The Class One Serves"

This movement away from Obama reflected remarkable ingratitude on the part of the financial elite. "The clever young man who recently made it to the White House," John Pilger noted in June 2009, "is a very fine hypnotist, partly because it is indeed exciting to see an African American at the pinnacle of power in the land of slavery. However, this is the 21st century, and race together with gender and even class can be very seductive tools of propaganda. For what is so often overlooked and *what matters above all, is the class one serves.*"[35]

FOX News–informed Tea Partiers might have mouthed paranoid, neo-McCarthyite fantasies about the new president's "socialism" and "Marxism," but serious investigators had little reason to doubt *which class the new president served.* "Our black president," as progressive commentator Matthew Rothschild mistakenly called Obama in October 2010,[36] had governed in accord with the wishes of Wall Street and corporate America from the start, making his first term a case study in reach of what left commentators Edward S. Herman and David Peterson call "the unelected dictatorship of money." That hidden regime "vets the nominees of the Republican and Democratic parties," Herman and Peterson note, "reducing the options available to US citizens to two candidates, neither of whom can change the foreign or domestic priorities of the US imperial regime."[37] Examples of this harsh reality include the following White House actions—and inactions:

- Expansion of the monumental $14 trillion bailout of the very hyper-opulent financial overlords who crashed the global economy in 2008 and 2009, combined with a steadfast refusal to consider nationalizing or breaking up the nation's giant financial institutions.
- Advance and passage of a health "reform" bill that was aptly described by liberal journalist and author Matt Taibbi as "a massive giveaway to private, profit-making corporations"[38]—a measure that only the big insurance and drug companies could love.
- The cutting of an auto bailout deal that raided union pension funds and slashed entry-level wages while rewarding the export of jobs.
- The cold-blooded undermining of global carbon emission reduction efforts at Copenhagen and the green-lighting of escalated strip mining and hazardous offshore drilling projects.
- The disregarding of key promises to unions to work for labor law reform and new trade legislation with stronger worker protections and a failure to embrace a historic public worker rebellion in Wisconsin, Ohio, and Indiana in early 2011.
- The appointment of a conservative Deficit Reduction Commission headed by avowed enemies of Social Security.[39]

As the venerable progressive commentator Bill Greider noted in the *Washington Post* in mid-March 2009, reflecting on popular outrage over how the American Insurance Group (AIG)—a leading force behind the financial manipulation that contributed to the 2007–2008 economic crisis—had recently paid out $165 million in bonuses to its top managers after receiving tens of billions of dollars in assistance from the federal government, "People everywhere [have] learned a blunt lesson about power, who has it and who doesn't. They [have] watched Washington run to rescue the very financial interests that caused the catastrophe. They [have] learned that government has plenty of money to spend when the right people want it"[40]—but little if anything for the millions thrown out of work and their homes by the depredations of the rich.

"Despite all the criticism that President Obama has received lately from Wall Street," the *New Yorker*'s perceptive economics writer John Cassidy noted in November 2010, "the Administration has largely left the great money-making machine intact. A couple of years ago, firms such as Citigroup, JPMorgan Chase, and Goldman Sachs faced the danger that the government would break them up, drive them out of some of their most lucrative business lines—such as dealing in derivatives—or force them to maintain so much capital that their profits would be greatly diminished." None of these things materialized, reflecting the moneyed elite's success in defining "realistic" policy options for a president who wanted a second term.[41]

Cassidy's sentiments were echoed two years later, on the eve of Obama's reelection, by the global business journalist Chrystia Freeland, an up-close chronicler and occasional consort of the ultra-rich. In a *New Yorker* essay titled "Super-Rich Irony," Freeland observed the curious incongruity of "the growing antagonism of the super-wealthy toward Obama" when "Obama has served the rich very well" by "support[ing] the seven hundred billion dollar TARP rescue package for Wall Street and resist[ing] calls from the Nobel Prize winners Joseph Stiglitz and Paul Krugman and others on the left, to nationalize the banks in exchange for that largesse."[42]

Men of Overgrown Estates

So what was the financial aristocracy's problem with the young president? By Freeland's subsequent account one day after the election, Obama had failed to sufficiently *stroke the egos of Wall Street's super-rich* even as he had done their bidding. Obama may have served the "most affluent Americans" and the "financial sector," Freeland reported, but he was "a severe disappointment when it came to the softer side of serving his wealthy supporters. The hand-written letters, White House photos and private policy discussions that are the accustomed quid pro quo for major donors did not happen," causing the "business community's ... leaders to [feel] personally disrespected." Obama had "chafed at the idea that he needed to kiss the ring of Wall Street," liberal Yale political scientist Jacob S. Hacker told Freeland. And that "drove many of the president's political supporters to despair—would it be so hard, they wondered, for him to write a few thank-you notes?"[43]

In her 2012 book *Plutocrats: The Rise of the New Global Super Rich and the Fall of Everyone Else*, Freeland reflected on the discomfort of many super-rich donors with Obama. A top "Wall Street Democrat" who had held key positions at America's top financial institutions told her the president had "alienated the business community" by *"speaking about 'the rich.'"* It would have been "best," the banker said, *"not to refer to income differences at all,* ... but if the president couldn't avoid singling out the country's top earners, he should call them 'affluent.'"[44] It wasn't enough for the wealthy few to receive the policy outcomes they desired from the new president. It was also important for him to "kiss their ring" and help keep their opulence invisible.

The remarkable arrogance behind their indignation would have been appreciated by Montesquieu. "To men of overgrown estates," the eighteenth-century philosopher noted, "everything which does not contribute to advance their power and honor is considered by them as an injury."[45]

At the same time, the wealthy election funders may have sensed danger in the popular hopes and progressive expectations raised by the rhetoric of a Democratic president who had no choice but to strike populist-sounding chords to rally the votes necessary to prevail in the next election. Such rhetoric carries a dangerous underside for the rich and powerful: the risk of raised and then dashed popular expectations, leading to popular activism of the sort that the Occupy Movement promised.[46] With the likes of the arch-plutocrat Mitt "Mr. 1%" Romney in the White House, the potential for radicalizing disappointment was nil. He would raise no progressive expectations to dash and crush.

Hope of a Different Kind (2011)

More than a "blunt lesson about power," the Obama presidency had been something of an advanced national seminar in who actually governs the country beneath and beyond time-staggered election spectacles—what Noam Chomsky called "personalized quadrennial electoral extravaganzas"[47]—and on the futility of seeking progressive change through the reigning electoral and party institutions. The real rulers, the Obama experience taught, were the wealthy few, those who would become known as "the 1%" in the late summer and fall of 2011. The apparently not so great and powerful Obama came to look to some of his former young supporters as something like the Wizard of Oz. He seemed a creature less of real power and principle than of deceptive marketing and imagery, his progressive-sounding bluster providing deceptive cover for his allegiance and/or captivity to the corporate and financial elite.[48]

It wasn't just the executive branch that seemed hopelessly in Wall Street's pocket, to be sure. In May 2009, Obama's former fellow US senator from Illinois Dick Durbin (D-IL) offered an interesting reflection from the nation's elite representative body on the leading financial institutions' power in Congress. "The banks," Durbin told a Chicago radio station, "are still the most powerful lobby on Capitol Hill," something he found "hard to believe in a time when we're facing an economic crisis that many of the banks created. . . . And *they frankly own the place*," Durbin added.[49]

"The Comic Opera in Washington"

By the late summer and early fall of 2011, the tutorial the Obama years were giving America on *who really owned and ran the country* created a serious popular rebellion. The elite-manufactured "debt-ceiling crisis" that took center media stage in July and August 2011 was the last straw for many. The corporate-backed hard-right Republicans threatened the federal government's credit rating and its ability to continue to fund core operations by refusing to let the corporate-backed Democratic president carry out the previously routine policy of raising the nation's borrowing limit until he agreed to undertake draconian cuts in government spending to reduce the federal deficit. The right designated this as "the defining issue of our time" and the cause of the economic downturn—even as the Republicans opposed even modest tax increases on the nation's corporations and rich, whose low tax rates were an important factor behind the deficit.

Majority opinion seemed irrelevant in the debt-ceiling drama. With good reason during a continuing vicious "human recession" that lived on beneath a "statistical recovery" that summer, most of the population believed that the nation's leading economic problem was unemployment and that the government's top priorities should be job creation and expanding the social safety net, not "deficit reduction." They felt that the rich had too much wealth and power and that the best way to reduce the deficit—insofar as that might be a relevant goal—would be to increase taxes on the wealthy.

None of that majority sentiment was remotely represented in Washington during the debt-ceiling fiasco. In his initial effort to cut a historic "grand [deficit reduction] bargain" with the Republicans, Obama had proposed large long-term cuts in Medicare and Social Security—cuts that defied majority public opinion support for those programs and went beyond anything the rightmost party proposed.

Also seemingly irrelevant amid the national media and political elites' obsession with the federal budget deficit was the basic fact that, as 2012 Green Party presidential candidate Jill Stein has explained, the deficit "is simply a symptom of the bigger disease: the recession (caused by Wall Street malfeasance), which led to the massive 2008 drop in tax revenues [and was] exacerbated by Wall Street bailouts, the Bush/Obama tax giveaways to the rich, private medical insurance inflation, and the disastrous $6 trillion military boondoggles in Iraq and Afghanistan."[50]

As Chomsky commented in early August 2011, "The comic opera in Washington this summer, which disgusts the country and bewilders the world, may have no analogue in the annals of parliamentary democracy.... Corporate power's ascendancy over politics and society—by now mostly financial—has reached the point that both political organizations, which at this stage barely resemble traditional parties, are far to the right of the population on the major issues under debate."[51]

The "comic opera" ended with Obama agreeing to a "deal" that cut social spending without any tax increases for the wealthy or their corporations. It was yet another example of the "hope" and "change" many Americans had felt in connection with the 2008 election coming up against the cold reality of the corporate and financial elite's *unelected dictatorship*.

"A Feedback Loop That Cannot Be Broken by the Usual Means"

One didn't have to be a leftist to see American democracy as trumped by plutocracy. Reflecting on "American decline" in the wake of the Occupy

Movement's emergence, the centrist *New Yorker* staff writer George Packer observed in the establishment journal *Foreign Affairs* in the fall of 2011 that

> the persistence of [a] trend toward greater inequality [inside the United States] over the past 30 years suggests a kind of feedback loop that *cannot be broken by the usual political means*.... The more wealth accumulates in a few hands at the top, the more influence and favor the well-connected rich acquire, which makes it easier for them and their political allies to cast off restraint without paying a social price. That, in turn, frees them up to amass more money, until cause and effect become impossible to distinguish. Nothing seems to slow this process down—not wars, not technology, *not a recession, not a historic election.*[52]

Embracing the venerable popular spirit of mutual aid, an Occupier named Justin Hardy epitomized this sense of deep democratic frustration on the widely read "We Are the 99 Percent" blog just before Christmas in late 2011. "We have looked to our government to help," Hardy wrote, "but alas *the system has failed.* Our children's futures are being taken away, our own futures are uncertain.... If our government chooses not to help then we must help ourselves by helping each other."[53]

"The Power of Hope"

The Nobel Prize–winning liberal economist Joseph E. Stiglitz has written about what produced the Occupy rebellion and why that rebellion only came three years after the onset of the Great Recession:

> That the young would rise up against the dictatorships of Tunisia and Egypt was understandable. The youth were tired of aging, sclerotic leaders who protected their own interests at the expense of the rest of society. They had no opportunity to call for change through democratic processes. But electoral democracy had also failed badly in Western democracies. US president Barack Obama had promised "change you can believe in," but he subsequently delivered economic policies that, to many Americans, seemed like more of the same....
>
> Years after the breaking of the bubble, it became clear that our political system had failed.... It was only then that protestors turned to the streets....[54]
>
> The strength of faith in democratic processes, however, is remarkable. One interpretation for why it took so long for the Occupy Wall Street protests to emerge was that many hoped that the political process would "work" to rein in the financial sector and redress the country's economic problems. It was only when it was evident that they did not that protests

became widespread. The strong voter turnout in 2008 (the highest since 1968) reflects the power of hope.[55]

"Something Bigger Than Electoral Wins"

Hope of a particularly electoral kind, that is. The finance-captive corporatism of the Obama administration encouraged many young and other Americans to pursue "change from the bottom up" (a recurrent Obama campaign mantra in 2007 and 2008) through social movements and protest rather than through elections and faith in politicians. A systematic survey of the OWS protestors in New York City's Zuccotti Park by Fordham University political scientist Costas Panagopoulos and a team of fifteen interviewers in October 2011 found that many of the activists were "disgruntled Democrats." A quarter said they were Democrats, but 39 percent did not identify with any political party. Eleven percent called themselves socialists and 11 percent said they were members of the Green Party.[56] A different poll (a survey of 1,619 respondents polled through the website occupywallst.org) conducted by another academician determined that 69 percent of the movement's supporters considered themselves "Independents."[57]

But polling on party identification may have missed a key and bigger point. Among the many ways in which the Occupy Movement was not "the tea party of the left," as some claimed, was that it was largely outside and hostile to major party politics. The Age of Obama had educated Occupiers not merely on the limits of the current president and the Democrats. It had demonstrated the deeper limits of a narrow money-soaked and corporate-managed political culture focused on candidates, elections, and politicians. A WNYC radio report from Zuccotti Park in early October captured the protestors' broader dissatisfaction with US electoral politics in general:

> In contrast [to the Tea Party], at the Wall Street protests in New York, there's been *little focus on turning widespread dissatisfaction with the status quo into results at the polls.*
>
> "The cold fact … is that people are aware that *our votes are meaningless. It's a whole charade* because it's the lobbyists that count," said Kenny Ladd, a construction worker from Staten Island.
>
> He still counts himself as an Obama supporter, but he said the president didn't really have a chance when money and corporate power reign in Washington.
>
> "Once you join the mechanism, you're part of the machinery," Ladd said. …
>
> That was also the take of Elizabeth Starcevic, a retired CUNY professor who came to the protests after an afternoon union meeting this week: "I think this is a bigger picture. I think this is an intention by the youth to

say it doesn't matter who's in charge. There has to be a fair shake," she said.

That wasn't the case three years ago, when young activists were certain it mattered who was in charge, and they worked for candidate Obama. New Yorker Alyssa Vinnik, now 26, was one of them. She knocked on doors for the campaign in Pennsylvania and Brooklyn, but is not sure she'd be great at it this time around. "I felt very, very convinced in 2008, and think it would be a little bit harder to do that for other people who are skeptical because I feel a little skeptical myself," she said. "I think it's going to be a harder sell."

Wall Street protestor Heather Long, 18, is among the unconvinced. "I'm neither here nor there on Obama," she said.... Long drove up to the protests from Jacksonville, Florida. She's a freshman in college, the first in her family to go—and she's felt the brunt of the bad economy up close. Her dad works construction, and was unemployed for a four-year stretch.... While Long says she's excited to vote for the first time, she doesn't have much hope that a single election will change much.

So many find themselves at Occupy Wall Street, demonstrating for something *bigger—more abstract—than electoral wins* that could alter the balance of power in Washington.[58]

As the OWS "kids" got it that American "democracy" was no less crippled by the dark cloud of high finance and corporate rule when Democrats held the White House, they took the fight beneath the ruling business parties and candidates to the economic root of social, environmental, and political decay. The lesson that the Democratic Party was part of the nation's plutocracy problem was further driven home by the repression meted against protestors by police operating at the command of local urban political machines run mainly by Democrats.

The Plutocrats Keep Their Shirts: Late 2012 and Early 2013

On the first Tuesday of November 2012, Barack Obama won a second term despite Romney's Wall Street fundraising advantage. Obama had run for reelection on the notions that the rich should be taxed more (an idea supported by 60 percent of US voters in an Election Day poll[59]), that Medicare and Social Security should be protected against corporate privatization, and that government had a positive role to play in creating opportunity and security for all Americans, not just the already well-off. The president's populist-sounding campaign tone (more than a little ironic given his first term's consistent service to the wealthy and corporate few) was launched in a December 2011 campaign speech in Osawatomie, Kansas (chosen since it was the site of Theodore Roosevelt's famous 1910 speech demanding a "Square Deal" from big business for working and middle-class Americans), where Obama called economic inequality "the defining issue of our time" and referred without criticism to the "people who've been occupying the streets of New York and other cities"[60]—this even after his Justice and Homeland Security departments had helped coordinate the armed force dismantlement of Occupy.[61]

For his part, Romney seemed straight out of central casting when it came to helping the 1%-friendly Obama pose as a caring and progressive man of the people. Besides advancing the privatization of Medicare and Social Security, the Romney–Paul Ryan ticket promised to drastically cut Medicaid, leaving 27 million poor Americans without health insurance while handing the rich nearly $5 trillion in tax reductions. Consistent with his early 2012 statement that "I'm not concerned about the very poor,"[62] Romney was caught on a cell phone video telling a group of wealthy campaign donors in Boca Raton in May of the same year that nearly half ("47 percent") of the American population were lazy, government-dependent moochers who took no responsibility for their own lives.[63]

Thanks in part to such rhetoric and to his related success in portraying Romney as the out-of-touch personification and agent of the 1%, Obama won 63 percent of voters from households that received less than $30,000 in income in 2011 and 60 percent of voters from households receiving less than $50,000. The polls also indicated that the president had won reelection with a significant popular mandate to increase taxes on the wealthy few, spend government dollars to create jobs, and strengthen the social safety net.[64]

Serious Concerns by International Observers

In his November 6 reelection night speech in Chicago, Obama made strong claims about "why [American] elections matter. It's not small," the president said, "it's big. It's important. Democracy in a nation of 300 million can be noisy and messy.... And when we ... make big decisions as a country, it stirs passions.... These arguments we have are a mark of our liberty, and we can never forget that as we speak, people in distant nations are risking their lives ... for *a chance to* argue *about the issues* that matter—the chance to cast their ballots like we did today."[65]

The Organization for Security and Cooperation in Europe (OSCE) had a much less sanguine take on US elections. A prominent international body of election monitors, it issued a report voicing serious concerns over voting rights, the accuracy of voter lists, and the degree of access given to international observers in the United States. In an assessment of the 2012 contests released one day after the election, the OSCE found much that violated international norms on universal suffrage, one-person-one-vote, and proportionality in voting and representation:

- 50 million of 237 million eligible US voters were unregistered to vote.
- Many voters were listed on multiple electoral lists in different states.
- 4.1 million citizens who are residents of US territories were ineligible to vote.
- 600,000 citizens who are residents of the District of Columbia (DC) could not vote for a US congressperson or a US senator.
- 6 million US citizens were disenfranchised due to a felony conviction, including 2.6 million Americans who had served their sentence.
- The presidential campaign "focused on undecided voters in only a few closely contested states," thanks to the Electoral College system, which awards the presidency not on the basis of the popular vote but through a significantly unrepresentative "winner take all" system that gives all of each state's electoral count to the candidate who polls a plurality in that state.
- Third-party candidates "received minimal attention" from a corporate "broadcast media" that "*dedicated the greater part of their electoral coverage to non-substantive issues* such as daily opinion polls and the holding of campaign events (64 percent), often at the expense of substantive discussion of policy (36 percent)" (emphasis added).
- The elections were "the most expensive to date" and there were "no limits to campaign spending, including from corporations," who were free (under the US Supreme Court's 2010 *Citizens United*) to make unlimited "independent expenditures" for or against a candidate.
- Much of the money spent on the election was "exempt from disclosure requirements, raising transparency concerns."
- There were "instances of long queues of voters and shortages in polling station staff that caused delays in voting."
- A number of states including the key battleground state of Ohio prevented the OSCE from fully monitoring the election.
- The competitiveness of election contests in many US congressional districts was low thanks to the role of state-level "partisan considerations" in the drawing of congressional districts.[66]

The OSCE report was a far-from-shining appraisal for the nation that claims to be the exceptional global homeland and headquarters of freedom and democracy. The problems discovered by the European observers help explain why just 126 million Americans voted, a comparatively low turnout rate of 57.5 percent—hardly what one would expect from a beacon to the world of popular self-governance.[67]

"The Plutocrats Lost Their Shirts"

"Among the losers in the United States are the super-rich, who spent unprecedented millions to evict President Barack Obama from the White House. On Tuesday night," Freeland declared the day after the election, "the plutocrats lost their shirts." Esteemed liberal Yale political scientist Jacob S. Hacker told Freeland that the election's outcome means "that your vote matters. If you can mobilize your votes, that is a pretty strong antidote to the role of money in politics."[68]

These judgments were premature and a bit naïve. Obama was able to succeed in mobilizing voters because he had once again drunk deeply at the big money political finance well (the Obama campaign raised more than $1 billion through September 2012[69]) and attended more elite fundraisers than the last five incumbent presidents combined by the end of April 2012[70] and because he tapped the power of the advertising and public relations industries to conduct history's most audacious and sophisticated voter marketing and data mining operation—a political market research and sales operation that left Romney's handlers awestruck.[71] To make matters worse for Hacker's judgment, big corporate money and media had combined to keep numerous issues of great significance off the table of the campaign and election. Among the problem and policy areas that were pushed aside, consistent with the OSCE's findings on the media's election coverage: economic inequality and its many negative consequences, including plutocracy; the climate catastrophe; mass poverty; mass structural unemployment; endangered civil liberties; the persistent dangerous underregulation of the financial sector; besieged union organizing rights, corporate media monopoly, and the ecological risks of rampant and expanded offshore drilling and domestic hydraulic fracturing ("fracking").[72]

From Electoral Extravaganza to "Fiscal Cliff"

As if all this wasn't sufficient to take the democratic risks out of the 2012 election, the unelected dictatorship had made sure to fix the terms of the postelection political and policy debate. It preinstalled the next great elite-manufactured budget crisis—the so-called fiscal cliff drama—as the mass media's top leading domestic news story in the immediate wake of the election. Literally overnight, the nation's politicians and leading news and commentary media became outwardly obsessed again with US government debt—with "the deficit." A coalition of ninety-five powerful, deep-pockets corporate and financial CEOs who called themselves "Fix the Debt" exhorted the nation to slash social expenditure and "entitlement programs" (Social Security and Medicare) in the name of *"shared sacrifice."*[73] It was a remarkable demand after three-plus decades in which American middle- and working-class incomes and benefits had stagnated and declined while (as we shall examine in the following chapter) the wealth and income of the very rich skyrocketed into "New Gilded Age" levels. It was also irresponsible in a country plagued by mass unemployment, endemic job insecurity, and related widespread poverty. As numerous liberal economists including Nobel laureates Krugman and Stiglitz pointed out, deficit spending was required as a stimulus to recovery and deficits are overcome by the growth that follows. This occurred after World War II, when the deficit was much larger.[74]

Populist- and progressive-sounding presidential campaigns and elections aside, a highly organized and class-conscious section of the economic elite seemed determined to roll back ordinary Americans' sense that they deserved decent treatment now and in their senior years, after decades of hard work and contribution to public retirement programs. "You're going to have to do something," Goldman Sachs CEO Lloyd Blankfein told CBS News in mid-November 2012, "to lower peoples' expectations of what they're going to get, the entitlements and all people think they're going to get, because you're not going to get it."[75] It was a fascinating if awkward comment from a super-entitled $16 million-per-year executive who sat atop a leading financial firm that had helped push the national and global economy (and the federal budget, it's worth noting) over *the cliff*—and then profited handsomely from that collapse with help from billions of dollars in federal taxpayer bailout money. Blankfein was a leading spokesman for Fix the Debt, which had raised more than $60 million to lobby for a "debt deal" that would make significant long-term cuts in so-called entitlements—Social Security, Medicare, and Medicaid—in return for some very mild increases in income taxes on the nation's richest 2 percent of income "earners."[76] Progressive commentator Roger Bybee captured the plutocratic essence of the "grand bargain" offered by the captains of corporate and financial America: "For the top 1% of mega-millionaires and billionaires, the ... 'sacrifices' [are] so minor that they will not even notice, especially when they rake in the gains from ... new corporate tax breaks for which they are pressing.... Blankfein holds out the tantalizing prospect of a vast wave of new corporate investment in America once the CEOs' demands are met. All this requires is ... draconian, life-shattering changes in Social Security and Medicare."[77]

Why were Blankfein and other Wall Street "deficit scolds"[78] going after the nation's public pension system, Social Security, a well-managed and widely popular program that didn't feed the dreaded federal deficit since it was self-funded? Beneath an ocean of deceptive bluster about the system's supposed crisis (a long-standing Wall Street propaganda myth), the financial elite didn't want to pay taxes for lesser Americans' pensions and (more important) wanted to cash in on the privatization of the masses' retirement accounts, which promised to provide a fee and investment bonanza for those expert at raking in profits from others' savings. There was deep self-interest behind the "millionaires' movement" for what Blankfein and other Fix the Debt leaders called "fiscal responsibility" and "shared sacrifice." And if they didn't get what they wanted, Blankfein et al. warned, then the economy would collapse into a new recession under the terms of the "fiscal cliff" agreement worked up between the president and the heavily Wall Street–supported right-wing Republican House of Representatives to end the summer 2011 "budget ceiling" drama—another elite-manufactured crisis.

Meanwhile, a study released by the Institute for Policy Studies (IPS) in late November 2012 showed that fifty-four CEOs on Fix the Debt coalition's Fiscal Leadership Council had together accumulated pension assets of more than $649 million from their firms' executive retirement plans. Seventy-one CEOs affiliated with Fix the Debt sat atop publicly traded companies. Of those seventy-one companies, less than sixty offered pension plans to their employees. Among the forty-one companies that did provide pension systems, IPS found, all but two had failed to contribute enough to their employees' pension funds to pay out their expected obligations. The total deficit among these thirty-nine companies' pension funds was more than $100 billion. The IPS study bore a clever and devastating title: *A Pension Deficit Disorder: The Massive CEO Retirement Funds and Underfunded Worker Pension Funds at Firms Pushing Social Security Cuts.*[79]

Like the fake Social Security crisis, the postelection talk of an imminent economic crisis resulting from the "fiscal cliff" was fear-mongering propaganda. It was based on a crass exaggeration of the extent to which the tax and spending changes promised if the "cliff" was breached would undo the economic recovery. It drastically understated the extent to which other, far more important factors (declining household income, continued underlying contraction of business investment, European recession, global trade contraction) could produce a return to recession.

Behind the notion of an impending fiscal disaster lay the real agenda of the nation's super-elite: preserving tax cuts for the rich and their corporations, increasing the tax burden on the middle class, and "taking back the accumulated social wages of tens of millions of Americans that is sometimes called 'entitlements'—i.e., Social Security benefits and Medicare." All "the hype and talk about a Fiscal cliff," progressive economist Jack Rasmus noted in early January 2013, was "just a cover for what will be the introduction of America's version of an austerity program" including "cuts in spending and entitlements backloaded to the out years of a ten-year agreement of about $4 trillion ... reducing deductions and credits now enjoyed by the middle class.... More out-of-pocket costs for Medicare. Age eligibility, disability eligibility, and cost of living hits to Social Security retirement benefits. Defense cuts limited to Afghan war drawdowns that were going to happen anyway."[80]

Déjà Vu: A Fiscal Gift to the 1%

The reelected president was once again to betray working and poor people to please the rich in the "deal" he cut with Republicans to avert a government shutdown at the end of December 2012. By making most of George W. Bush's tax cuts for the rich permanent, Obama frittered away the big bargaining chip he could have used to preserve safety-net social programs in subsequent negotiating rounds. The December 31 "deal" extended unemployment insurance, but that temporary relief for the nonaffluent was considerably outdone by giant long-term giveaways to the wealthy few. Estate taxes were repealed for all but the wealthiest 0.1 percent, with a giant exemption of $10.5 million per couple. The agreement retained a corporate tax loophole that permitted multinational firms to avoid taxes on their foreign subsidiaries even as it hit workers with a big increase in their Social Security payroll taxes. The "bargain" also put in place painfully low capital gains and dividend rates of 15 to 20 percent, "ensuring," as Jill Stein ruefully observed, "that billionaire bosses everywhere will pay lower tax rates than their secretaries."[81] Sue Sturgis, an economic researcher with the Institute for South Studies, gave an interesting title to her reflections on the year-end agreement between Obama and congressional Republicans: "For the 1 Percent, a Fiscal Gift from Congress."

The "fig leaf" Obama used to "cover this surrender" was "a token increase" on wealthy households "earning" over $450,000 per year. This was a "brazen retreat from his promise to raise taxes on those earning over $250,000, a meager reform to begin with in a tax system already rife with favors to the rich.... If you're having political déjà vu as Obama's second term in the White House gets underway," Stein wrote, "you're not alone. The supposedly populist candidate—who won re-election promising to tax the rich, protect Social Security and make the economy fair—has morphed backed into an invaluable ally of the economic elite. Yet again, he's willing to let people fall under the bus."[82]

In his 2012 "fiscal cliff" negotiations as in his 2011 debt-ceiling dealings, Obama proposed distressing cuts to core safety-net programs in the supposedly urgent name of "deficit reduction"—cuts to be considered in subsequent negotiations. In doing so, he betrayed his core campaign promise to protect Social Security. It was an alarming performance on behalf of the rich in a time when, as Stein noted, nearly one in three Americans was either officially poor or low-income and more than one in three senior US citizens relied on Social Security to stay out of poverty.[83]

The Real Program

So what if, as the leading liberal Katrina vanden Heuvel noted, "Americans have just voted to reelect the president with clear priorities," including

"Washington ... get[ting] to work creating jobs ... [and] rais[ing] taxes on the richest two percent ... to invest in areas vital to our future, as he pledged repeatedly across the country?"[84] And so what if, as numerous liberal and progressive economists led by Stiglitz noted, the US economic situation called for the government to spend more, not less, so as to reduce joblessness, in the short term?[85] So what if austerity (slashed spending) would increase the likelihood of renewed recession and if deficits are best overcome with the growth that follows significantly increased spending, as occurred after World War II, when the deficit was much larger? And so what if the contemporary federal deficit is itself primarily a product of the recession, caused by the misbehavior and hyper-opulence of the financial and corporate elite, whose insistence on enjoying low taxes feeds inequality, the deficit, and economic stagnation?[86]

American major party election contests and campaign rhetoric are largely for show, cloaking the real mechanisms of policy and power. As Rasmus all-too-easily foretold just three days after Obama's 2012 victory,

> the *real economic program* for the next four years is about to be revealed.... The economic promises of both candidates during the election were *only talk, both candidates telling their constituencies what they thought they wanted to hear*. Now *the real thing*—the economic program—is about to appear.... Stay tuned for the next few weeks, as the political fog called US national elections slowly burns off and the *true outlines of the real program* being cooked behind the scenes ... by the powerful economic and political elites of both parties becomes clear.[87]

The real and bipartisan program was austerity for the poor and the rest, alongside record-setting profits for the few and their leading corporations and financial institutions.[88] Serving the broad populace and the common good was not on the nation's real masters' agenda, whatever the progressive-sounding election-time rhetoric of politicians. "At a time when the federal government should be supporting its citizens by providing them with the tools to survive in a global economy," the liberal, multiple Pulitzer Prize–winning investigative journalists Donald L. Barlett and James B. Steele noted earlier in the year, "the government has abandoned them. It is exactly what members of *the ruling class* want. The last thing they want is an activist government.... Their attitude is 'let the market sort it out'.... Now that same *ruling class* and its cheerleaders in Congress are pushing mightily for a balanced budget at any cost."[89]

Inauguration for Sale

In early January 2012 it was reported that the plutocratic penetration of presidential politics extended even to the president's forthcoming second inauguration. In 2009, Obama's Presidential Inaugural Committee raised $53 million to host 1.8 million visitors to the nation's capital. The money was garnered from individuals only, with no corporate contributions accepted and donations capped at $50,000. This time, with half the previous number of visitors expected, the Presidential Inaugural Committee sought to raise the same amount but this time with no limits on corporate donations or on the size of donations. The committee solicited commitments as high as $1 million and was working with large corporations who participated in the hope of enhancing "access" to the administration in its second term.[90]

Nobody Home

Nearly a month after the president's second inauguration, an estimated 30,000 to 50,000 people marched in front of 1600 Pennsylvania Avenue. They came to ask Obama to refuse to approve the Keystone XL pipeline—a project that, if completed, would carry more than 700,000 barrels of dirty Canadian tar sands oil a day from Alberta to the southern US Gulf Coast. As numerous environmental scientists including leading climate expert James Hansen (director of NASA's Goddard Institute for Space Studies) warned, Alberta's giant stash of tar sands oil is an epic "carbon bomb" whose release promised to push Earth's climate past the tipping point of irreversible runaway warming. If all the crude in the deforested tar sands region were burned, Hansen calculated, the quantity of carbon dioxide in the atmosphere would rise from its current 390 parts per million to 600 ppm, pushing Earth over the climate cliff, leading to what Hansen called "Game Over" for the planet.

Many of the demonstrators mistakenly believed they had good reasons to expect Obama to side with the majority of Americans who thought it was time to act in defense of the climate. "For the sake of our children," the president had said in his February 2013 State of the Union address, "we must do more to combat climate change." But Obama had done little to back up those words with any meaningful action, and the chances he would act to block Keystone were slim. And moments after noting in his address that "the 12 hottest years on record have all come in the last 15," Obama boasted that his "administration will keep cutting red tape and speeding up new oil and gas permits." He wasn't about to defy "the fossil fuel lobby, which certainly isn't as big as half the US population, but makes up for it in spending power."[91]

Indeed, the president wasn't at home when Hansen and his fellow climate demonstrators came calling. Obama was out socializing with a fossil fuel plutocrat, tellingly enough. He was "in Florida, golfing with Houston Astros owner Jim Crane, who has interests in fracking and natural gas pipelines, and who even invested in the Deepwater Horizon drilling platform that dumped oil into the Gulf of Mexico in the spring and summer of 2010."[92]

The Grim Grand Bargain vs. the Invisible Green New Deal

The austerity advanced by the rich and powerful in defiance of public opinion and national economic common sense in the wake of Obama's second "progressive mandate" marched forward on March 1, 2013. That's when significant across-the-board federal budget cuts mandated by the Budget Control Act—the legislation agreed to by Obama and Congress to end the debt-ceiling crisis in the summer of 2011—went into effect as a result of the president and Congress's failure to sign a comprehensive "deficit reduction deal" at the beginning of 2013. The $85 billion in automatic spending reductions were inflexibly imposed on domestic social programs—no small problem in the United States, home to the highest poverty rate and most extreme inequality among all rich nations. To name one terrible consequence, 70,000 poor preschool children were slated for removal from the successful Head Start program in the name of this regressive "sequestration."[93]

The following month Obama released his Fiscal Year 2014 budget proposal. Claiming to offer an alternative to sequester, the White House led the charge to roll back Social Security and Medicare, the crown jewel liberal-Democratic safety-net programs of the 1930s and 1960s. Promoting the "Grand Bargain" with ruthless corporate Republicans that Obama had talked about for years, the president's budget called for $400 billion in Medicare and other health care cuts, requiring senior citizens to increase their payments or face reduced coverage. Obama advocated the "means testing" of Medicare, a long-standing elite strategy for reducing public support for social programs by limiting their benefits to the nonaffluent. Obama also advanced the reduction of Social Security benefits by calling for a "chained CPI" method to determine cost-of-living increases to those benefits. Under the dubious market calculations proposed by the White House, average US retirees would lose more than 2 percent of their incomes, "more than three times the burden imposed by Obama's nominal tax increase on the rich last year." Obama targeted Social Security in brazen defiance of a February 2013 Pew survey showing that just one in ten Americans wanted to cut Social Security while more than four in ten actually wanted to increase Social Security benefits. He did so despite the modesty of US Social Security payment levels (an average of just $1,480 per month per retiree) and despite the facts that nearly two-thirds (65 percent) of US seniors relied on Social Security for the majority of their cash income, that more than one-third (36 percent) relied on it for 90 percent of their income, and that more than 40 percent of elderly Americans would have incomes below the federal poverty line without Social Security.[94]

Reflecting on the plutocratic absurdity of it all last April, the eloquent but officially invisible presidential candidate Jill Stein offered an excellent statement of what was called for to address both the economic crisis and the climate crisis—putting millions to work while attacking the urgent problem of global warming and guaranteeing reasonably priced health care for all:

> The real solution to the recession is to jump start the economy through a massive job creation program.... An alternative to the grim Grand Bargain is offered by the Green New Deal, a package of emergency reforms proposed by the Green Party. This approach would end both the economic crisis and the climate crisis in one fell swoop. It would create 25 million jobs in green energy, sustainable agriculture, public transportation and infrastructure improvements—as well as jobs that meet our social needs, including teachers, nurses, day care, affordable housing, drug abuse and violence prevention and rehabilitation. It would be funded by scaling back the oversized military budget to year 2000 levels, adopting a Medicare-for-All insurance system that would save trillions of dollars, requiring Wall Street gamblers to pay a small (0.5%) sales tax, taxing capital gains as income, and taxing income more progressively. These key provisions of the Green New Deal enjoy majority public support in poll after poll.
>
> The Green New Deal addresses the concocted deficit/debt problems by solving the bigger, underlying crises of an unraveling economy and accelerating climate catastrophe.[95]

It was characteristic of the unelected dictatorship's hold that Stein's powerful and synthetic reflection and alternative proposal was thoroughly ignored in the nation's dominant corporate mass media, like her candidacy. (We shall return to the Green New Deal in Chapter 6.)

The plutocrats had *kept their shirts and more.* The latest presidential election spectacle was in the books as another monument to what author Christopher Hitchens cleverly described as "the essence of American politics": "the manipulation of populism by elitism."[96]

CHAPTER 2

Richistan and the Rest of Us
The Second Gilded Age and Why It Matters

If there was a gold medal for inequality, the United States would win hands down.

—Harvard economist Richard B. Freeman, 2007[1]

The Great Compression

You wouldn't know it from the characteristically amnesiac way in which America mass media covered the Occupy Rebellion, but large-scale popular fear and anger directed at concentrated wealth have a long and rich history in the United States.[2] That fear and anger have always been rooted in harsh class disparities that have defied the nation's reigning "land of equality" mythology. The problem of socioeconomic inequity goes back to the beginning of the American historical experience but reached its peak in the late nineteenth century. By the early twentieth century, following the notorious inequality of the Gilded Age, when most of the nation's stupendous new "robber baron" fortunes grew out of heavy industry and railroads, wealth inequality had become as great in the United States as in France or Prussia, though still less drastic than in England.[3] A contemporary analysis in 1890 argued that the nation's top 1 percent owned more than half the nation's wealth, up from 26 percent in 1860.[4] A generation later, in 1922, more reliable data showed that the richest 1 percent controlled 37 percent of the nation's net worth. That percentage rose to its twentieth-century peak of 44 percent in 1929,[5] on the eve of the Great Depression and after a decade in which the top 5 percent garnered half the growth in US income and (thanks largely to a remarkable stock market boom) the number of US millionaires rose from 5,000 to 35,000.[6] Poverty was nonetheless rampant in the Roaring Twenties, when two-thirds of US households lived on annual incomes below $2,000, understood to be the minimum family budget for a decent and healthy standard of living. Hardship reached epic levels during the 1930s, of course, when food lines and mass hunger were widely visible and unemployment never fell below 14 percent, peaking at 25 percent in 1933.[7] In his second inaugural address in 1937, Franklin Roosevelt spoke with reason of "one-third of a nation still in poverty."[8]

Though disparities in wealth have been present throughout American history, the contours of that inequality have shifted significantly over time. As economic historians Jeffrey Williamson and Peter Lindert have noted, "The inequality of [US] wealth has not been an eternal constant." Inequality declined during the 1860s, when overall national inequality was reduced by slave emancipation and as new inequalities were opened up between North and South. Inequality also fell "briefly but sharply" during World War I and then for five decades between the onset of the Great Depression and the onset of the Reagan era.[9] The biggest and by far the longest decline in American economic disparity took place during these years. Across the long post–World War II boom from 1945 through the early 1970s, during the so-called golden age of US-led Western capitalism, the rich actually lost ground relative to the rest of America as much of the nation's middle- and working-class majority went on an unprecedented mass shopping spree for cars, homes, appliances, and more. In what economists Claudia Goldin and Robert Margo call "the Great Compression" and the historian Judith Stein calls "the Age of Compression,"[10] the share of the nation's wealth owned by the top 1 percent fell strikingly, from 36 percent in the late 1930s to 20 percent in the middle 1970s. Already by the middle 1950s, the Nobel Prize–winning economist Paul Krugman notes, the post-tax incomes of the nation's top 1 percent were 20 to 30 percent lower than they had been a generation before. The after-tax incomes of the top one-thousandth had fallen by more than half since the 1920s. Over the same period real median US income doubled, so that "the majority of Americans were able, for the first time, to afford a decent standard of living," with a majority of families owning a car and 70 percent possessing telephones by 1955. At the same time, the wage difference between unskilled and skilled workers and the pay premium enjoyed by professionals fell considerably.[11] "For thirty years after World War II," Joseph Stiglitz notes, "America grew together—with growth in income in every segment, but with those at the bottom growing faster than those at the top."[12]

The point should not be exaggerated. The stubborn and related problems of poverty and inequality continued through the booming 1960s. Across the entire postwar period (1945–1971), Howard Zinn noted in 1973, the bottom tenth of the US population—20 million Americans—experienced no progress whatsoever in increasing their share of national income (a paltry 1 percent).

Corporate profits and CEO salaries rose significantly across the 1960s boom, but deep poverty remained deeply entrenched in "the golden age" of Western and American capitalism.[13] As Zinn elaborated,

> Being rich or poor was more than a statistic; it profoundly determined how an American lived. In postwar United States, how much money Americans had determined whether or not they lived in a home with rats or vermin; whether or not their home was such that their children were more likely to die in a fire; whether or not they could get adequate medical and dental care; whether or not they got arrested, and, if they did, whether or not they spent time in jail before trial, whether they got a fair trial, a long or a short sentence, whether or not they got parole. How much money Americans had determined whether or not their children would be born alive. It determined whether or not Americans had a vacation; whether they needed to hold down more than one job; whether or not they had enough to eat; whether or not they could influence a congressman or run for office; whether or not a man was drafted, and what chances a man had that he would die in combat.[14]

As the nation spent billions to put astronauts on the moon, millions of Americans remained ill-clad, ill-fed, and ill-housed. A *New York Times* report on July 13, 1969, at the height of postwar prosperity, captured the dark irony during the week when the first moon-landing flight was launched:

> Within the shadow of the John F. Kennedy Space Center, the hungry people sit and watch.
>
> They sit on wooden porches near Highway 520 each evening and watch as the out-of-state cars crammed with tourists stream into Cocoa Beach and surrounding towns of Brevard County.
>
> They sit and watch the early morning crush of cars filled with engineers and technicians moving toward "the Cape," 18 miles north, in the feverish days before the Moon launching on Wednesday morning.
>
> "The irony is so apparent here," said Dr. Henry Jerkins, the county's only Negro doctor. "We're spending all this money to go to the moon and here, right here in Brevard, I treat malnourished children with prominent ribs and pot bellies. I do see hunger."[15]

It wasn't just the officially poor whose material reality did not jibe with the much-ballyhooed notion that America had entered an age of mass affluence. As historian Judith Stein notes, "Affluence was as much as an ideology as a description of US society [in the 1950s and 1960s]. Politicians and academics forgot that the non-poor included many who were non-rich." The median

US family income in 1968 was $8,362, significantly up from its 1947 level ($3,031) but less than what the Bureau of Labor Statistics defined as a "modest but adequate" income for an urban family of four. The bureau found that 30 percent of the nation's working-class families were living in poverty and another 30 percent were living above poverty but still below the following austere "intermediate" family budget:

> a toaster that will last for 33 years, a refrigerator and a range that will each last for 17 years, a vacuum cleaner that will last for 14 years, and a television set that will last for 10 years … a two year old car that [will last] 4 years [with a] tune up once a year, a brake alignment once a year every 3 years, and front end alignment every 4 years…. The husband will buy one year round suit every 4 years, 1 top coat every 8.5 years … take his wife to a movie once every 3 months…. The average family's 2 children are each allowed one movie every 4 weeks. A total of two dollars and fifty-four cents per person is allowed for admission to all other events, from football and baseball games to plays or concerts. The budget allows nothing whatsoever for savings.[16]

Yet if it was too much to say that post-WWII America had replaced capitalism and its class distinctions with "mutualism" or "industrial democracy"* or to claim (as many leading social scientists believed[17]) it had moved into a postmaterial age of abundance, it nonetheless remains true that millions of Americans had reason to feel that the United States had emerged from the traumas of the Great Depression and World War II as something of a "middle-class nation." Between 1947 and 1973, real annual income for American families grew on average nearly 3 percent, with the highest increases going to those at the bottom.[18] As Krugman notes,

> America in the 1950s *was a middle-class society, to a far greater extent than it had been in the 1920s—or than it is today.*… Ordinary workers and their families had *good reason to feel that they were sharing in the nation's prosperity as never before.* And, on the other side, the rich were a lot less rich than they had been a generation earlier.… Somehow, Franklin Roosevelt and Harry Truman managed to preside over a dramatic downward redistribution of income and wealth that made America far more equal than ever before.…

---

* This claim was made in the widely read weekly magazine *Readers' Digest* and reported favorably in a best-selling American book published early in the postwar era: see Frederick Lewis Allen, *The Big Change: America Transforms Itself, 1900–1950* (New York: Bantam, 1952).

The postwar generation was a time when almost everyone in America felt that living standards were rising rapidly, a time in which ordinary Americans felt that they were achieving a level of prosperity beyond their parents' wildest dreams.[19]

With the material fortunes of many millions of working Americans improving while those of the rich fell in comparative terms, a real sense of economic and social democratization took hold in postwar America. As Krugman notes, in a reflection drawing on personal memory as well as empirical research,

F. Scott Fitzgerald's remark that the rich "are different from you and me" has never, before or since, been less true than it was in the generation that followed World War II.... The rich might have had bigger houses than most people, but they could no longer afford to live in vast mansions—in particular, they couldn't afford the servants necessary to maintain those mansions. The traditional differences in dress between the rich and everyone else had largely vanished, partly because ordinary workers could now afford to wear (and clean) good clothes, partly because the rich could no longer afford to dress in a style that required legions of servants to help them get into and out of their wardrobes. Even the rich man's advantage in mobility—to this day high-end stores are said to cater to the "carriage trade"—had vanished now that most people had cars ... [and] all this contributed to a new sense of dignity among ordinary Americans.[20]

Across what Krugman calls "the Long Gilded Age" (from the late nineteenth century through the 1930s), US society was pervaded by a top-down class consciousness wherein the rich considered themselves "the betters" of everyone else and working people cringed in fear of "the bosses."[21] In 1997 the pioneer neoconservative Irving Kristol recalled an older, pre–World War II America where "distinctions of social class were still quite visible. Industrial workers still wore cloth caps, drank beer and rye whiskey. Their 'betters' wore fedoras and drank Scotch or wine."[22] Such sentiments and cultural signifiers of class disappeared to no small extent in postwar America, when "a worker protected by a secure union, as many were, had as secure a job and often nearly as high an income as a highly trained professional."[23] It helped that real wages rose consistently for fifteen straight years, underpinning the most explosive growth in mass consumption in American or world history. By 1956 the real income of the average American was more than 50 percent higher than it had been in 1929. In 1960 that income was 35 percent higher than it had been at the end of World War II.[24] (It also helped, as I will suggest in the following chapter, that the United States dominated the international economy to an unprecedented degree during these years.)

The New Gilded Age

A New Oligarchy Arises

The equalizing trend did not last more than a generation. "In contrast with the previous periods of wealth-leveling," Williamson and Lindert wrote in 1980, "the [mid-]twentieth century leveling has not been reversed.... From 1929 until mid-century, wealth inequality seems to have undergone a permanent reduction, ... paralleling the movement in income inequality."[25] These observations were obsolete the minute they hit the page they were written on. The Great Compression did not survive into the final fifth of the previous century. As Hedrick Smith notes, "The explosive Jack-and-the-Beanstalk growth of a new economic oligarchy took off in the late 1970s ... spawning the third wave of great private wealth in US [modern] history" after the Gilded Age (1880s–1890s) and the Roaring Twenties.[26]

In 1980 the top 1 percent of Americans had 9 percent of overall national income, roughly the same level it had received since the end of World War II. By 2007 the top one-hundredth's take was 23 percent—an income disparity "not seen in the United States since 1928, a time of Robber Baron wealth, stock manipulation schemes, and vast poverty."[27] Meanwhile, wealth concentrated back to near-1920s levels, with the top 1 percent controlling 38 percent of the nation's net worth by 1998—the highest percentage since, again, the end of the 1920s. Between 1983 and 2001 the top 1 percent gobbled up 28 percent of the rise in American income, 33 percent of the gain in national wealth, and 52 percent of the growth in financial net worth.[28]

The disparities deepened in the new millennium. During the nation's weak expansion between 2002 and 2007, the top 1 percent (3 million people) received fully *two-thirds of the nation's income growth*. The other 99 percent got "one-third of the gains to divide among 310 million people."[29] As US senator Bernie Sanders (I-VT) noted in the wake of the Occupy Movement's emergence, the top 1 percent by 2005 received more income than the bottom 50 percent of Americans—"with the top 300,000 earners making more money than the bottom 150 million."[30] By 2007, Stiglitz reports, "the average after-tax income of the top 1 percent had reached $1.3 million, but that of the bottom 20 percent amounted to only $17,800. *The top 1 percent get in one week 40 percent more than the bottom fifth receive in a year; the top 0.1 percent received in a day and a half about what the bottom 90 percent received in a year*; and the richest 20 percent of income earners earn in total after tax more than the bottom 80 percent combined."[31] In 2010, the leading inequality analyst and economist Emmanuel Saez determined, the top 1 percent garnered fully 93 percent of the nation's income gains.[32]

By the time Occupy Wall Street arose, *the 400 richest Americans possessed more wealth than the entire bottom half of the US population—150 million US citizens.*[33] *The top 1 percent possessed as much as the bottom 90 percent,*[34] a reflection among other things of the fact that the lowest two US wealth quintiles (the bottom 40 percent) of the United States controlled *an astonishingly paltry 0.3 percent of the nation's net worth, essentially nothing.*[35]

By the account of labor economist Sylvia Allegretto in December 2011, six Waltons—five children and one daughter-in-law of Sam and James "Bud" Walton (the founders of Wal-Mart, whose previously unimaginable profits flowed from the import of cheap goods manufactured abroad and especially in China) had a total net worth of $69.7 billion in 2007. This was equal to the total wealth of the entire bottom 30 percent, Allegretto found, citing the triennial Survey of Consumer Finances. It was a remarkable finding given reports that Wal-Mart was cutting back health care coverage for part-time workers and raising premiums for many full-time staff and in light of the fact that Wal-Mart wages were so low that nearly a third of the company's workforce received public assistance.[36]

In July 2012, Senator Sanders told his Twitter followers that the Waltons now owned "more wealth than the bottom 40 percent of America." His stark observation was judged accurate by the *Tampa Bay Times*'s Pulitzer Prize–winning fact-checking website PolitiFact.com, which noted that typical US families lost an astonishing 39 percent of their wealth between 2007 and 2010, with median family net worth falling from $126,400 to $77,300 during those years. Across the same period, the wealth of the Walton family members rose from $73.3 billion to $89.5 billion, a nearly 22 percent increase.[37]

Consider also executive pay. In 1980 the CEOs of major American companies received "earnings" equal to average American wages multiplied by forty. Ten years later, the typical US big firm CEO took home 100 times more than the typical US worker. In 2007, on the eve of the Great Recession, the total CEO package had blown up to 350 times the income of that worker. In 1968, to make the change especially crystal clear, the CEO of General Motors (GM)—the largest US company at the time—received roughly sixty-six times the wages and benefits of the typical GM worker. Just more than a generation later, in 2005, the CEO of America's largest company, Wal-Mart, "earned" 900 times the pay and benefits of the typical Wal-Mart worker.[38]

This historic hyperconcentration of wealth and income began in the late 1970s, gathered force in the 1980s, and went stratospheric (with a brief lull during the late 1990s) between 1990 and 2007. By the latter year, the United States was home to more than 10 million millionaire households and to more than half a million households worth in excess of $10 million—more than double the numbers in 1990. Never before had so many Americans become so wealthy so fast. The upward distribution was without historical parallel in terms of the number of super-wealthy Americans created and (as we shall see below) in terms of the nation's position in global rankings for inequality. The original Gilded Age and the stock market boom of the 1920s may have generated richer single individuals relative to the overall economy (John D. Rockefeller was estimated at the turn of the twentieth century to possess wealth equal to 1.5 percent of the American GDP), but "the Second Gilded Age" that took off in the 1980s and expanded through the 1990s and 2000s has "eclipsed all others," Robert Frank notes, "when it came to the sheer number of new millionaires and billionaires. The combined annual incomes of the top 1 percent exploded to $1.7 trillion, *greater than the annual GDP of Canada.* Their wealth topped $21 trillion at its peak in 2007."[39]

Frank's observation is echoed in what the financial heiress and novelist Holly Peterson told Chrystia Freeland in 2010, as millions of Americans reeled from the devastating effects of an epic recession caused to some degree by the manipulations of the heiress's father—a hedge fund titan. "There's so much money on the Upper East Side right now," Peterson said. "If you look at the original movie *Wall Street,* it was a phenomenon where there were men in their 30s and 40s making $2 and $3 million a year, and that was disgusting. But then you had the Internet age, and then globalization, and you had people in their 30s, through hedge funds and Goldman Sachs partner jobs, who were making $20, $30, $40 million a year. And there were a lot of them doing it. *I think people making $5 million to $10 million definitely don't think they are making enough money."*[40]

"A Parallel Country of the Rich"

In the mid-2000s, Robert Frank became the first *Wall Street Journal* reporter to focus full time on the lives of the nation's super-rich. Frank went into the American aristocracy's world. His research involved "hanging around yacht marinas, slipping into charity balls, loitering in Ferrari dealerships, and scoping out the Sotheby's and Christie's auctions." Frank "studied up on trust law, high-end investing, and the latest trends in charitable giving. [He] grilled the top luxury realtors, jet brokers, party planners, and escort managers" and "asked [rich people] endless questions," getting them "to talk openly about their money and their lives."[41] His journey into the upper-crust was eye-opening, to say the least. He discovered what he described as a *separate nation within the nation*—"a parallel country of the rich" that he labeled "Richistan." By Frank's account,

Today's rich had formed their own virtual country. They were, in fact, wealthier than most nations. By 2004, the richest 1 percent of Americans were earning about $1.35 trillion a year—greater than the total national incomes of France, Italy, or Canada ... and with their huge numbers, they had built a self-contained *world unto themselves*, complete with their own health-care systems (concierge doctors), travel network (Net Jets, destination clubs), separate economy (double-digit income gains and double-digit inflation), and language ("Whose your household manager?"). They didn't just hire gardening crews; they hired "personal arborists." The rich weren't just getting richer; they were becoming financial foreigners, creating their own *country within a country, their own society within a society, and their economy within an economy.*[42]

"Richistan," Frank observed, was itself divided into three levels of millionaire distinguished by levels of net worth and spending, values, and source of wealth:

	Lower Richistan	Middle Richistan	Upper Richistan
Household Net Worth	$1 million–$10 million	$10 million–$100 million	$100 million–$1 billion
Population	7.5 million households	More than 2 million households	In the thousands
Chief Source of Wealth	Salaries, small business, equity	Business ownership, equity, salaries	Business ownership, equity
Average 2006 Spending	Watches: $2,100	Watches: $71,000	Watches: $182,000
	Cars: $44,000	Cars: $158,000	Cars: $311,000
	Jewelry: $9,200	Jewelry: $126,000	Jewelry: $397,000
	Spa services: $5,300	Spa services: $42,000	Spa services: $169,000
Value of Primary Residence	$810,000	$3.8 million	$16.2 million

Source: Robert Frank, *Richistan: A Journey through the American Wealth Boom and the Lives of the New Rich* (New York: Crown, 2007), 8.

The lower one stood in the Richistan schema, Frank found, the more one derived one's wealth from employment-based professional income and the more likely one was to be politically conservative, in debt, and susceptible to anxiety over one's own economic and social status. At the top ("Upper Richistan"), Frank determined, families worth $100 million or more possessed so much personal wealth that their households required "family offices—large companies dedicated entirely to serving a family's day-to-day needs, from investments and legal work to travel plans and hiring house staff. Upper Richistanis rarely open their own mail or pay their own bills, which may help explain why the average annual spa bill in Upper Richistan is $170,000."

The peak of the wealth pyramid was held by the nation's 400 to 1,000 billionaires, whose "personal lives are more like companies. Their homes are like hotels, purchasing budgets and legions of staff. Ask a billionaire for his or her bank statement and you'll get a five-level flowchart of interlocking subsidiaries, holding companies, investments funds, and foundations."[43] Here is the 2005 expense statement for one billionaire household that shared its financial information with Frank:

Mortgages	none
Real Estate Taxes	$900,000
Insurance	$500,000
Utilities	$700,000
House Staff and Personal Assistants	$2,200,000
Annual Maintenance of Real Estate	$900,000
Charity, Philanthropic Events	$3,000,000
Restaurants/Bars	$250,000
Cars	$1,000,000
Personal Beauty/Salon/Spa	$200,000 (includes $80,000 for massage)
Clothing	$300,000
Air Charters/Private Jet	$3,000,000
Club Memberships	$500,000
Political Contributions	$100,000
Yacht(s) (purchased new boat last year)	$20,000,000 ($1,500,000 for salaries alone)
Entertaining (at house)	$2,000,000

Consider also the reporting of leading wealth consultant Larry Samuel, described by *Slate* as "the anthropologist of the plutocrats." In the late 1990s, Samuel noted that America's "richest technobarons" were "engaged in a my-whatever-is-bigger-or-better-than-yours competition that would have made tycoons of an earlier century proud." Charles Simonyi, the chief software designer of Microsoft, for example, built "a Xanadu right out of *Citizen Kane*, a 21,000-square-foot techno-temple (Villa Simonyi) on Seattle's Gold Coast that had everything from a heliport to an art museum to a video arcade. [Microsoft cofounder] Paul Allen ... bought himself an island near Seattle." A new wave of "mega-houses" built for the very rich during the late 1990s included kitchens with three cooking areas (one each for him, her, and the cook); master bedrooms with sitting areas, his-and-her baths, her-and-her dressing rooms, and rooms just for packing; libraries; bars; gyms; massage rooms; meditation rooms; hair salons; home theaters; and more.[44]

The opulent excess of the wealthy few was particularly evident on Manhattan's Upper East Side, "a peculiar world to anyone who [isn't] part of it but perfectly normal to those who are." By Samuel's account of the neighborhood at the fin de siècle:

Half the dads of kids in private schools there were or seemed to be investment bankers, their chauffeur-driven Town Cars lined up at Dayton, Brearly, and Spence like a funeral procession every weekday morning and afternoon. Kids were wearing $3,000 watches and diamond necklaces to gym class; they never experienced the horror of flying commercial. Two C-notes were often stuffed into birthday cards for friends, with boys and girls sometimes taking their whole class down to Disney World to celebrate. In their parents' circle, $100 million (nicknamed "a Hunge," while $1 billion was a "Bill") was now the measure for "real money."[45]

The ultimate power possession for people with "real money" by the late 1990s was the $35 million Boeing Business Jet, which "eclips[ed] the much smaller Gulfstream V ('The Five' to private jet-setters) as the way to make a grand entrance and departure."[46]

"Richistanis" who wanted to dine without any chance of encountering their socioeconomic subordinates took their meals at "velvet rope clubs" like Frederick's in New York and Casa Casuarina in Miami—highly exclusive VIP establishments that were beyond the reach of the nonwealthy.[47] Those who wished to eat even more safely removed from the hoi polloi occasionally enjoyed "helicopter delivery of favorite meals from one's favorite Manhattan, Los Angeles, or Florida restaurant."

The wealth culture extended to hospital stays. By 2000, "a dozen US hospitals had luxury wings, some with antiques, designer fabrics, catered meals, and prices to match."[48]

On the eastern end of Long Island, the apex of super-wealthy living, *Business Week* writer Bruce Nussbaum beheld the ultra-rich in the same years. They were engaged in an epidemic of "tear-down[s] (demolishing that 20,000-square-foot perfectly nice house to put up a 40,000-square-foot edifice that is more truly 'you')." They owned multiple expensive vehicles—"both a Land Rover with a black steel ramming grill in front plus a Porsche in your garage (O.K., maybe a cute new Beetle, too, for your daughter who attends the Dalton School)." They hired a many-sided retinue of personal servants—personal fitness trainers, massage therapists, jewelers, nutritionists, chiropractors, and so on—for moms, dads, and children as well.[49]

Hollowing Out the American Dream

According to the reigning "neoliberal,"* so-called free market economic theory and ideology that accompanied the transition from the Great Compression to the New Gilded Age, increased wealth at the top "trickles down" to the rest of the populace, demonstrating a glorious identity of interests between the investing class and the broad populace. Quite to the contrary, however, the resurgent plutocracy (or "plutonomy") of the Second Gilded Age brought "trickle up," with languishing incomes for the majority alongside skyrocketing wealth and income for the rich. Over the three-plus decades connecting the Reagan era to the age of Obama, the annual wages of the typical American worker stagnated, averaging only $280 more than thirty years ago—a less than 1 percent gain over a third of a century. During the same period, political scientist Lane Kenworthy has shown, the bottom quartile (25 percent) of American households got just 20 cents of every new dollar of income from earnings on a job. The rest—80 cents—came from federal social programs, including Social Security, unemployment insurance, Medicare, Medicaid, the earned income tax credit, and the child

---

* The words *neoliberal* and *neoliberalism* as used throughout this volume refer to the ruling corporate and political ideology in post–New Deal America (1980 to the present). The classic, bourgeois, "liberal," free market political-economic doctrine of the nineteenth century held that the "free market" and possessive-individualist economic rationality were the solutions to social, political, and even personal problems. Recycling this doctrine in opposition to socialism, social democracy, government regulation, and the welfare state in the late twentieth and early twenty-first centuries, neoliberals believe that "the market should be allowed to make major social and political decisions," that "the state should voluntarily reduce its role in the economy," that "corporations should be given total freedom," and that "trade unions should be curbed and citizens given much less rather than more protections." (I quote from Susan George, "A Short History of Neoliberalism," Conference on Economic Sovereignty in a Globalizing World, March 24–26, 1999.) As numerous left thinkers note, neoliberals are not really "antigovernment." They are opposed to government action on behalf of the common good, working people, social justice, equality, and the poor, but they are not opposed to government action on behalf of corporate power, the upward concentration of wealth and power, and the punishment and disciplining of the poor and those who resist existing wealth and power centers. To paraphrase the late French sociologist Pierre Bourdieu, neoliberals (and bourgeois/state-capitalist actors more generally) are only opposed to "the left hand of the state." They welcome and encourage the "right hand of the state"—the parts of government that serve the rich and control and punish the rest. There is also a mass cultural and ideological neoliberal project—a culture of neoliberalism sold to the populace that will be discussed at some length in Chapter 5. For useful discussions of the origins, nature, and contradictory practice of neoliberalism, see Noam Chomsky, *Profits over People: Neoliberalism and Global Order* (New York: Seven Stories, 1999), 65–120; Henry A. Giroux, *The Terror of Neoliberalism: Authoritarianism and the Eclipse of Democracy* (Boulder, CO: Paradigm Publishers), xiii–xviii and passim. See also Paul Street, *Empire and Inequality: America and the World since 9/11* (Boulder, CO: Paradigm Publishers, 2004), xiii–xiv, 150–151.

tax credit. Americans in the second quartile from the bottom did just barely better, with two-thirds of their new income coming directly from the federal government. "The only protection" the bottom half of Americans "have had from a complete collapse in their standard of living," economist Jeff Madrick notes, "has been government social programs"—this in a country with a considerably less generous social and governmental safety net than those in Europe. Beginning in 2001, the US median wage actually began to drop.[50]

The American middle class has shrunk during the New Gilded Age. As the esteemed Pew Research Center reported in an August 2012 study titled *The Lost Decade of the Middle Class*, "51 percent of all [US] adults were middle class in 2011, compared to 61 percent in 1971." Between 1971 and 2011, Pew also determined, the middle class's share of the nation's income fell from 62 to 45 percent.[51]*

It was not for a lack of effort on the part of working people. The numbers on middle-class decline and wage and median and average income stagnation seem all the more remarkable when we realize that American households are working considerably longer hours today than they did during the late 1970s. During the Second Gilded Age, the wages of full-time male workers have stagnated and the income of those without a college degree have fallen. To stop family incomes from falling further, total family working hours rose primarily because more women joined their husbands in the labor force. Working-age married couples with children increased their total number of hours of employment by more than ten work weeks (406 hours) per year over the last two decades of the twentieth century.[52] "These people never stopped working hard," Madrick notes. "The problem is that wages stopped growing—and that good jobs became harder to find."[53]

To make matters significantly worse, the benefits granted to American workers have declined significantly since the end of "the golden age." American employees are significantly less insulated against health care costs and more burdened by increased medical prices than they were a generation ago. Fewer workers are covered by health insurance and by pensions, and most pensions are now offered on far less favorable terms than was common during the post-WWII period. Most retirement benefits used to come to workers via "defined-benefit" systems whereby retired workers were certain of what they would receive while their former corporate employers bore the risk of the pension funds' stock market fluctuations. In the New Gilded Age, by contrast, most workers are given "defined-contribution" schemes that require them to manage their own retirement accounts and bear the risk of market shifts and

---

* Pew defined the middle class ("middle-income" group) as households with an income ranging from two-thirds of median national household income to double the median national household income.

inflation. With the bursting of the real estate market bubble and the stock market bubble based on inflated housing values in 2007 and 2008, tens of millions of ordinary Americans saw their net worth and retirement incomes devastated—no small part of how the 2000s became a "lost decade" for the middle and working classes.[54]

It all amounted to the culmination of a historical departure—the end of the middle-class American Dream, which came closest to realization in the post-WWII era. As Madrick observes,

> The American dream has never been the rags-to-riches fable of the Horatio Alger stories. But there once was a real American dream, and it went like this: If you work hard, your income will rise consistently and will enable you and your family to have a decent life, a good life—even a secure life.
>
> No more. For at least half of all Americans … that dream has been dead for more than thirty years. Their household incomes have hardly risen since the glory decades after World War II. In many cases their incomes have actually fallen.[55]

Welcome to the Plutonomy

Yes, but … so what? So asked a leading Citigroup economist and equity analyst named Ajay Kapur in a report to his bank's shareholders in the fall of 2005. In what was destined to become a notorious formulation (thanks in part to the clever liberal-populist film documentarian and provocateur Michael Moore), he devised the theory of what he called "the plutonomy" economies—rich nations, including above all the United States, where consumption was dominated by the wealthy few. Prior to his "discovery," Kapur had been trying to determine why recently rising oil prices and resulting spiking costs at the gas pump were not significantly depressing US consumption. The explanation, he determined, was that the United States had become a nation dominated by the spending of the wealthy and that such nations exhibited economic behavior different from countries dominated by "the middle class." High gas prices might have suppressed middle-class spending, but they did not matter that much in a plutonomy because wealthy consumers were not as affected as the less well-off by higher gas prices.

"There are rich consumers, few in number but disproportionate in the gigantic slice of income and consumption they take," Kapur noted. And then "there are the rest, the 'non-rich,' the multitudinous many … accounting for a surprisingly small bite of the national pie." Thus it was, Kapur explained to investors, that a listing he called the Plutonomy Index—breaking out stocks that catered only to the wealthy—had significantly outperformed the market since the mid-1980s. "The world is dividing into two blocs," Kapur added, "—the plutonomy and the rest. The US, UK, and Canada are the key plutonomies—economies powered by the wealthy" and divided between the ever more opulent few and "the rest."[56]

Five years later, as many among the "multitudinous many" struggled with the worst poverty and joblessness in decades, a *Wall Street Journal* report suggested that Kapur had underestimated the degree of American plutonomy. In his 2005 research Kapur guessed that the top fifth of Americans accounted for as much as 50 percent of the nation's consumer spending. By 2010, however, the leading economic research firm Moody's Analytics determined that the top 20 percent of Americans accounted for 60 percent of all US consumption and indeed that the top twentieth—the upper 5 percent of income "earners"—accounted for more than a third (37 percent), significantly up from 25 percent in 1990.[57]

"A Club We Do Not Wish to Join"

In accord with these developments, the United States in the Second Gilded Age became for the first time the most unequal, wealth-top-heavy nation in the industrialized and/or postindustrialized world. As recently as the 1970s the top 1 percent in the United States garnered a smaller share of their nation's riches than the top 1 percent in France, Germany, Switzerland, and Canada. "We were economically more democratic than the Europeans," Hedrick Smith notes. By 2000, however, "the picture had reversed" as "America's ultra-rich had pulled away from the world." In terms of the few's share of their nation's wealth and income, "the US [now] easily outpaced their peers in Germany, Great Britain, Canada, Australia, France, Japan, and Switzerland" as America became "the most unequal society among industrialized countries in the West."[58]

In fact, the American economic pyramid by the turn of the twenty-first century was more comparable to the historically steep hierarchies of developing nations in Latin America than it was to the comparatively social-democratic developed nations of Western Europe and Japan. A common accepted measure of national inequality is the Gini coefficient (G). If income in a society is shared equally across a population, its G is zero—perfect equality. If all the income went to a single person, its G would be 1—perfect inequality. In the real world today, the most egalitarian societies have Gini coefficients of 0.3 and less. The most uneven, top-heavy societies include numerous nations in Africa (especially South Africa, thanks to its long history of extreme racial disparity) and Latin America, long notorious for extreme class division. These nations are scarred by Gini coefficients of 0.5 and above. As Stiglitz notes, the United States "hasn't made it yet into this 'elite' company, but it's well on the way." Between 1980 and 2011, the US Gini coefficient rose from just barely 0.4 to 0.47. The United Nations reports that the United States is "just slightly more unequal than Iran and Turkey, and much less equal than any country in the European union." Stiglitz notes, "We are now approaching the level of inequality that marks dysfunctional societies" (another term for the same problem is "failed states"). The United States is close to entering "a club we would distinctly not want to join, including Iran, Jamaica, Uganda, and the Philippines."[59]

"If there was a gold medal for inequality," the Harvard labor economist Richard B. Freeman wrote in 2007, "the United States would win hands down.... Standard measures show that the United States *more closely resembles a developing country than an advanced country* on this measure of economic performance."[60]

"Inequality," the leading global economists Uri Dadush and Kemal Dervis note, "is generally higher in developing countries than in advanced countries, though the United States has levels of inequality comparable to that of many developing countries."[61]

The Hedge Fund Republic

In some cases, it appears, the United States became considerably more unequal than developing Latin American nations during the New Gilded Age. In the fall of 2010 liberal *New York Times* columnist Nicholas Kristof commented that "if you want to see rapacious income inequality, you no longer need to visit a banana republic. You can just look around [the United States]." His point was that "the wealthiest plutocrats now actually control a greater share of the pie" in what he called "The Hedge Fund Republic" than they do in "historically unstable countries like Nicaragua, Venezuela, and Guyana." Responding to critics who found his language and comparison unfair, Kristof investigated further and found that the United States had traded places with Argentina when it came to inequality over the past seven decades. "The truth," Kristof determined, "is that Latin America has matured and become more equal in recent decades, even as the distribution in the United States has become steadily more unequal."[62]

Most disturbing of all, perhaps, are the findings of the United Nations Development Program (UNDP) on comparative international "human development." The UNDP's authoritative measure combines basic statistical measures of income, health, and education. Prior to adjustment for inequality, the United States ranks fourth—behind Norway, Australia, and the Netherlands—on the UNDP's Index of Human Development. Once inequality is factored in, however, America's ranking falls to *twenty-third, behind every single one of the European countries*. The contrast between its ranking with and without inequality is unmatched in the industrialized world.[63]

The Inequality Tax and the Resurgence of Mass Poverty

The new American inequality has torn asunder the positive relationship that had prevailed between economic growth on one hand and poverty reduction and median income on the other during the post-WWII "golden age." "If the relationship between overall GDP growth and poverty that prevailed between 1959 and 1973 had held up," economist Josh Bivens calculates, the US poverty rate "would have been driven to zero by the late 1980s. Sadly, it didn't hold up and instead progress in reducing poverty was halted in its tracks."[64]

Thanks to what Bivens calls the nation's "inequality tax," official American poverty rose to 15.1 percent in 2010. But the notoriously inadequate and excessively low federal poverty rate does not come close to fully capturing how poor the officially impoverished are in the United States. Between 1996 and 2011, the number of US families living on two dollars or less a day per person—the World Bank's measure of poverty for developing nations—rose from less than 800,000 to 1.5 million. The "poverty gap," the percentage by the which the average (mean) income of a nation's poor falls below that nation's official poverty line, is quite high in the United States (37 percent), making the United States "one of the worst-ranking [poverty-gap] countries" in the developed world and "in the same league as Spain (40 percent), Mexico (38.5 percent), and Korea (36.6 percent)." The ubiquity of poverty in the United States is illustrated by the remarkable fact that one in seven Americans depends on the government to meet basic food needs and that many millions still go to bed hungry at least once a month.[65]

Why does the United States, the self-described "world's richest nation," rank fortieth in the world in terms of life expectancy, just below Cuba? Why are its infant and maternal mortality rates "little better than in some developing countries" and "worse than Cuba, Belarus, and Malaysia, to a name a few"? Lack of health insurance, especially among the poor, is a leading factor. So, more broadly is the "dismal condition" of the US poor, who "have a life expectancy that is almost 10 percent lower than that of those at the top."[66]

As a further indication of the *inequality tax* imposed on American incomes over the preceding generation, Bivens and the Economic Policy Institute find that median US family income today would be $9,220 higher if economic growth had been as equitably distributed during the past three decades as it had been between 1948 and 1973.[67] In a similar vein, political scientists Jacob Hacker and Paul Pierson have calculated how much more money eight different US income segments would have earned in 2006 if each segment had received the overall average rate of income growth—if growth was making the income distribution neither more equal nor less (as was the case from 1945 through the early 1970s)—between 1979 and 2006. As the table on the following page shows, the results of Hacker and Pierson's exercise are stark, with the top 1 percent "earning" $694,298 more and the bottom three quintiles

The Price and Gain of Unequal Growth for Eight US Income Segments, 1979–2006

Income Segment	Average Household Income in 2006	2006 Household Income if All Groups Had Experienced the Average Rate of Income Growth between 1979 and 2006	How Much Less or More Annual (2006) Household Income Would Have Been Received if All Groups Had Experienced the Average Rate of Income Growth between 1979 and 2006
Bottom/Poorest Quintile (bottom 20%)	$16,500	$22,366	+$5,866
Second Quintile	$35,400	$45,181	+$9,781
Middle Quintile	$52,100	$64,395	+$12,295
Fourth (second richest) Quintile	$73,800	$84,209	+10,409
80th–90th Percentile	$100,915	$106,696	+$5,781
90th–95th Percentile	$132,258	$128,714	−$3,544
95th–99th Percentile	$211,768	$181,992	−$29,776
Top 1 Percent	$1,200,300	$506,002	−$694,298

Source: Jacob Hacker and Paul Pierson, *Winner-Take-All Politics* (New York: Simon and Schuster, 2010), 25.

getting roughly $6,000 (bottom quintile), $10,000 (second from bottom), and $12,000 (middle quintile) less than they would have gotten in 2006 if income had been distributed equally (as it was during the postwar era).

The Mobility Myth and the Great Gatsby Curve

According to a long-standing and widely disseminated conservative myth, the stark portrait of contemporary US inequality just presented is beside the point since America is the great "land of opportunity" and upward mobility—where yesterday's poor and working class are tomorrow's middle and upper classes. This Horatio Alger story line has never come remotely close to accurately describing American social and economic reality, but the narrative has become increasingly impossible to defend with empirical data in the New Gilded Age. For many years now, the Economic Policy Institute's annual *State of Working*

America reports have documented how distinctively durable poverty is in the United States, with the American poor experiencing much less success in rising out of low economic status than their counterparts in other advanced industrialized states.[68] A recent rigorous study by the Economic Mobility Project of the Pew Charitable Trusts finds a stronger link between parents' education level and their children's income and education in the United States than in any other country researched, including England, France, Germany, Italy, Sweden, Finland, Denmark, Canada, and Australia.[69] "Social mobility," Dadush and Dervis report, "is now much lower in the United States than in European countries."[70]

National comparisons aside, a recent study by the centrist Washington think tank the Center for American Progress finds that US children born into the bottom fifth of the nation's income pyramid have just a 1 percent chance of entering the top 5 percent.

The distinguished Princeton economist and former chairman of President Obama's Council of Economic Advisers Alan Kreuger reports that the relationship between US parents' income and that of their children is like the relationship between parents' height and that of their children: "The chance of a person who was born into the bottom 10 percent of the [US] income distribution rising to the top 10 percent as an adult is about the same as the chance of a dad who is 5'6" tall having a son who grows up to be over 6'1". It happens but not often."[71]

Those at the bottom have a significantly better chance of staying there in the United States than they do in other industrialized democracies. Fully 42 percent of Americans born into the bottom 20 percent stay there—a much smaller percentage than in Denmark (25 percent) and even relatively hierarchical England (30 percent). "And when they do move up," Stiglitz notes, "they tend to move up only a little. Almost two-thirds of [American parents] in the bottom 20 percent have children who [stay] in the bottom 40 percent." Just 8 percent of Americans born into the bottom 20 percent make it into the top quintile—far less than in England (12 percent). At the same time, and by the same token (the other side of the hierarchical coin), "once one makes it to the top in the United States," Stiglitz notes, "one is more likely to remain there."[72]

This harsh inequality of opportunity is intimately related to inequality in fact—to inequality in outcomes. This is because, as Stiglitz notes, in "a pattern [that] has been observed across countries—countries with more inequality [in fact] systematically have less equality of opportunity. *Inequality persists*" (emphasis added).

Kreuger has an interesting name for the prevailing positive relationship between high inequality and low upward intergenerational economic mobility in the United States: *The Great Gatsby Curve.*[73]

Inequality more than merely persists across generations in the United States. It expands, with the disadvantages of one generation producing deeper barriers to advancement for subsequent generations. Inequality in fact—in outcomes—*is* inequality in opportunity and in chances for upward mobility. This is something leading US politicians never really acknowledge when they give voice to the nation's long-standing "free labor ideology" by proclaiming that all Americans deserve an "equal shot" at enjoying "the American dream"—a frequent and recurrent theme in President Obama's rhetoric for many years.

Inequality and Slow Growth

What about the promise of growth—the "rising tide that lifts all boats"—that Western capitalism has long offered as the answer to those who bemoan inequality and joblessness under the profits system? The harsh reality is that economic disparity on the scale of the Second Gilded Age reduces the system's capacity for responding with "more" for all. In fact, the poverty, middle-class decline, joblessness, and the broader inequality they reflect are a central part of the answer to why average annual US economic growth rates declined precipitously with the shift from the post-WWII Great Compression to the New Gilded Age in the 1970s and 1980s.[74]

Pro-rich, neoliberal economists are wrong when they argue that making rich people richer relative to the rest expands national economies. "Trickle-down economics" works in the opposite way. It reduces the purchasing power of ordinary people, who spend a considerably higher portion of the money they receive than do the wealthy. Unlike the rich, ordinary working and poor people necessarily expend all or nearly all of their income on consumption. That is why more unequal countries experience slower growth on average and why individual countries grow more rapidly in periods when incomes are more equally distributed.[75] That is certainly the case in the United States since World War II. America "enjoyed considerable equality from the 1940s through the 1970s," Kristof notes, "and growth was strong. Since then inequality has surged, and growth has slowed."[76]

Sharing out wealth and income more equitably would help spark growth, especially during a recession. "In an economic downturn," the liberal British economist Ha Joon Chang notes, "the best way to boost the economy is to redistribute wealth downward, as poorer people tend to spend a higher portion of their incomes. The economy-boosting effect of the extra billion dollars given to the lower-income households through increased welfare spending will be bigger than the same amount given to the rich through tax cuts." Give ordinary folks more money and they quickly buy necessities, stimulating the economy. By contrast, extra money for the rich often funds numerous activities that have little stimulus effect and some that are quite contrary to the growth and wages promised: the purchase of back-stocked luxuries, mergers and acquisitions that actually cut jobs, storage of surplus wealth in offshore tax havens, the hiring of management consultants who advise on how to shrink payrolls and eliminate unions; the hiring of lobbyists who push for cutting public sector programs, jobs, and unions; the hording of cash reserves; the purchase of sophisticated financial instruments that cannibalize the economy; and numerous other forms of parasitism that "mark profits without hiring anyone."[77]

This inequality is a major problem for the US economy for a simple, timeworn reason: declining income for the working class is a drag on demand—on the market for goods and services. The problem has systemic roots that go beyond policy. The economy's growth capacity is capped by what US analysts affiliated with the Marxist journal *Monthly Review* have long shown to a timeworn contradiction of capitalism: on one hand, private accumulation (savings and investment) depends on suppressing wages; on the other hand, economic growth and investment ultimately rely on wage-based consumption.[78]

Debt and Crisis

That contradiction has given rise to another less-than-novel problem in the neoliberal era: the deadly overexpansion of household debt. Remarkably enough given the relative stagnation of wages for the majority, household consumption continued to rise during the Second Gilded Age. But how that happened is not a pretty story, either for American workers or for the broader economy. Consumer capacity was fed by a continued expansion in the number of two-earner households, people working longer hours and taking extra jobs, the cheapening of goods permitted by multinational corporations' shifting of production to the super-exploited periphery of the world economy, and *above all by an ever-increasing and ultimately unsustainable expansion of consumer debt*. Between the early 1960s and 2007, household debt rose from roughly 40 percent to more than 100 percent of GDP and surged to 127 percent of peoples' incomes. By the end of the last long neoliberal boom (2007), Americans paid 14 percent of their disposable income *just to service their debt*.[79]

The expansion of debt allowed workers to buy more than they would have been able to afford otherwise. During the George W. Bush years, it was fueled by an unprecedented housing bubble—a dramatic rise in housing prices fed by remarkably low interest rates and the determination of Wall Street to provide an increasingly wide array of home mortgage products to an ever-widening segment of the populace. The recipients included many lower-income black and Latino households, sucked into the real estate bubble, despite their own stagnant and declining wages, by an explosion of super-exploitative subprime loans. In what economic commentators called "the wealth effect," rising real estate prices provided homeowners with collateral for taking out more credit to fuel consumer purchasing. The country was living and spending far beyond its means, with finance capital raking in billions of dollars in credit card and mortgage fees and profits from the sale of exotic new financial instruments—collateralized debt obligations (CDOs) and other complex derivative securities that bet on the performance of housing stocks and bundled mortgage debt for mass institutional purchase.

The slowly growing US economy of the early twenty-first century was plagued by two serious flaws. The first flaw was a classic 1920s-like capitalist disconnect between the artificially inflated value of the securities market and the actual value produced by the real economy. The second was growth's reliance on the ability of an ever wider and poorer segment of the nation's wage- and salary-squeezed populace to pay their mortgages. The process came to a halt in 2007 and 2008. That's when the housing bubble popped, deflated by a wave of foreclosures among marginal new owners, whose frozen wages did not permit them to carry their rising mortgage debt burdens. The reckoning came *like no time since 1929.* The fall in prices led to millions of homeowners owing more on their houses than they were worth, something that fed a vicious downward cycle of defaults. Banks seeking to shore up their profit-loss sheets began to hold back on the extension of credit card debt. Consumption fell as jobs and credit retreated. Capital investment was delayed and suspended, causing more job loss and feeding a downward spiral. The more jobs disappeared, the more foreclosures occurred (by 2009, 60 percent of foreclosures were the direct result of job losses). Since the nation's small number of giant "too-big-to-fail" financial institutions had invested heavily in housing securities, the resulting panic claimed a number of Wall Street's leading firms and called for massive government assistance to keep the rest afloat.[80]

For a time, people can consume beyond their income by taking on debt, something Americans did at a record rate prior to the onset of the Great Recession. Ultimately, however, the borrowing boom could not last without comparable wage and salary gains. The gains did not occur, and the crash inevitably came.[81]

"Richistan Seems More Foreign Than Ever"

The Great Recession of 2007–2009, itself a product of the Second Gilded Age's inequality, only deepened the chasm between "Richistan" and the rest of America. "As millions of non-rich Americans lose their jobs," Robert Frank noted in his 2011 book *The High-Beta Rich*, "many of the rich are already recovering from the financial crisis, thanks in part to the government bailout of Wall Street and the Federal Reserve's support of financial markets and cheap money." As a reader of Frank's *Wealth Report* blog wrote in early 2011,

"The rich have gotten back what they lost and the rest of America is still in the purple fart cloud of the last bust."[82]

Consistent with that observation, a *New York Times* article published at the height of the elite-manufactured debt-ceiling crisis in the summer of 2011 reported that the rich and super-rich had resumed their ways of conspicuous and opulent consumption. "Even Marked Up," the *Times*'s headline ran, "Luxury Goods Fly Off Shelves." *Times* readers learned that

> Nordstrom has a waiting list for a Chanel sequined tweed coat with a $9,010 price. Neiman Marcus has sold out in almost every size of Christian Louboutin "Bianca" platform pumps, at $775 a pair. Mercedes-Benz said it sold more cars last month in the United States than it had in any July in five years.... Even with the economy in a funk and many Americans pulling back on spending, the rich are again buying designer clothing, luxury cars and about anything that catches their fancy. Luxury goods stores, which fared much worse than other retailers in the recession, are more than recovering—they are zooming. Many high-end businesses are even able to mark up, rather than discount, items to attract customers who equate quality with price.... The luxury category has posted 10 consecutive months of sales increases compared with the year earlier, even as overall consumer spending on categories like furniture and electronics has been tepid.

The retail experience was different on the other side of the American class divide. The "success luxury retailers are having in selling $250 Ermenegildo Zegna ties and $2,800 David Yurman pavé rings—the kind encircled with small precious stones," stood in "stark contrast to the retailers who cater to more average Americans." The *Times* reported that middle-class clothing stores were holding fire sales to coax spending. Wal-Mart was "selling smaller packages because some shoppers do not have enough cash on hand to afford multipacks of toilet paper."[83]

Harsh economic realities for millions among "the rest of us" underlay such reports. The statistical signs of misery at the bottom were unmistakable two years into Obama's "change" presidency:

- By 2010, the total number of Americans living in official poverty reached a historic high of 46.2 million. Over 15 percent of the nation's population (one in seven US citizens) lived below the federal poverty line—$22,314 for a family of four.[84]
- A Census report commissioned by the *New York Times* in the fall of 2011 showed that one in three Americans lived either in official poverty or in "near poverty," either officially poor or at less than 150 percent of the poverty level.[85]

- CBS News reported in December 2011 that "a record number of Americans—nearly one in two—have fallen into poverty or are scraping by on earnings that classify them as low income." Half the population—150 million—was either officially poor (50 million) or living at less than double the federal government's notoriously inadequate poverty level (100 million).[86]
- The 2010 Census revealed that a record-setting one in fifteen Americans now lived in deep poverty—at less than half the federal government's notoriously inadequate poverty measure (less than $11,157 for a family of four).[87]
- Four of every ten US blacks experienced unemployment in 2008 and 2009.
- The real combined unemployment rate for black and Latino workers (including workers who were involuntarily underemployed) in 2010 was 25 percent.
- The black poverty rate rose to 26 percent, double that of white poverty.[88]

By early 2012, reflecting the Great Recession's economic toll, the Pew Center found that the percentage of Americans who said they were in the lower-middle or lower class had risen from a quarter of the adult population to about a third over the past four years. Among those Americans who put themselves in the lower classes, nearly half felt that "hard work and determination" were "no guarantee of success" in the United States.[89]

In March of the same year, another indication of the poverty that had spread across the nation came in a *New York Times* article on the Obama reelection campaign's sprawling headquarters in downtown Chicago. The center of operations "looks more like a company than a campaign," the *Times* reported. "For the last year, an office that appears nearly as long and as wide as a football field has steadily grown, with more than 300 workers now sitting bunched together ... a payroll of $3 million in January suggests the staff is larger than any ever assembled for a presidential race." The *Times* added that the workers were having a hard time raising money from the "small donors who gave early and often [to Obama] in 2008." This was because "some of the volunteers who went to work enlisting friends and neighbors [in 2008] have been *turned off by unmet expectations*" and because "they have literally lost track of many reliable Democratic voters, *particularly lower-income people who have lost their homes or their jobs or both,* and can no longer be reached at the addresses or phone numbers the campaign has on file."[90] No doubt some of the onetime small givers the president's campaign could no longer reach due to jobs and/or home loss had joined in the crowd of 1 million or so who gathered in and around Chicago's downtown Grant Park to celebrate Obama's election in November of that year.

One of the things that was striking about this remarkable explosion of poverty was the considerable number of formerly working- and middle-class people who had been knocked down into the "underclass." As the PBS talk show host and commentator Tavis Smiley and Princeton philosopher Cornel West reported in their 2012 book *The Rich and the Rest of Us: A Poverty Manifesto*, written after they conducted an eighteen-city US Poverty Tour that began in August 2011, on the eve of the Occupy Wall Street movement,

> In 21st-century America, the poor are no longer just the permanently unemployed, the recently incarcerated, or the mentally ill. Disheveled vagrants who push overstuffed, wobbly wheeled carts down abandoned streets, who sleep across sidewalk grates, or who stay in overcrowded shelters are no longer the reigning face of poverty.... While many whom we met fit what some define as the "old poor" (people who were impoverished before the "Great Recession" in late 2007), we were also gathered with shockingly large numbers of the "new poor"—citizens who were once bona fide members of America's middle class.... They are the grandchildren and great-grandchildren of ... generation[s] that embodied artist Norman Rockwell's *American Dream*. They once possessed relatively predictable and reasonably comfortable lives until they were inexplicably cast into a maelstrom of economic dispossession and spiritual despair. When the bottom fell out ... the formerly lower, middle, and upper-middle classes found themselves recast in the nightmares of the downtrodden.[91]

Such "new" twenty-first-century poor people provided some basis for the curious title of a CNNMoney report that came out in February 2011: "How the Middle Class Became the Underclass."[92] The title overstated things, but it was a bracing reminder of how close many in the formerly secure middle classes had come to falling down the "greased chute" into destitution and of how many middle-class Americans had in fact experienced "sudden downward mobility."[93]

"Richistan seems more foreign than ever," Frank notes, "as many Americans lose hope of ever getting rich themselves. In our post-TARP, deficit-ridden age, many see the rich as the winners in a zero-sum game of global wealth. Richistan and America are viewed more like Disraeli's 'Two Nations,' 'between whom there is no intercourse and sympathy ... as if they were dwellers in different zones ... and not governed by the same laws.'"[94]

In the early fall of 2012, *Forbes* magazine published its annual list of the 400 wealthiest Americans, showing that the cumulative net worth of the wealthiest 400 Americans had risen by $200 billion over the previous year. That compared with a 4 percent decline in median household income over the same period, the Census Bureau reported.[95]

Wealth consultant Larry Samuel called it. Writing in early 2009, after the richest Americans had lost billions in the stock market crash, Samuel noted that "the rich are incredibly adaptive, quite familiar with the natural ebb and flow of economic cycles and how to ride them out." He expected the recession to "further separate the have-nots from the haves, with the most elite of the ultra-rich ... pulling further away."[96] Consistent with that prediction, the top 1 percent garnered more than 90 cents on every new dollar of US income during 2010, the first full year of technical economic recovery.[97]

"Mass Affluence Is Over"

The following year, a study from the American advertising industry's top trade journal *Advertising Age* (*AA*) reported that the American middle class had become economically irrelevant. The great global recession, *AA* found, had shined "a spotlight on the yawning divide between the richest American and everyone else," signaling that "mass affluence is over." Since "the incomes of most American workers have remained more or less static since the late 1970s" even as "the income of the rich (and the very rich) has grown exponentially," *AA* explained, a "small plutocracy of wealthy elites drives a larger and larger share of total consumer spending and has outsize purchasing influence—particularly in categories such as technology, financial service, travel, automotive, apparel, and personal care.... More than ever before, the wealthiest households will be the households with significant disposable income to spend."[98]

Liberal commentator Sam Pizzigati noted a curious historical development—a reversal of the scenario portrayed in *Mad Men*, the hit cable TV series set on Madison Avenue during the early 1960s, when the mass market was all about ordinary working folks:

> The chain-smoking ad-agency account execs of *Mad Men* ... all want to be rich some day. But these execs, professionally, couldn't care less about the rich. They spend their nine-to-fives marketing to average Americans, not rich ones.
>
> *Mad Men*'s real life ad agency brethren, 50 years ago, behaved the exact same way—for an eminently common-sense reason: In mid-20th-century America, the entire US economy revolved around middle-class households. The vast bulk of income sat in middle class pockets.... The rich back then, for ad execs, constituted an afterthought, a niche market.
>
> Not anymore. Madison Avenue has now come full circle. The rich no longer rate as a niche.... Marketing to the rich—and those about to gain that status—has become the only game that really counts.[99]

It was a curious and telling reflection on the long transition from the "golden age" and Great Compression to the New Gilded Age of Inequality.

The American people, *AA* observed, had yet to catch up with this harsh reality straight out of the "plutonomy" thesis. Americans "like to believe in an egalitarian idea of affluence" wherein "everyone has an equal shot" at "amassing a great fortune through hard work and ingenuity," *Advertising Age* noted. But this was sheer fantasy for all but a few Americans now. As a result, *AA* argued, corporations would have to write off the fading American middle class and cater exclusively to the super-rich and to the affluent and rising middle classes in other countries like China, India, and Brazil.[100]

The Broken Society

If It Doesn't Matter ...

On October 24, 2011, the elitist *Newsweek* columnist, CNN commentator, and best-selling author Fareed Zakaria posted on his CNN blog an old essay penned by the onetime pioneer neoconservative Irving Kristol. Zakaria gave his post a provocative title: "Irving Kristol: Why Inequality Doesn't Matter." As Zakaria explained beneath a picture of a "We Are the 99 Percent" poster, "economic inequality is once again at the forefront of American public debate. . . . We feel it useful to resurrect a skeptical perspective on the subject from a previous era." A remark at the bottom of the post online offered a clever rejoinder. "If it 'doesn't matter,'" one of Zakaria's readers reflected, "then I'm sure the rich won't mind trading places with the people they've been looting all these years."[101]

Inequality vs. Growth, Mobility, and Democracy

Inequality matters a great deal on numerous levels. We have already dealt in this chapter with the two most common "conservative" objections to those who present data showing that the United States is the most unequal society among the world's affluent countries: (1) the notion that supposedly high upward mobility pushes poor people regularly into the middle and upper classes in the United States; and (2) the notion that giving the people at the top what they want creates wealth that trickles down to benefit the rest through employment and other opportunities resulting from growth. The difficulty with these narratives, we have seen, is not simply that neither upward mobility nor economic growth is strong enough to ameliorate the negative socioeconomic results of inequality in the contemporary United States. The deeper problem is that inequality on the contemporary "hedge fund republic" scale undermines both mobility and growth.

It also (no small matter!) *undermines* democracy—something that has been well understood by leading Western and American thinkers, activists, and policymakers from Aristotle through Thomas Jefferson, James Madison, Henry George, Upton Sinclair, John Dewey, Eugene Debs, Louis Brandeis, Franklin Roosevelt, Martin Luther King Jr., Mario Savio, and Noam Chomsky. Brandeis's notion that we *must choose between democracy on one hand and "wealth concentrated in the hands of a few" on the other* arises from these and other thinkers' understanding that disproportionate political, cultural, ideological, and policy influence flows to those who possess large concentrations of money and worldly goods. Those with little of either exercise little power in the absence of remarkable, difficult-to-achieve-and-sustain mass solidarity and organization. For this reason, the prolific left author and commentator Chris Hedges noted in July 2013 that "you can't sustain a democracy in an oligarchy."[102]

We shall examine some of the different and interrelated ways in which the rich translate their wealth into wildly disproportionate political power and policy influence in Chapters 3, 4, and (especially) 5. The remainder of this chapter (all too) briefly examines economic inequality's further and related disastrous impacts on US social health and on livable ecology at home and abroad.

Degrading Societal, Mental, and Physical Health

In early 2003, on the eve of the US invasion of Iraq, the prestigious US Council on Foreign Relations (CFR) released a document bearing the interesting title *Iraq: The Day After.* The CFR study contained a fascinating comment from a leading US policy thinker named James Dobbins, then director of the Pentagon-affiliated Rand Corporation's Center for International Security and Defense Policy. He was a former special US envoy during US interventions in Somalia, Haiti, Bosnia, Kosovo, and Afghanistan. "The partisan debate," Dobbins proclaimed, "is over. Administrations of both [US political] parties are clearly prepared to use American military force *to repair broken societies.*" Broken societies, Dobbins explained, give rise to terrorism, including the jetliner attacks of September 11, 2001. It is in America's national interest, Dobbins argued, to find and fix "broken societies" around the world in places like Afghanistan, Iraq, and Sudan.[103]

Leaving aside both the fact that US foreign military and economic policy are leading forces behind societal fracturing abroad and the dubious prospects of fixing societal problems with military force, Dobbins might have wanted to take a closer look at the United States itself if he and other US elites were searching for *a broken society to repair.*[104]

In 2010 the leading British public health researchers Richard Wilkinson and Kate Pickett published *The Spirit Level: Why Greater Equality Makes Societies Stronger*, a comprehensive and widely read study of economic inequality's many dire consequences for public, social, and individual health in the late twentieth and early twenty-first centuries. Wilkinson and Pickett processed a remarkable amount of comparative national and international data to show definitively that the more unequal societies are, the more medical, mental, and social problems they experience. The authors determined that high levels of socioeconomic disparity correlate with low levels of social trust and mental health, the weakening of community life, high levels of obesity and drug use, high levels of personal narcissism and aggression, elevated teenage pregnancy rates, low child well-being, high homicide and violence rates, low rates of happiness, high anxiety levels, reduced life expectancy, high infant mortality, high incarceration, elevated high school dropout rates, reduced friendship levels, reduced upward economic mobility, overwork (long working hours), unemployment, and household debt.[105]

Across the world's rich ("developed") countries, Wilkinson and Pickett found an extremely high statistical correlation between inequality and their index of health and social problems. When it came to mental illness, homicide, incarceration, infant mortality, obesity, teen pregnancy, and low social mobility, they determined that fully three-fourths of the inter-country differences could be statistically explained by inequality. By their calculations, the United States is not only the most unequal nation among the world's rich nations—it is also and not coincidentally the most dysfunctional, unhealthy, and alienated society among those nations. Wilkinson and Pickett further note that inequality contributes to economic instability, feeding capitalism's long-standing boom-and-bust propensities by concentrating massive amounts of surplus wealth without productive investment outlets in the hands of a few while encouraging deadly mass indebtedness among the many. At the same time, they observed that high levels of inequality are correlated with a heavy "weight of downward prejudice" against those at the bottom. As Wilkinson and Pickett explain, "We maintain social superiority to those below. Those deprived of status try to regain it by taking it out on more vulnerable people below them.... The English say, 'The captain kicks the cabin boy and the cabin boy kicks the cat,' describing the downward flow of aggression and resentment."[106] This "bicycling reaction" of downwardly displaced aggression may help explain why the United States, the self-advertised "land of freedom," criminally marks and locks up a globally unmatched percentage of its population in prisons and jails—an indignity that is very disproportionately imposed on poor people of color.[107]

Wilkinson and Pickett find that the differences between more equal (say, Sweden) and less equal national societies (the United States above all) are quite large. The many social and health problems they investigated across nations "are anything from three times to ten times as common to the more unequal societies." Significantly, the differences apply to whole national citizenries, not just to the poorest within each nation: "these ... are not differences between high- and low-risk groups within populations which might apply only to a small proportion of the population, or just to the poor. Rather, they are differences between the prevalence of different problems which apply to whole populations."[108] The vast majority of people in the United States are harmed by the nation's extreme level of inequality, not just the poor. On numerous health indicators, in fact, research shows that more highly educated middle-aged American males experience considerably more problems than their middle-class counterparts in England. They also experience more sickness and disease than their age and race counterparts *in the English working class.* "Even if you take the death rates just of white Americans," Wilkinson and Pickett note, US citizens "still do worse than the populations of most other developed countries."[109] For what it's worth, no nation has more index entries in *The Spirit Level* than the United States, with forty-three entries. The next closest is the United Kingdom at twenty-five.[110]

The 1% and the Fate of the Earth

The arguably single greatest problem resulting from inequality—a problem that clearly impacts the whole of society, including even the very rich—receives relatively minor attention in *The Spirit Level*: climate change.* Beneath the regular drumbeat of current events the primary threat to a decent and desirable human future is the destruction of the environment. By any reasonable account, the planet is threatened by environmental collapse on many fronts but most particularly by catastrophic climate change resulting from excessive human-generated carbon emissions—anthropogenic global warming (AGW).[111] According to new research released in the spring of 2012 by the science journal *Nature*, humanity is now facing an imminent threat of extinction—a threat caused by its reckless exploitation of the natural environment. The report reveals that AGW is pushing our planet's biosphere steadily and ever more rapidly toward a fateful/fatal "tipping point," meaning that all of the planet's ecosystems are nearing sudden and irreversible change that poses a menace to the species. "The data suggests that there will be a reduction in biodiversity and severe impacts on much of what we depend on to sustain our quality

---

* The rich, to be sure, make special efforts to insulate themselves from the consequences of climate change. Some elites with pricey homes in wooded mountain areas have secured private fire protection services—privatized fire departments who will come to put out the flames only in homes with whom they have contracted for service. Others have signed up with private "four-star hurricane evacuation" plans that let you escape the next global warming–fueled super-storm in style. Still, there is no complete escape from a poisoned planet, even for the most privileged plutocrats. They are not, after all, the extraterrestrials portrayed in John Carpenter's *They Live*, habituated to a different sort of climate on a distant home planet and able to hop from one depleted planet to another in an endless galactic quest for more wealth.

of life, including … fisheries, agriculture, forest products, and clean water. This could happen within just a few generations," wrote lead author Anthony Barnosky, a professor of integrative biology at the University of California at Berkeley. "My colleagues who study climate-induced changes through the Earth's history are more than pretty worried," co-researcher Arne Mooers, a professor of biodiversity at Simon Fraser University in British Columbia, said in a statement. "In fact, some are terrified."[112]

It appears that even many of the most pessimistic climate scientists under-estimated the risks when they started sounding alarms about anthropogenic (human-generated) global warming in the late 1980s and early 1990s. The experts seemed to think that the "tipping point" beyond which human life was gravely threatened was 550 carbon dioxide parts per atmospheric million (double the historical norm of 275 parts per million). The more accurate tip-ping point measure, recently discovered, is closer is to 350, a benchmark we have actually passed. We are currently at 390 parts per million and projected to hit 650 before final collapse without fundamental changes in our patterns of energy use.[113]

Ecocide and Inequality

These excessive carbon emissions are intimately linked to New Gilded Age inequality and the 1%'s power and influence in numerous and interrelated ways. The connections include the special political and ideological influence (garnering weak environmental regulations on, and large public subsidies to, carbon-emitting corporations) exercised by 1%-owned fossil fuel extract-ing (coal, gas, and oil) and fossil-fuel using (utilities, facilities management, manufacturers) corporations; heavy 1% sunk-cost fixed capital investment in the vast fossil fuel infrastructure (what we might call carbon-industrial "asset inertia"); the reluctance of elite investor classes in different nations (the United States included) to agree to global carbon emission limits that might (they fear) disadvantage them relative to rival capitalists from other nations in terms of energy use; the heavy reliance of 1%-owned corporations on waste-ful production processes crafted in accord with the perverse logic of built-in obsolescence; and the way that the great economic downturns encouraged and triggered by extreme inequality and by elite financial power and manipulations tend to undermine popular support for governmental policies and practices deemed antithetical to economic reexpansion.[114]

No connection between contemporary inequality and environmental col-lapse is more relevant, perhaps, than that suggested by the power of "the growth ideology." The holy grail of "growth" has long been Western capital-ism's "solution" for the inequality that capitalism creates. "A rising tide lifts all boats," the conventional Western growth ideology proclaims, supposedly rendering irrelevant popular anger over the fact that an opulent minority sails in luxurious yachts while millions struggle on rickety dinghies and leaking rowboats. As *Le Monde*'s ecological editor Herve Kempf noted in 2008, "the oligarchy" sees the pursuit of material growth as "the solution to the social crisis," the "sole means of fighting poverty and unemployment," and the "only means of getting societies to accept extreme inequalities without questioning them…. Growth," Kempf explained, "would allow the overall level of wealth to arise and consequently improve the lot of the poor without—and this part is never spelled out [by the economic elite]—any need to modify the distribution of wealth."[115]

"Growth," the liberal economist Henry Wallich explained (approvingly) in 1972, "is a substitute for equality of income. So long as there is growth there is hope, and that makes large income differentials tolerable."

"Governments love growth," British environmental writer and activist George Monbiot noted in the fall of 2007, "because it excuses them from dealing with inequality…. Growth is a political sedative, snuffing out protest, permitting governments to avoid confrontation with the rich, preventing the construction of a just and sustainable economy."[116]

When growth stops, William Greider notes, "the political system loses its cover. The safety valve is off. The comforting mythology about growth loses its power to distract the public from anger and to discourage critical inquiry into how the system actually functions."[117] The Occupy Movement and the broader wave of anti-austerity protest (of which Occupy was a somewhat belated manifestation) that emerged around the world in the wake of the Great Recession is a case in point.

The pressure to keep the "safety valve" on comes at an unsustainable price, setting up a devil's choice between jobs and income for proletarianized masses on one hand and livable ecology for humanity (and other living things) on the other. The wealthy few's reliance on growth to cloak inequality and keep dangerous "populist" sentiments at bay is at the heart of *How*, to use the title of Kempf's most recent book, *the Rich Are Destroying the Earth*.*

Another key connection between the 1% and the fate of the earth is provided by what Wilkinson and Pickett call "the Veblen effect." Consistent with the writings of the brilliant late nineteenth and early twentieth-century US economist and iconoclast Thorstein Veblen, the very existence of the rich and super-rich encourages untold millions of less-well-off Americans to engage in excessive mass consumption that helps push the biosphere to the limits of decent habitation. As Veblen explained in his classic 1899 text *Theory of the*

---

* It should be added, however, that growth is more than only an ideological requirement for the 1%. It is also very much a material and economic requirement for the 1%'s profits system (capitalism), something that is very ably discussed in John Bellamy Foster, Brett Clark, and Richard York, *The Ecological Rift: Capitalism's War on the Planet* (New York: Monthly Review Press, 2010).

Leisure Class, "Each class envies and emulates the class next above it in social scale.... Our standard of decency in expenditure, as in other ends of emulation, is set by those next above us in reputability; until, in this way, especially in any community where class distinctions are somewhat vague ... all standards of consumption are traced back by insensible gradations to the usages and habits of the highest social and pecuniary class."[118]

Writing in advance of the full flowering of the modern mass consumer advertising industry, Veblen anticipated the "keeping up with the Joneses" mentality that industry helped inculcate in the American populace, at no small cost both to household budgets and to a natural environment that has had to absorb a deluge of heavily packaged, mass-marketed waste sold to masses struggling to align their consumption patterns with dominant notions of "decent" living that spread from the top of the 1% down. Research confirms the existence of a ubiquitous and long-standing "Veblen effect" in the United States and other rich societies—a widespread tendency to purchase and use consumer goods more for their perceived social and status value than for their actual usefulness. As Wilkinson and Pickett note, "Our almost neurotic need to shop and consume is ... a reflection of how deeply social we are. Living in unequal and individualistic societies, we use possessions to show ourselves in a good light, to make a positive impression, and to avoid appearing inadequate or incompetent in the eyes of others."[119]

Can we put appropriate environmental limits on this system of unremitting increase and epic squander? Doing so requires a public and collective commitment to long-term social, economic, and environmental planning that contradicts the short-term priorities of the 1% and its profits system. As the leading progressive economist and author Jeff Faux notes, a sustainable US energy future would require "a national commitment to electric cars, mass transit, solar and wind power, and clean coal, with the jobs and benefits designed to stay in the United States. This in turn demands that the country's governing class abandon its ... notion that the energy future can be left to the market."[120] But the elite US business class has never taken kindly to those who would impose long-term and socially responsible criteria on how it might employ the surplus it has accumulated on the backs of society and nature. Its time frame does not generally extend beyond quarterly and annual earnings and profit-loss statements. This is particularly true in the current age of financialized and global capitalism, when wealth is tied like never before to speedy and speculative transactions and when "American" capital is less concerned than ever with the long-term economic and related social development of the United States—topics we shall examine in some detail in Chapter 4.

American politicians, for their part, think mainly in terms of two-year (congresspersons in the House and House candidates), four-year (presidents and presidential candidates), and six-year (senators and Senate candidates) election cycles, paying special attention to their need to win the approval of the big 1% interests that fund viable campaigns and own the media corporations that cover and sell elections. Elected officials feel compelled to demonstrate their contribution to "growth" and hence to "jobs" and "security" over the course of their terms.[121]

No Planet B: Our Pass-Fail Moment

The climate crisis—and the related broader ecological crisis of which it is currently one if not the most urgent parts—is unlike other problem areas linked to inequality by Wilkinson and Pickett (and many others) in a critical way. When it comes to most contemporary policy issues (health care is a perfect example), progressives can at times reasonably choose to win what little they can, split the difference, and then gather resources for future gains on the path to full reform, knowing that failure to win a really big victory in the present does not make progress unattainable in the future. Things are different with the climate because, as the leading climate activist and author Bill McKibben observes, "Global warming ... is a negotiation between human beings on the one hand and physics and chemistry on the other. Which is a tough negotiation, because physics and chemistry don't compromise."[122]

Tipping points are forever—or at least for a very, very long time. As the Marxist writer Ricardo Levins-Morales noted a few years ago, the cautious "one small step at a time" approach to progressive change loses credibility when the existing order is posing imminent radical threats to survival. "If the road we are on leads to a precipice," Levins-Morales wrote,

> then a shift in ... orientation is overdue.... If we envision ourselves ... advancing across an expanse of open field, then we can measure our progress in terms of yardage gained and be satisfied that we are least moving in the right direction. If, instead, a chasm has opened up which we must leap across to survive, then the difference between getting twenty percent versus forty percent of the way across is meaningless. It means we have transitioned from a system of political letter grades to one of "pass/fail." We either make the leap or not.[123]

As Chomsky argued in a widely read 2012 essay, "If the [environmental] catastrophe isn't ... averted—[then] in a generation or two, everything else we're talking about won't matter."[124] It's a cautionary comment for Occupiers and other progressives: Who wants to turn the world upside-down only to find that it is irredeemably riddled with disease and decay? What good is it to inherit a poisoned Earth from the 1%? What's the point of more equally sharing out a poison pie? If livable ecology is one among many patients in the crowded emergency room of inequality's victims—this is how it appears in *The Spirit Level*—it is a patient of a very odd and critical sort in that if it dies, so do all other patients waiting for care.

Humanity and the struggle for justice can and will survive to fight another day if we fail to solve the poverty or debt or unemployment or health care disparity problem in the next three decades. Failure to solve AGW is not like that. "There is," a bumper sticker reminds us, "no Planet B."

We shall return in this book's final chapter to what could and indeed must be done to address this fateful problem.

CHAPTER **3**

Political Economy
How They Got So Rich

It is not that the economy has been broken for the last 30 years or so, but rather that it is working as it has been designed to work.... For 30 years, policy levers have been pulled to help the well-off, and this policy orientation worked spectacularly on its own terms.
  —*Laurence Mishel, president of the Economic Policy Institute, 2011*[1]

In researching the ironic hostility of many super-rich Americans toward Barack Obama in 2012, Chrystia Freeland interviewed a sixty-nine-year-old Bronx-born billionaire and hedge fund founder named Leon Cooperman. A leading figure behind the false charge of many plutocrats that the president was "anti-business" and "anti-wealth," Cooperman told Freeland of how he had recently been visited by a "world-renowned cardiologist" seeking financial advice on the eve of his retirement. The elite heart surgeon and his wife (herself one of the country's experts in women's medicine) had what Cooperman considered an unimpressive net worth of "just" $10 million. Cooperman was "shocked" at how "tight" this top-flight medical couple would have to be in their retirement. "You know," Cooperman added, *"I lost more money today than they spent a lifetime accumulating"*[2]—a remarkable statement on the difference between a by no means impoverished couple who spent their careers at the highly skilled top of the healing profession and a man who dedicated his working life to the analysis and manipulation of financial securities on behalf of his own economic lust and that of other investors.

The Victim-Blaming Skills Gap Smokescreen

How did the Great Compression (1929–1970s) give rise to the New Gilded Age, creating such outrageous fortunes for filthy rich plutocrats like Leon Cooperman while a rising mass of ordinary Americans have faced stagnation, decline, and insecurity? Mainstream US economists, business elites, pundits, and politicians (including President Obama) love to portray the rising inequality of the neoliberal era as the inexorable outcome of underlying market forces and related technological changes that have placed a growing premium on skill and education in determining earnings from employment—especially in an ever more connected global system, "where technology goes worldwide in a nanosecond."[3]

This "skills gap" explanation of contemporary US inequality is belied by nine basic facts. First, the current American workforce is more educated than the workforce was in 1979. More than one of every three (34 percent of) US workers had a college degree in 2010, compared with less than one in five (19 percent) in 1979.[4] The economy today has nearly twice as many workers with advanced degrees as it did in 1979.[5]

Second, there is remarkably little evidence linking educational levels to national economic performance. This is thanks in part to the fact that, as Ha Joon Chang notes, "with increasing de-industrialization and mechanization, the knowledge requirements may have even fallen for most jobs in rich countries."[6]

Third, while the earnings premium accruing to the possession of a college degree has risen in recent decades, rising income inequality "is not," as Jacob Hacker and Paul Pierson note, "mainly about the gap between the college-educated and the rest. It's about the pulling away of the very top. Those at the top are often highly educated, yes, but so, too, are those just below them who have been left increasingly behind." Indeed the household income of the 80th percentile has grown just one-fourth as quickly per year as the income of the top 1 percent across the Second Gilded Age.[7]

Fourth, those with college degrees have pulled away from the bottom not so much due to their own rising income as because of the remarkable stagnation of income among the less educated in an age of neoliberal and global restructuring. As economic historian Judith Stein notes, "Changes in government labor policies, which led to declining minimum wages and union membership, were more responsible [than educational- or skills-requirement changes] for the [stagnating and often declining] wages of high school graduates." So were "structural factors such as the shift from high-paying manufacturing to low-paying service industries—steel to fast-food restaurants—and increased trade competition with low wage countries."[8] The latter factor has been critical across recent decades, with the US international "goods deficit" increasing from $19.6 billion in 1979 to $97 billion in 1992 and to a remarkable $838 billion in 2006.[9]

Fifth, if skills-intensive technological change was significantly driving socioeconomic change in the New Gilded Age, then, the Center for Economic and Policy Research (CEPR) notes, "we would expect that a higher—probably substantially higher—share of workers with a four-year college degree or more would have good jobs [defined by CEPR as jobs paying at least $37,000 per year and offering an employer-provided health insurance plan and an employer-sponsored retirement plan] today. Instead, at every age level, workers with four years or more of college are actually less likely to have a good job now than three decades ago."[10] A typical American entry-level employee with a bachelor's degree or more made just $1,000 more for full-time year-round work in 2006 than he or she did in 1980. That 2006 worker was also much less likely than his or her 1980 counterpart to get health insurance on the job. "So much," Hacker and Pierson note, "for the enormous general rewards of a college degree."[11]

Sixth, if it were all about education and technology, then a very different group of people would comprise America's super-rich today. In fact, as Hedrick Smith notes, "Some of the most highly educated people in America, PhD physicists, astroscientists, top heart, brain, and cancer surgeons, and brilliant engineers, earn only a fraction of the astronomical pay of CEOs and Wall Street's top bankers. Bank traders earn far more than 'quants'—the mental geniuses who dream up the derivatives that traders use to make money."[12] Since 1989, CEO "earnings" have risen 100 percent while compensation for jobs in math and computer science rose just 4.8 percent and actually fell 1.4 percent in engineering.[13]

Seventh, England, France, Germany, and other European countries along with Japan and a host of other nations have all experienced advanced techno-logical change without experiencing anything remotely like the remarkable upward redistribution of wealth and income seen in the United States—the global "gold medalist" of inequality.[14]

Eighth, skilled and educated workers' wages and overtime would increase in response to an authentic shortage of skilled workers. Neither has occurred.[15]

Ninth, labor market researchers subjecting the skills gap theory to rigorous empirical testing discover no large pool of high-skill job openings waiting to be filled. To the contrary, they find that the greatest job growth is found precisely in low-wage occupations that require only a high school degree or less and that the percentage of college-educated workers stuck in jobs where they are clearly overqualified (as retail clerks and bartenders and the like) has risen sharply (60 percent of retail clerks in the Milwaukee metropolitan area have at least some college education, for example).[16]

Reflecting these facts, progressive journalist Roger Bybee notes, a grow-ing "consensus of prestigious economists, think tanks, and workforce experts rejects the skills gap [theory] as [a] baseless" narrative that diverts attention from the real problem—the shortage of good jobs. It would be preposterous, of course, to blame the sharp increase in US joblessness in 2008 and 2009 on the "skills gap"—as if the problem behind mass joblessness was some sort of sudden endemic skill loss on the part of American workers instead of an epic economic meltdown generated by the financial elite.

Why does the skills gap explanation nonetheless retain central influence in the national political discourse? Bybee explains the narrative's appeal to business, media, and political elites quite well. Thanks to the US labor market's abject failure to provide a reliable and sufficient supply of good jobs, Bybee notes, recent public opinion polls show a widespread loss of faith on the part of ordinary Americans in the ability of the "free enterprise system" and the "free market" to meet their economic needs. "The skills gap version of reality shifts the spotlight from the deficiencies of US capitalism in generating jobs with family-sustaining wages and benefits, to the alleged deficiencies of the workers themselves.... Not only does the skills gap story displace media coverage of the daunting problems faced by working Americans, it also activates a self-blaming reflex among workers conditioned their entire lives to ascribe structural failures to their personal shortcomings."[17] The skills gap myth diverts responsibility from the 1% and its profits system to the system's working-class subjects. It is another version of the timeworn upper-class game of blaming one's own victims.

Because Others Are Worse Off

The Second Gilded Age has much less to do with the supposedly inexorable logic of market and technological forces (and related purported skills gaps) than it does with the more human and malleable realms of greed and politics. Let us turn briefly to the Republican National Convention (RNC) that took place in September 2012 in Tampa, Florida. Amid the standard surfeit of arch-plutocratic and white-nationalist rhetoric displayed at that traditionally elite and exceedingly Caucasian gathering, one particularly revealing moment came with a speech given by US senator Marc Rubio (R-Florida) as he introduced his party's fantastically wealthy presidential candidate, Mitt Romney. Interweaving personal and national narcissism to toxic perfection, Rubio's speech wedded his family's supposedly heroic story of hard work and escape from socialism (the Cuban Revolution) to a standard "American exceptionalist" narrative proclaiming that the United States was the world's leading land of opportunity and freedom and the strident claim that "faith in our Creator is the most important American value of all."

Another striking moment came when Rubio launched a stinging accusation at the incumbent president, Barack Obama—a claim that echoed the sentiments of Republican plutocrats like Leon Cooperman. "Instead of ... reminding us of what makes us special," Rubio intoned, Obama "tells Americans they're worse off because others are better off. That people got rich by making others poor."[18] By the way Rubio lodged this complaint, it was clear that he viewed the notion that some US citizens have enriched themselves at the expense of others as something close to an un-American thought-crime.

Curiously enough, the supposedly unthinkable thing Rubio accused the president of believing happens to be *precisely what has been going on in the United States during the New Gilded Age*. Ever since the late 1970s, the data clearly show, American economic growth has been both slow and unequally distributed. The combination of slow and unequal growth—by no means just coincidental as we have seen—has proven a deadly combination as the rich have appropriated so much of the wealth and income expansion that there has been little left over for the rest. Examining how this happened in his valuable 2011 book *Failure by Design: The Story of America's Broken Economy*, economist Joshua Bivens reminds us that "one person's *wage* is another person's *cost*." As Bivens explains,

> A key reason why, for example, lawyers and surgeons saw rapidly rising living standards over the past three decades is *precisely because* the wages and salaries of the majority of American workers did not rise as rapidly. Because the wages of autoworkers and landscapers grew slowly, cars and lawn-care services became relatively cheap, boosting the living standards of workers not concentrated in those professions. Lawyers, surgeons, and financial professionals could enjoy goods and services that were made cheap because the workers producing them saw such slow wage growth, all while seeing their own salaries move briskly ahead.... In short, having the already privileged grab a growing share of the pie over time simply leaves less of it for everybody else, and given the overall rate of income growth over the last 30 years, the only way that low- and middle-income families could have seen more income growth is if very high-income families saw less.... More at the top means less at the middle and bottom.[19]

The Second Gilded Age hasn't involved everybody getting rich with the rich just getting rich faster. It's been a matter of the rich getting richer and more numerous at the expense of everyone else and especially the increasingly numerous and more deeply poor. In the words of a rebel in Shakespeare's *Coriolanus*, "our misery" is a source of "their abundance; our sufferance is a gain to them."[20]

The New Rentier/Robber Class Rigs the Game

The liberal Nobel laureate Joseph Stiglitz says something similar. "Those at the top have learned how to suck out money from the rest of us.... To put it baldly," Stiglitz adds, "there are two ways to become wealthy—to create wealth or to take wealth away from others. The former adds to society. The latter typically subtracts from it, for in the process of taking away, wealth gets destroyed."[21] The formulation is technically inaccurate since capitalist wealth creation always involves the appropriation of a surplus value and profit taken from others—from workers above all. That basic reality of exploitation does not disappear in periods when the profits system generates a large amount of economic development and societal wealth. Still, as Stiglitz makes clear in his epic volume *The Price of Inequality*, the neoliberal Second Gilded Age has been very much about capitalists taking away from others while adding nothing at all. It's about what mainstream economists call "rent-seeking" and what the leading Marxist analyst David Harvey considers capitalism's significant return to its original reliance on "accumulation by dispossession"—a rediscovery on the part of "the American bourgeoisie ... that, as [Hannah] Arendt has it, 'the original sin of simple robbery' which made possible the original accumulation of capital, had eventually to be repeated lest the motor of accumulation suddenly die down."[22]

The contemporary versions of "the original sin" are often far from simple. Stiglitz mentions a number of the elaborate rent-seeking techniques whereby the very rich have enhanced their fortunes in ways that appropriate from society and contribute nothing to the broader community:[23]

- Corporate CEOs setting their own compensation levels with the help of stacked corporate boards and powerless shareholders—a reflection of weak corporate governance laws that reflect the political influence of the rich.
- The use of political influence to receive and enjoy giant taxpayer-funded government giveaways and subsidies—that is, gifts. Under one current gift scheme, the Federal Reserve System "lends unlimited amounts of money to banks at near zero-interest rates" and "allows them to lend the money back to government (or to foreign governments) at much higher interest rates ... a hidden gift worth billions and billions of dollars."[24] Under another, a provision in the 2003 Medicare drug benefit bill actually prohibited the government from bargaining for lower prices on drugs—an at least $50-billion-per-year gift to the nation's leading pharmaceutical corporations.
- Targeting the poor and uninformed with deceptive and predatory lending and abusive credit card practices with exorbitantly high interest rates, late payment fees, exaggerated balloon payments, and the like.
- Making markets, financial institutions, and financial and other products nontransparent so that buyers and investors are unable to fully assess the risk involved in making deals with a bank or other financial institutions. The hyper-risky financial derivatives market—the cause of AIG's collapse and a leading player in the 2008–2009 financial crisis—was "kept in the shadows of the over-the-counter-market" in the early 2000s. Leading financial institutions sold real estate securities designed to fail, fully aware that buyers were ignorant of their doomed nature, while at the same time essentially *betting against those securities with derivatives.*
- Taking excessive financial risk with the knowledge that the federal government will rescue them on the theory that their corporate entities

are "too big to fail" without massive detrimental effect on the overall economy (AIG, for example, was bailed out at a taxpayer price of $150 billion).

- The use of political influence to undermine and prevent laws that would tax the rich progressively; promote strong social, labor, and environmental protections; prohibit anticompetitive/monopolistic behavior by corporations; prohibit giant taxpayer subsidies to corporations that serve no higher societal purpose; make markets and financial and other leading corporate institutions more transparent; and effectively regulate markets and leading corporations and financial institutions.

The rent-taking and robbery have not been achieved simply through the operation of market and technological forces, obviously. They have been attained through "a political system that gives inordinate power to those at the top," who "have used their power ... to shape the rules of the game in their favor."[25] In other words, it's been about *political economy* (to use the original eighteenth- and nineteenth-century term applied to the systematic study of production, exchange, and the distribution of national income and wealth) with a vengeance. It has reflected deliberate human design embodied in state policy crafted for, and captive to, the rich and corporate few.

Building on decades of research by the EPI, Bivens synthesizes and analyzes a wealth of economic information to show how the rich have benefited from a number of regressive policy choices that helped concentrate wealth and income upward. The problem, Bivens and other liberal and progressive economists show, has not been that "the economy" has been broken by the "invisible hand" of the market or other forces beyond human control. The real difficulty is that the "human-made" US economic system has been *working precisely as designed*: to distribute wealth, income, and power upward. Regressive outcomes have been deliberately crafted into a number of key, interrelated, largely bipartisan, and not-so-public policies across the long "neoliberal" era (from the mid-1970s to the present) that supplanted the long New Deal Era (mid-1930s to mid-1970s) during the Jimmy Carter and Ronald Reagan presidencies:

- Letting the value of the minimum wage be eroded by inflation.
- Slashing labor standards for overtime, safety, and health.
- Tilting the laws governing union organizing and collective bargaining strongly in employers' favor, feeding the epic decline of US union membership, union contract coverage, and labor political influence.
- Weakening the social safety net.
- Privatizing public services.
- Accelerating the integration of the US economy with the world economy without adequately protecting many workers from global competition.
- Shredding government oversight of international trade, currency, investment, and lending patterns.

- Deregulating the financial sector to an epic degree (above all the repeal during the late 1990s of the New Deal Glass-Steagal Act's separation or firewall between investment and commercial banking) along with numerous other industries.
- Privileging low inflation over full employment and abandoning the latter as a worthy goal of US fiscal and economic policy.
- Slashing taxes on corporations and the rich; for example, the top marginal tax rate fell from 70 percent under Carter to 28 percent under Reagan and to 35 percent under George W. Bush.[26]

American inequality in the Second Gilded Age is "the result of political forces as much as economic ones."[27]

Regarding the last policy bullet-pointed above (tax cuts on the rich and their business order), the most egregiously regressive aspect of recent US tax policy has been the cutting of the federal tax rate on capital gains, from 35 to 15 percent. First implemented under Bill Clinton and extended under George W. Bush, the current low capital gains rate means that "we have given the very rich, who receive a large fraction of their income in capital gains, close to a free ride." The bottom 90 percent of Americans get less than 10 percent of all capital gains, and less than 7 percent of households earning less than $100,000 per year receive any capital gains at all. By contrast, the nation's 400 richest income "earners" received 58 percent of their income as capital gains (salaries and wages accounted for less than 9 percent of that income). Slashing the capital gains levy to 15 percent granted these 400 an average per-household gift of $45 million in 2007 and $30 million in 2008, costing the federal government $18 billion in the former year and $12 billion in the latter. By Stiglitz's chilling accounting,

> The net effect is that the super-rich actually pay on average a lower tax rate than those less well-off; and the lower tax rate means that their riches increase faster. The average tax rate in 2007 on the top 400 households was only 16.6 percent, considerably lower than the 20.4 percent for taxpayers in general.... While the average tax has decreased little since 1979—going from 22.2 percent to 20.4 percent—that of the top 1 percent has fallen by almost a quarter, from 37 percent to 29.5 percent.[28]

"It doesn't make sense," Stiglitz laments, "that investors, let alone speculators, should be taxed at a lower rate than someone who works hard for his living, yet that's what our tax system does."[29]

Also egregious was the deregulation of the financial sector that began under Reagan and peaked late in Bill Clinton's administration. As Stiglitz notes,

> Good financial regulation helped the United States—and the world—avoid a major crisis for four decades after the Great Depression. Deregulation in

the 1980s led to scores of financial crises in the succeeding three decades, of which America's crisis in 2008–09 was only the worst. But these government failures were no accident: the financial sector used its political muscle to make sure that the market failures were not corrected, and that the sector's private rewards remained well in excess of their social contributions—one of the factors contributing to the bloated financial sector and to the high levels of inequality at the top.[30]

But is it really even "our tax system," or "our" federal government anymore, if it ever was? Harsh economic inequality is cause as well as effect of regressive government policy, reflecting a self-reinforcing cycle of disparity and plutocracy. It's a vicious circle. The more fortune concentrates in a few hands at the top, the more sway the organized and well-connected rich acquire over politics and policy in order to deepen inequality.[31]

"Blaming Simple Fate Absolves Those in Power"

The remarkable depth and degree of the recession that ultimately resulted from this harsh plutocratic reality—and from inherent crisis tendencies of the profits system[32]—were far from inevitable. They were not mandated by the mysterious "invisible hand of the market." If even just a fraction of the resources lost to "tax cuts aimed disproportionately at corporations and the very rich and at wars abroad" and "flagrant giveaways to pharmaceutical companies and other corporations" had "found their way into well-targeted interventions to boost the job market," Bivens notes, "the [2000–2010] decade could have been very different, with wage growth supporting living standards instead of debt[33].... Blaming simple fate," Bivens adds, "absolves those in power far too easily."[34] The terrible results were both predictable and in fact predicted—the unsurprising outcomes of an economy tilted by the visible hand of elitist policy choice.

The Real Conflict: Government for the Few vs. Government for the Many

The Second Gilded Age has been very much about politics and policy, not mysterious market or technical, much less natural, forces beyond human agency. Appropriately enough, liberal and progressive economists and activists have called for rational and democratic policies to "tip the balance of power away from the privileged few who have done so well for the past 30 years and back toward everyone else."[35] Proposals include an appropriately updated, inflation-adjusted minimum wage; union-friendly labor law reform; guaranteed pensions and health care; globalization protections; re-regulation of the financial sector; ambitious infrastructure investments; the re-enshrining of full employment as a legitimate policy goal; and action to shrink the nation's giant racial gaps in employment, wealth, and wages. If human-made economic policy can be designed and implemented to serve the few, it can also be designed and implemented to serve the working-class majority or "the many"—as we shall (in the next section of this chapter) see it did to no small degree during the Great Compression.

This might seem an elementary assertion, but it is a remarkably difficult point to advance through the fog created by neoliberal "free market" ideology and its hold over US political discourse today. Over the previous generation, the dominant US economic ideology has set up a fantasy struggle between the allegedly evil and capricious state on one hand and the supposedly virtuous and inexorable "free market" on the other. At the radical extremes, the ideology's proponents have proclaimed a desire to "starve the [government] beast" and "cut government down to the size where we can drown it in the bathtub" (Grover Norquist). Then the "invisible hand" of the market would be free to do its ultimately welcome and benevolent work, the theory goes.

But neoliberalism has never really wished to free economic elites or others from state policy. Beneath quasi-libertarian discourse about an epic conflict between "stultifying government" and the "free market," neoliberalism's corporate sponsors and beneficiaries have always sought to wield and profit from government policy of a particular sort. Reflecting their investment in a profit-based system that has always relied heavily on government protection and assistance, they have only targeted some parts of the public sector for malnourishment. They wish to de-fund and delegitimize what the French sociologist Pierre Bourdieu called "the left hand of the state": programs and services won by past popular struggles and movements for social justice, equality, and inclusion. They do not wish to axe the "right hand of the state": the parts that provide service and subsidy (corporate welfare) to concentrated wealth and dole out punishment and repression to the poor and to anyone among the rest who dares to resist (including rampant mass incarceration and felony-marking). They do not wish to dismantle America's military-industrial and imperial complex, a form of giant public transfer to the high-tech "private sector."[36]

The "antigovernment" rhetoric has worked to hide the actual core policy question. The real issue is NOT whether government can or should "work." It is rather the question of *whom government policy should work for—the public and the common good or the nation's leading centers of wealth and power.*

The New Deal Era and "the Golden Age"

During the Great Compression, that policy worked to no small extent for a broad segment of the populace. The trend toward greater equality in those years had nothing to do with any desire on the part of the rich to give up wealth and power and had everything to do with politics and policy during the Great Depression and World War II. Three key political factors were critical. The first was the federal government's decision to tax the rich and their corporations like never before (or since) in American history. The nation's top tax rate (currently 35 percent) rose from 24 percent in the 1920s to 63 percent during Franklin Roosevelt's first term, to 79 percent in his second term, and to 91 percent by the mid-1950s. In a similar vein, the average federal tax on corporate profits rose from less than 14 percent in 1929 to more than 45 percent in 1955. The top estate or inheritance tax rose from 20 percent to 77 percent during the same period. The nation's policymakers were in no mood for low tax rates on the rich, given the American plutocracy's egregious assault on the economy with the stock market collapse and the Great Depression and with the giant burden placed on government to pull the nation out of the Depression, win the Second World War, and match the Soviet Union across the globe in the Cold War.[37]

A second great leveling factor was the rise and consolidation of unions and regular collective bargaining agreements, aided and abetted to no small extent by the federal government. At the end of World War II, more than a third of American nonfarm workers were unionized—a drastic increase from the 1920s, when the nonagricultural union density rate (the percentage of the workforce enrolled in unions) was less than 10 percent. By the mid-1950s, union density reached 40 percent and most workers in the nation's leading industrial corporations (General Motors, Ford, Chrysler, General Electric, Westinghouse, John Deere, International Harvester) and extractive and transportation sectors enjoyed steadily rising wages, along with unprecedented job security and promotion ladders as well as an expanding package of benefits (health, pension, and more) codified in historic contracts meant to stabilize labor relations and underpin mass purchasing power. Many workers not enrolled in unions received increased wages high enough to match union wages and keep those workers content not to join unions. A number of developments produced the remarkable upsurge and consolidation of unionism in the United States during and after the interwar period, including immigration restrictions imposed by the federal government in the 1920s, a significant increase in worker militancy and solidarity resulting from anger over—and experience with—monumental capitalist injustice and dysfunction during the Great Depression, and significant organizational and political changes internal to the US labor movement during the mid-1930s. Also critical, however, was the pivotal 1935 National Labor Relations (Wagner) Act, which provided unprecedented protection to union organizing rights and required employers to bargain in good faith with workers who chose independent union representation through government-supervised union elections.[38]

Workers' gains were consolidated during World War II, when labor shortages enhanced workers' bargaining power and Roosevelt's National War

Labor Board raised substandard wages by decree and forbade employers from eliminating unions in an effort to buy labor peace and to ensure uninterrupted production. Under the existential pressure of the Great Depression, the global war against fascism, and the Cold War, the wealthy few's loathing of high taxes and unions took a backseat to the nation's larger priorities of survival and triumph. An especially critical federal measure was the 1944 Servicemen's Readjustment Act, known as the GI Bill of Rights (the "GI Bill" for short). "Even today," historian Ira Katznelson notes, "this legislation ... qualifies as the most wide-ranging set of social benefits ever offered by the federal government in a single, comprehensive initiative." Along with college tuition grants and the expansion of higher education, the GI Bill provided return- ing World War II veterans with low-interest mortgages and business loans, critically underwriting the growth of the suburbs and the growth of the small business sector. By 1957, 10 million veterans had received tuition and training subsidies under the legislation. Veterans Administration business loans totaled more than $50 billion in 1962. Between 1944 and 1971, Katznelson adds, "federal spending for this 'model welfare system' totaled over $95 billion," an expenditure that went a long way "to create a more middle class society." The long US-led postwar boom was fueled in no small part by the Wagner Act, the 1935 Social Security Act (providing federal and contributory old-age pensions and unemployment insurance for working Americans), and perhaps above all the GI Bill.[39]*

Across the US-led "golden age of Western capitalism" (1945–1973) the corporate elite settled in with the Keynesian notion that the expansion of mass purchasing power was consistent with high profit rates. The discomfort the captains of industry and finance may have felt with rising wages and labor power—and a welfare safety net that expanded partly under the pressure of social movement protests during the 1960s—was eased significantly by the remarkable profit-making opportunities afforded by the vastly expanded mass market created by the "middle class society" brought into being by the New Deal, World War II, and the emergence and consolidation of American mass production unionism. Also seductive for the rich was the widespread elite notion that the United States had found the permanent solution to its long-standing problem of social and class conflict "in abundance: not [just] in mere volume of production but in a system that would perpetuate prosperity and at the same time guarantee political harmony by distributing the consumption of goods so lavishly that it would not seem urgent to distribute them equally. In

---

* Katznelson's judgment in his important book *When Affirmative Action Was White: An Untold History of Racial Inequality in Twentieth-Century America* (2005) comes with a key caveat: "a more middle-class society, *but almost exclusively for whites.* Written under southern auspices, the [GI Bill, like the Social Security Act] was deliberately designed to accommodate Jim Crow. Its administration widened the country's racial gap. The prevailing experience for blacks was starkly differential treatment."

that way," the incisive British commentator Godfrey Hodgson observed (in a chapter on postwar America titled "Abundance"), "economic privilege could be left undisturbed. Social conflict could be made irrelevant, obsolete. The abundant society could short-circuit the quintessential questions of politics, the questions of justice and the question of priority: who gets what? What must we do first?" These questions had agitated Americans throughout their national history. Now the hope among many in elite economic, political, and intellectual circles was that these concerns would be marginalized for good by "full employment" (an official unemployment rate of less than 5 percent) and the provision of "dishwashers, nylon stockings, and automatic transmissions" to increasingly affluent and suburbanized masses.[40]

Elite concerns over the passing of the older pre-WWII class society were alleviated also by capitalists' sense of national mission—of contributing to victory over fascism, to a national economic miracle, and to a hoped-for victory in the Cold War—and by the remarkable new hegemonic position of the United States in the world economic system. The two decades following World War II marked the apex of what historian Charles S. Maier calls "the [American] Empire of Production." Fulfilling the potential for global mass-productionist dominance it had exhibited earlier in the century, the United States emerged from the war with its remarkable "Fordist" industrial apparatus intact and indeed expanded, remarkably free of foreign competition in an industrialized world that had been laid low by bombs and artillery beyond US shores. The United States emerged from the war boasting almost two-thirds of the planet's industrial production[41]—no small part of how the abundance myth could take off in the late 1940s and 1950s.

This favored position, the attendant myth of perpetual abundance, and the national allegiance of the elite—none of these would last. Also transient were the relative social and economic democratization and the sense of shared community and national identity across class lines that had preceded and fed the postwar boom. A Second Gilded Age harkened by the end of the 1970s, one in which many if not most members of an ever more financialized and globalist US elite seemed to have lost any sense of connection to the economy and society of the United States as such. Hodgson's "quintessential questions" were destined to return, with a vengeance.

The Power of and Incentive for Plutocracy in the Neoliberal Era

The shift in US policy from the comparative egalitarianism of the New Deal era to the savagely unequal New Gilded Age neoliberalism of the past thirty-plus years had nothing to with a shift toward alignment with big business and the rich on the part of the broad populace. As the perceptive radical economist Richard Wolff notes, "The last three decades of US politics did not see a change of political opinion from more left to more right. Rather, what happened was a relative withdrawal from politics on the part of those social groups that favored social-welfare and income-redistribution policies (the New Deal 'legacy') and a relative increase in the participation of business and the rich, who used their money to shift the tone and content of US politics [to the right]." Working- and lower-class participation in politics, already constricted by the 1970s, declined significantly under the pressure of stagnant wages, rising working hours, and increased levels of household debt. These burdens "all combined to leave working families with less time and energy to devote to politics—or indeed to social activities and organizations in general."[42]

This decline in popular engagement occurred as US labor unions' long and steep decline of membership and effectiveness accelerated under employer assault while soaring profits and wealth gave the rich massive resources to pour into shaping the nation's politics and political culture. The richer they got, the more the wealthy corporate and financial few were incentivized to influence politics. As Wolff explains,

> Rising economic inequalities are always a concern to those at the top because of the risks of envy, resentment, and opposition. There is always the possibility that the economically disadvantaged will seek to use political means to recoup their losses in the economy. The 99 percent might turn to politics to negate the economic gains of the 1 percent. Thus it became—and remains—more important than ever for the 1 percent to use their money to shape and control politics.[43]

We will turn in Chapter 5 to a more detailed analysis of precisely how the 1 percent does that (it's about more than campaign contributions, as we shall see).

"We Built It"

The rentier-robber rich, unsurprisingly, have a very different take on their own spectacular wealth. A standard narrative in elite circles holds that the wealthy deserve their opulence because they "earned" it through skill, brains, and hard work and that it is therefore "none of anyone's business" what they do with the riches they obtained because of their own special talents and efforts. It is "robbery," the narrative holds, to tax their wealth and "give it to someone else." It is also economically and socially dysfunctional to limit their wealth and regulate their economic activities, the storyline continues, because the rich are the source of economic development and employment for the rest. They are the benevolent, far-seeing "job providers" who have built the US economy, the engine of "American prosperity and freedom," and who would return the nation to full employment and broad affluence if only the government would "get out of the way" and let "the free market" work its magic.

These are standard claims in US business class boilerplate propaganda, honed over many decades. Along with the recurrent claims that the Democrats seek to "punish success," they were very much on display at the 2012 RNC, where one business-friendly speaker and politician after another returned again and again to the platitude that "We [the business class] built it,"[44] with "we" referring to the rich and "it" referring to the American economy.

None of Our Business?

This long-standing narcissistic fable of the elite is so full of holes that it is hard to know where to begin in tearing it apart. In terms of the disastrous consequences that contemporary economic inequality holds for democracy and human life (not to mention the lives of other species), it is neither here nor there whether the rich worked hard or well to attain their wealth. And it is *very much our business what they do with their fortunes, regardless of how those fortunes were acquired.* That said, it must also be noted that the 1% is loaded with people who are rich independent of any special effort or skill on their part due to simple facts of inheritance, luck, and greed. The passing on of net worth, connections, and other benefits across generations covers up the stupidity, decrepitude, and/or laziness of many rich people. Regardless of their different levels of skill, energy, and diligence, moreover, the modern-day "well-born" profit from the fact that success in the "free market" of the present and future depends significantly on how much accumulated economic and social capital you bring from the past. Bad behavior and poor skills can have remarkably little negative economic impact on those born into wealth; they typically stay rich regardless, just as most born into the lower and working classes remain there regardless of how hard, honestly, and skillfully they toil.

Social Capital and Private Fortunes

Even in cases of first-generation ascendancy into the wealthy elite without the benefit of inheritance, the notion that the rich "earn" their fortunes on their own is false. As the US ultra-billionaire investor Warren Buffett has acknowledged more than once, people can earn large amounts only when they live under favorable social circumstances. They certainly don't create those circumstances by themselves like mythical Robinson Crusoes. Society, Buffett admits, is responsible for his wealth. "If you stick me down in the middle of Bangladesh or Peru," he once said, "you'll find out how much my [special talent for smelling market opportunities] is going to produce in the wrong kind of soil." The Nobel Prize–winning economist and social scientist Herbert Simon has estimated that "social capital" is responsible for *at least*

90 percent of the income that people receive in rich nations. By social capital, Simon means not only natural resources but also technology, organizational skills, and "good [wealth-friendly] government.... On moral grounds," Simon added, "we could argue for a flat income tax of 90 percent."[45]

Exploitation

But this actually understates the case for confiscatory taxation of the rich today. The contemporary wealthy do not simply benefit from society; they accumulate fortunes at the expense of it. They profit from mass unemployment's depressive impact on wages, which cuts their labor costs; regressive tax cuts and loopholes, which increase with wealth while shutting down social services for the poor; the cutting and undermining of environmental regulations, which reduce their business costs while spoiling livable ecology; wars and giant military budgets, which feed the bottom lines of the "defense" corporations they own while killing and crippling millions and stealing money from potential investment in social uplift; a hyper-commercialized mass consumer culture that despoils the environment while reducing human worth to exchange value and destroying peoples' capacity for critical thought; dealings with corrupt dictators who provide natural resources at cheap prices while depressing wages and crushing democracy in "developing countries"; the closing down of livable wage jobs in the United States and the export of employment to repressive and low-wage peripheries; a health care system that privileges the profits of giant insurance and drug companies over the well-being of ordinary people; exorbitant credit card interest rates that lead to millions of bankruptcies each year; predatory lending practices that spread and perpetuate poverty and foreclosure; agricultural and trade practices that destroy sustainable local and regional food cultivation and distribution practices at home and abroad; the imposition of overly long working hours that keep employee compensation levels down while helping maintain a large number of unemployed workers; exorbitant public business subsidies and tax-payer incentives and bailouts of the rich paid for by the rest; and ... the list goes on and on.[46] Corporate and financial profits were restored in the wake of the 2008 financial crisis largely because the working-class majority paid for them, through taxpayer bailouts, slashed social services, layoffs, and reduced wages, hours, and benefits.

Wanting to Be Rich, Playing Unfair

Contrary to their claims of generous concern for the economic vitality and "freedom" of other Americans, part of what makes and keeps the rich rich is their willingness to put aside moral qualms about such harsh realities. "Modern capitalism," Stiglitz notes, "has become a complex game and those who win have to have more than a little smarts. But those who win at it often possess less admirable characteristics as well: the ability to skirt the law, or to shape the law in their own favor; the willingness to take advantage of others, even the poor; and to play *unfair* when necessary." Stiglitz quotes a leading capitalist who said that "the old adage 'Win or lose, what matters is how you play the game' is rubbish. All that matters is whether you win or lose." More importantly, he cites a key recent experimental study showing that people of higher income are far more likely than others to be driven by self-interest, far more likely to cheat, far less likely to have misgivings about breaking the rules, and generally more prone to behave in ways that are widely viewed as unethical.[47] The nation's sociopathic 4 percent[48] would appear to be significantly overrepresented among the nation's economic 1 percent. Part of what gets and keeps the rich rich is not only the hardly universal[49] desire to become and/or stay rich, but a willingness to bend and break rules and compromise ethics to achieve or sustain hyper-affluence.

Capitalists and Most of Us: C-M-C vs. M-C-M' and M-M'

The rich, it should be recalled, are capitalists for the most part, something that makes their dealings with the market very different from the rest of us. As David McNally explains in his important volume *Global Slump*, most of us engage with the market primarily by renting out our core human capacity for work to more privileged others in order to survive—to purchase use values that make life possible. Capitalists are different, by economic definition. Economically speaking, they and (above all) their highly organized concentrations of profit-seeking capital—corporations—care about little beyond exchange value and profit. They engage the market in order to exploit the world and its people and are in a competitive race to do so more effectively than their capitalist rivals. There would be no capitalist point to their investment without exploitation. There would be no point in paying us wages and salaries without surplus value—extra labor value going to them beyond the commodity price of our labor power—or in lending us money without interest or in selling us goods or services without a margin. When profit and its critical ingredient surplus value are deemed unattainable, they toss us into the metaphorical and sometimes all-too-literal gutter, where, as members of the "reserve army of labor" (Marx's still-relevant term), we help them bid down the commodity value of labor. Here are McNally's reflections (utilizing Marx's famous "money-commodity-money prime" schemata for illustrating the inner logic of exchange and production under the profits system) on the difference between capitalists and the rest of us when it comes to how and why we engage the market:

As a rule, when capitalists enter the market, their purpose is entirely foreign to the motivations of most people. For most of us, money is a means to get commodities that sustain life. We sell a commodity (usually our labor [power]), get money in return, and use that money to buy commodities to consume. Put as a simple formula, we are regularly engaged in the cycle C-M-C, where C represents commodities and M stands for money. The whole point of engaging in the market, therefore, is to procure the commodities that make life possible. But things are very different for a capitalist enterprise. For a business, the operative formula is M-C-M'. The capitalist begins with money (M) then buys commodities, such as machines, raw materials, and labor power, with which to produce new commodities (like bread or jeans) that are sold for money (M'). Money, not commodities for consumption, becomes the end goal of production. But that only makes sense for a capitalist if the second sum of money is bigger than the first, which is why it is designated as M'. Otherwise the capitalist would be simply going through the whole cycle of investment only to come out with the same sum of money with which he began. Clearly, something else is going on: the drive for profit, the drive to accumulate greater wealth.[50]

It should be noted that McNally presents one of the different ways in which capitalist enterprises have historically engaged the market to accumulate profit and power for investors. The paragraph just quoted describes the behavior and circuits of manufacturing and industrial capital, where companies invest in raw materials, means of production, and labor power (the latter providing more value than its price—what Marx called "surplus value"). Fully written out, this formula is M-C (raw materials)-C (means of production)-C' (labor's hourly price plus unpaid work)-M'. But Marx also wrote about a simple "merchant capitalist" formula of M-C-M' where the enterprise never invests in production at all, simply profiting from the price rent it affords from its ability to transport and market commodities made, grown, or otherwise provided by and purchased (or taken) from others and/or from nature. A different one of Marx's formulas is that of finance/money capital, whereby the investor profits without making or selling any tangible thing or use value at all: M-M'. The simplicity of the formula, we shall see, can be deceptive, for the methods by which M' is extracted from M are often highly, even maddeningly, complex.[51]

From colonial origins through the 1850s, the dominant capitalist enterprises in British colonial North America and the early and antebellum United States were caught up primarily in the cycles of merchant capital (M-C-M').[52] The industrial or manufacturing cycle (M-C-C-C'-M') defined the nation's leading firms (including General Motors, Ford, General Electric, Westinghouse, US Steel, International Harvester, and other vast, vertically integrated manufacturing firms) from the aftermath of the Civil War through the 1960s, a period when the United States reached industrial maturity and became the leading industrial power on the planet. But the "Empire of Production" was short-lived. Over the course of the post-WWII "golden age," and emerging with undeniable force in the 1970s, foreign industrial competition rebounded with the latest, most highly efficient technologies and production systems, its new economic muscle ironically nurtured by the United States government in accord with Washington's imperial and geostrategic imperatives during the Cold War.[53] With the world market for manufactured goods increasingly crowded, reflecting a classic overaccumulation of capital and feeding a related declining rate of profit in manufacturing, the American investor class sought to restore high returns through a number of interrelated strategies that reflected and advanced a much more short-term, regressive, and transactional mindset than the sort of business orientation that is linked to the building and maintenance of a strong domestic industrial base. The strategies included a major "top-down class war" on unions and collective bargaining, on progressive tax rates, on government regulation, on the welfare state, and on democratic processes and public opinion—a topic we will turn to in Chapter 5. At the same time and in complementary ways, the investor class increasingly moved American production outside the United States to lower-wage zones of the global economy and shifted surplus capital into an ever more globally footloose and unregulated financial sector, which had no particular strong connection to the making of real things within, or even beyond, the United States but was more predisposed to overseas production than to domestic manufacture.

As the smoke cleared on this brave new "neoliberal" order, it was evident that M-C-C-C'-M' had moved largely beyond US shores. The commanding heights of the American economy were now held by firms who sought to make money off money—in various complex elaborations on the M-M' formula—with no material production or related broad economic and societal development required within the United States itself. The age of financialized state global capitalism was upon us.

CHAPTER 4

Dismantling Domestic Development
The Global Age of Finance

US Steel is in business to make profits, not to make steel.
—*David Roderick, chairman of US Steel, 1979*[1]

For years the most profitable industry in America has been one that doesn't design, build, or sell a single tangible thing.
—*John Cassidy,* New Yorker, *November 2010*[2]

There's nothing new in American, Western, or global history about economic exploitation, elite rent-seeking, plutocracy, or the use by the rich of the state to increase their fortunes even as they complain about overreaching government power. Also less than novel are mass joblessness, endemic poverty, widespread economic insecurity resulting from the power of greedy profit-accumulators, and deceptive claims of compassion and benevolence on the part of greedy wealth-accumulators whose enterprises are dedicated to extracting wealth from the populace and the broader community—regardless of the cost to fellow humans and the Earth. Regarding the last pattern, the late eighteenth-century philosopher and economist Adam Smith (a founder of the field that was once properly called "political economy") denounced what he called the "vile maxim of the [merchant-capitalist and financier] masters of mankind: 'All for ourselves, and nothing for other people.'" Writing of England, the world's first great capitalist power, Smith observed that "the principle architects" of policy were the great merchants and manufacturers who essentially owned the nation, and they made sure their own interests were "most particularly attended to," regardless of how "grievous" the effects on others, including the people of their own supposedly beloved land of England.[3] "Power," John Adams once said, "always thinks it has a great soul and vast views beyond the comprehension of the weak; and that it is doing God's service when it is violating all his laws."[4]

Vicious Circle I: Financialization and "De-Industrialization"

At the same time, there *is* something novel in the American experience during the Second Gilded Age—something that sets it apart from previous long eras of upward wealth concentration in US history. A major underlying change came in the 1970s. Prior to that "pivotal decade" (business and labor historian Judith Stein's term and the title of her latest book[5]), the United States "had been," in Noam Chomsky's words, "with ups and downs ... a developing society, not always in pretty ways, but with general progress toward industrialization, prosperity, and expansion of rights."[6] During and since the 1970s, however, the United States has moved from "several hundred years of progress towards industrialization and development" toward what Chomsky called in the fall of 2011 "a process of de-industrialization and de-development ... a significant shift of the economy from productive enterprise—producing things people need or could use—to financial manipulation."[7]

The first major shift was the change of investors' domestic preference from industrial production to "FIRE": finance, insurance, and real estate—a transformation that tripled financial institutions' share of total US corporate profits.[8] Before the 1990s those institutions rarely made more than 20 percent of those profits. But the "financial services industry's" share rose from 10 percent in the early 1980s to 40 percent on the eve of the Great Recession that industry largely caused in 2007, when nearly a quarter of the "Forbes 400" (the 400 richest Americans) gained their fortunes in finance (up from less than a tenth in 1982).[9] During one quarter in 2001, finance's share of US profits reached nearly half (46 percent). The financial sector received nearly a third of those profits after the technical end of the recession, posting a record-setting $57.7 billion profit in the fourth quarter of 2010.[10]

Over the Second Gilded Age, the number of Americans employed in finance ballooned from 5 million to 7.5 million. Financial sector earnings skyrocketed to the point where Wall Street became "the preferred destination for the bright young people who used to want to start up their own companies, work for NASA, or join the Peace Corps." Even after the financial meltdown, a third of Harvard's seniors with secure jobs in the spring of 2010 were headed to the financial sector.[11]

Finance has even taken over within firms that are historically identified with manufacturing. In early 2011 many of President Obama's liberal fans applauded his appointment of General Electric's CEO Jeffrey Immelt to head the White House's new "Council on Jobs and Competitiveness" on the grounds that Immelt represented a company that actually manufactured goods rather than being simply a manipulator of financial wealth. But this praise was somewhat misplaced since General Electric (GE) earned "more revenue from its financial operations than it does from manufacturing."[12]

A second and related change (and another reason not to applaud Immelt's appointment) was another GE specialty—the global "outsourcing" or "offshoring" of production. Like many "US companies," GE employs most of its workforce outside the United States.[13] The mass export of formerly US-based manufacturing jobs across the neoliberal era is a reminder that big "American" capital has not been interested in deindustrialization per se, only in the deindustrialization of the "high wage" United States. US corporations and their investors have been happy to promote industrialization in "developing nations" where lower wages and weaker government protections and regulations promise higher profits.

The global flight of manufacturing capital and the related end of the post-WWII "assumption that [American] capital and [American] labor should prosper together"[14] were intimately connected to financialization. Reflecting on what she calls the post-1970s "Age of Inequality," Judith Stein notes the central involvement of leading Wall Street institutions in the trade-based undermining and dismantlement of US industry, which accelerated with the emergence of vast new cheap labor supplies abroad and fed the housing bubble that blew up in 2007 and 2008:

> The Fed, to counter the bursting of the stock bubble [in 2001], lowered the interest rates eleven times, producing the lowest rates in fifty years. Too much of that money was going into the housing sector because US policy over the last twenty years had outsourced the manufactured goods that Americans consumed. The goods deficit had skyrocketed during the 1990s.... The collapse of the Soviet Union and the opening up of China and India doubled the global labor force. The American financial services industry bankrolled factories that employed these workers, weakening organized labor and sending a flood of cheap imports to the United States.... Funds from China and other east Asian countries resulted from their huge trade surpluses with the United States.... East Asians purchased US Treasury and other government bonds with their dollars [gained from huge trade surpluses with the United States], which kept interest rates low. Cheap money made it easier for Americans to buy houses, despite stagnant incomes.... Economist Paul Krugman noted in 2005, "these days, Americans make a living by selling each other houses, paid with money borrowed from the Chinese."[15]

It wasn't just that the 1%'s capital shifted from factories to finance. The New Gilded Age's enlarged and highly profitable financial sector preyed upon the nation's disappearing manufacturing and productive base, actively shutting it down in favor of production abroad in ways that helped generate a deadly, unsustainable real estate bubble.

From General Motors to Wal-Mart

At the end of it all stands the displacement of General Motors (GM) by the low-price and low-wage leader and militantly anti-union company Wal-Mart as both the nation's largest corporation and the nation's "business template." In the 1950s, at the height of the Great Compression, the revenues of the heavily unionized automaker GM comprised 3 percent of US GDP. GM was the nation's leading company, its payroll so vast and its products so commonplace and central to daily life that it was common for pundits and citizens to repeat former GM CEO Charles Wilson's once purported belief that "what's good for General Motors is good for America." By the early twenty-first century, Wal-Mart had supplanted GM with a nonunion workforce of 1.5 million and revenues equivalent to 2.3 percent of US GDP. But, as the late world systems analyst and historical sociologist Giovanni Arrighi noted in 2007,

> the two templates differ in fundamental ways. GM was a vertically integrated industrial corporation, which established production facilities throughout the world *but remained deeply rooted in US economy*, where the bulk of its products were manufactured and sold. Wal-Mart, in contrast, is primarily *a commercial intermediary between foreign (mostly Asian) subcontractors*, who manufacture most of its products, and US consumers, who buy most of them. The change of guard between the two corporations ... can ... be taken as a symbol and a measure of transformation of the United States from *a nation of producers to a nation whose role as global financial entrepot* enables it to [like turn-of-the-twentieth-century England] ... "share in the activity of brain and muscles of other countries."

The "rise of Wal-Mart and its anti-labor strategies," Arrighi observed, "are manifestations of the crisis of the previously dominant industrial corporations on one side, and the financialization of US capital on the other."[16]

The Auto Bailout as Anti-Industrial
and Ecocidal Finance Capitalism

The same can be said of the manner in which General Motors was "rescued" by the Obama administration in 2009. Obama's bailout of GM is an epitome of what the progressive economist and author Jeff Faux calls "the transactional Wall Street mindset, with its obsession with the short-term bottom line"—opposed to any notions of a long-term economic, environmental, and industrial policy. Instead of appointing people with industrial backgrounds, the president put a Wall Street–leveraged buyout expert named Steve Rattner in charge. It was *deemed irrelevant that Rattner knew nothing about automobiles, energy, manufacturing, or transportation.* Appointed simply to save GM from bankruptcy at the lowest possible political and financial cost, Rattner treated General Motors like a typical quick Wall Street "equity-capital" fix. As Faux notes in his book *The Servant Economy: Where America's Elite Is Sending the Middle Class*,

> Rattner ... fired the [GM] CEO [Rick Waggoner] and forced concessions from the unions, the suppliers, and the car dealers. Ed Whiteacre, the new CEO, knew nothing about the industry. Rattner hired him for his toughness....
>
> Whiteacre ... was then replaced by a managing director of another leveraged buyout firm, the Carlyle Group. In his five months as auto czar, Rattner made one trip to Detroit, and it lasted just one day, on which he was briefed by officials at GM and Chrysler, gawked at a modern assembly line, and flew back to Washington....
>
> At the end of 2010, GM initiated a new stock offering in which the government sold about half its shares.... During that time, 21,000 more workers were laid off, at least 14 [US] factories and 3 warehouses were closed, Rattner's ... plan ... *shifted more production to China, South Korea, and Mexico.*[17]

When the United Auto Workers wrote to Congress protesting Rattner's plan to boost car imports, the White House "shrugged off" the complaint. "The Obama administration," the *New York Times* reported, "sees interference in such plans as *crossing a line into industrial policy*"[18]—a revealing statement. The administration's view was hardly surprising since the president had put Wall Street elites in charge of his administration's economy policy from the start.[19] Consistent with that choice, the White House imposed a two-tier wage system, reducing entry level wages from $28 to $16 an hour, as "the price of bailing out GM and Chrysler"[20]—*a price borne by workers, not investors.* Entrusted to financial wizards with no special knowledge or concerns in relation to industry, technology, ecology, labor, or national planning, the much-ballyhooed auto "rescue" (highly touted in Obama's 2012 reelection campaign) amounted to a leveraged-buyout operation, with taxpayers providing the equity. "The bailout of GM was just that and nothing more," Faux notes. "It was unconnected to the long-term transportation and energy needs of the country, US industrial redevelopment, or the kinds of autos that Americans should be producing and driving in the future."[21]

Regarding energy and ecology, it is important to note that the previous GM CEO, Rick Waggoner, had begun preparations to produce an all-electric car along with the Chevy Volt, the company's gas-electric hybrid. But Rattner wasn't interested. "The bottom line," he wrote in a memoir of his five months as the nation's "car czar," was "there was no way for the Volt or any other next generation car to have a positive impact on GM's finances any time soon. Certainly not within the five-year framework that private equity firms typically use to evaluate investment opportunities."[22]

That reflection speaks volumes on finance capitalism's short-term fixation and inability to plan and set limits in accord with environmental needs. As Faux explains, "The dismantling of the New Deal [in the neoliberal era] profoundly affected the way in which the private corporate sector treated the future. Time itself became increasingly monetized as deregulation dramatically shortened the horizons of US business. . . . Management was now judged solely by the quarterly bottom line it delivered to the shareholders of record, who would most likely be different by the next quarter."[23]

"Worse Than the Great Depression"

The Lost Multiplier

In the postindustrial financialized and globalized capitalism of the Second Gilded Age, when most goods Americans consume are produced abroad (especially in East Asia), government stimulus measures like the one passed in early 2009 have lost much of their onetime power to increase employment by boosting consumer demand. The once heralded "multiplier effect" of Keynesian spending no longer redounds solely or even primarily to American industry. Perhaps as much as half of every dollar spent at Wal-Mart is what Mike Davis calls a "stimulus to the Chinese or the Korean economies," reflecting what Davis calls "the huge difference between the situation today and the 1930s: . . . in the 1930s the United States had the largest, most productive industrial machine in the world. It could make almost anything. The question was how to put the workers and machines back to work."[24]

"These Jobs Aren't Coming Back"

This evisceration of the domestic industrial job base is a key part of why the economic crisis that broke out in 2007 and 2008 can actually seem to some individuals as more terrible than the worst economic collapse in American (and world) history. The Great Depression of the 1930s might have created higher unemployment and more widespread poverty than what resulted from the Great Recession of 2007–2009. The earlier crisis was accompanied, however, by an accurate and realistic sense that jobs and prosperity would return for working-class people at some point in the not-so-distant future. Things are very different for political as well as economic reasons with the more recent collapse. As Chomsky noted in May 2012, in terms that reflected his observation of the American experience over eight decades,

> I'm just old enough to remember the Great Depression. After the first few years, by the mid-1930s—although the situation was objectively much harsher than it is today—nevertheless, the spirit was quite different. There was a sense that "we're gonna get out of it," even among unemployed people, including a lot of my relatives, a sense that "it will get better." ... There was militant labor union organizing going on, especially from the CIO (Congress of Industrial Organizations).... Also New Deal legislation was beginning to come in as a result of popular pressure. Despite the hard times, there was a sense that, somehow, "we're gonna get out of it."
>
> It's quite different now. For many people in the United States, there's a pervasive sense of hopelessness, sometimes despair.... And it has an objective basis.... In the 1930s, unemployed working people could anticipate that their jobs would come back. If you're a worker in manufacturing today—the current level of unemployment there is approximately like the Depression—and current tendencies persist, those jobs aren't going to come back.[25]

The notion that America's manufacturing job loss is permanent has been widely shared by American capitalists and investors during the Second Gilded Age, consistent with a haunting lyric in Bruce Springsteen's hit 1985 song "Your Hometown": "They're closing down the textile mill down by the railroad tracks. Foreman says these jobs are going away and they ain't coming back." But it isn't just blue-collar manufacturing workers (a declining share of the American workforce since the 1920s) who feel hopeless at the current peak of the Second Gilded Age. Millions in the service and professional sectors have good reasons to wonder if anything remotely close to the once vaunted American Dream will ever again be within their reach. The aforementioned "We Are the 99 Percent" blog began collecting and posting notes detailing personal experience of economic difficulty from thousands of Americans since October 2011. The accounts told difficult, often heartbreaking stories of eviction, job loss, indebtedness, worthless educations, daunting student loan debts, fractured families, and shattered dreams from all walks of the American educational and occupational terrain.

Vicious Circle II: Political Financialization

To the vicious circle of financialization and domestic deindustrialization and de-development must be added the related one of wealth accumulation and political corruption. The more wealth accumulated in the financial sector, the more capital that sector possessed for investment in the political process, pushing the costs of US elections ever higher and "driving political leaders ever deeper into the pockets of wealthy backers, increasingly in financial institutions.... Naturally," Chomsky notes, "the funders were rewarded by the politicians they put into office, who instituted policies favorable to Wall Street: deregulation, tax changes, relaxation of rules of corporate governance, and other measures that intensified the concentration of wealth and carried the vicious cycle forward."[26]

"Beyond Insane"

Already in place before the Reagan era, American capital's decision to "trade factories for finance" (Stein's evocative phrase in the subtitle of her aforementioned book) was richly encouraged by key legislation and policy changes that Wall Street successfully campaigned and lobbied for during the Clinton administration. The Financial Services Modernization Act (1999) abolished key provisions of the 1933 Glass-Steagal Act, tearing down the last firewalls between investment banks, commercial banks, securities companies, and insurance firms. "Now," the muckraking financial journalist Dylan Ratigan notes, "a single bank could take your money for safekeeping, and use it as collateral to fund investments in high-risk securities with no supervision, all the while insuring itself against losses the taxpayers must pay if the bets the banks made with our money went bad.... Banks could actually make more money from bonds that defaulted than from those that were paid," since they kept the price customers paid for failed securities and collected insurance paid on those securities.[27]

The Commodity Futures Modernization Act (2000) ensured that there would be no regulation of key nonproductive, parasitic, and destructive "financial products,"[28] including credit default swaps and other derivatives*— "contracts that would encourage risky investment practices at Wall Street's most venerable institutions and spread the risks, like a virus, around the

---

* A derivative is a financial instrument that derives its value from something else, termed the "underlying" or "referenced" bond, stock, or other financial tool. A "stock index" is a derivative based on a collection of "underlying stocks." Purchasers of a stock index do not buy the stocks that comprise the index. Still, the buyer's "index security" rises and falls in accord with the value of the stocks it tracks. "Think," the progressive nonprofit director Les Leopold writes, "of fantasy baseball. It's a derivative game of betting based on statistics based on the behavior of real major league players. You don't own the players, or even a piece of them as in a mutual fund. When you own a fantasy baseball team, you don't really own anything except your derivative statistics compiled for you by a service. Your bet has value because other players and their derivative teams are willing to bet with you. There can be thousands of fantasy baseball leagues based on only two major league teams. Similarly, there are tens of thousands of derivative securities based on combinations of the same underlying real securities."

world."[29] The bill proclaimed that derivatives required no oversight since they were deals between "sophisticated parties" who knew what they were doing. Officially unregulated, the derivatives market operated without transparency, capital reserve requirements, fraud prohibitions, and other protections for buyers and the broader economy. Along the way, the new financial products received triple-A ratings from the top bond and credit rating agencies (AAA and Standard & Poor's) since those agencies were "paid by the companies they're supposed to regulate."[30]

The heavily Wall Street–supported crafters of the second bill were not content merely to prohibit a regulator from touching derivatives, regardless of how dangerous they became to the US and global economy. They also "gave derivatives claims 'seniority' in the event of bankruptcy. If a bank went under," Joseph Stiglitz explains, "the claims on the derivatives would be paid off before workers, suppliers, or other creditors saw any money—even if the derivatives had pushed the firm into bankruptcy in the first place"[31]—an epitome of the Second Gilded Age's privileging of elite financial manipulation over human labor in the "homeland."

Wall Street power brokers also moved to increase the amount of other people's money they could legally use to bet on risky investments that ultimately crashed the US and global economy. As Matt Taibbi noted two years after the onset of the financial collapse that triggered the Great Recession,

> The banks that had been bailed out by Bush and Obama had engaged in behavior that was beyond insane. In 2004, the five biggest investment banks in the country (at the time, Merrill Lynch, Goldman Sachs, Morgan Stanley, Lehman Brothers, and Bear Stearns) had gone to then-SEC chairman William Donaldson and personally lobbied to remove restrictions on borrowing so that they could bet even more of whatever other peoples' money they happened to be holding on bullshit investments like mortgage-backed securities.
>
> They were making so much straight case betting on the burgeoning housing bubble that it was no longer enough to be able to bet twelve dollars for every dollar they actually held, the maximum that was then allowed under a thing called the net capital rule.
>
> So people like Hank Paulsen (at the time, head of Goldman Sachs) got Donaldson to nix the rule, which allowed every single one of those banks to jack up their debt-to-equity ratio above 20–1. In the case of Merrill Lynch, it got as high as 40–1.... This was gambling, pure and simple, and it got rewarded with the most gargantuan bailout in history.[32]

Under these and other changes high finance pushed through Washington, Ratigan notes, "Cheating was no longer a side game, it was the primary game."[33]

The corruption cut across major party lines, with both of the official political organizations captive to the moneyed elite, something that had been clear to careful observers since at least the Carter administration.[34] It was the Clinton administration that did the most to shred the regulatory methods that shielded ordinary citizens from rapacious financiers. The George W. Bush administration shredded the federal revenue base with hideously tilted tax cuts for the rich. The Obama administration carried the bailout of "too big [and powerful] to fail" banks to record-setting levels and permitted predatory financial criminals to continue to profit unchecked after it instituted supposed "reforms" in the wake of the 2008 collapse.[35]

Viewing it all from the venerable perspective of American democratic populism, the socialist US senator Bernie Sanders (I-VT) could not contain his disgust. "They produce worthless, illegal products that nobody understands, make huge amounts of money for themselves, and when their Ponzi schemes collapse," Sanders lamented, "they get the American taxpayers to bail them out."[36]

"To Help Us Quell the Mob"

In his important book *Confidence Men: Wall Street, Washington, and the Education of a President* (2011), the Pulitzer Prize–winning author Ron Suskind tells a remarkable story from March 2009. Three months into Barack Obama's supposedly progressive, left-leaning presidency, popular anger at Wall Street was intense, and the nation's leading financial institutions were weak and on the defensive in the wake of the onset of the epic 2008–2009 financial collapse and economic recession they had essentially created. The new president called a meeting of the nation's top thirteen financial executives at the White House. The banking titans came into the meeting full of dread, with reason. As Suskind notes,

> They were the CEOs of the thirteen largest banking institutions in the United States.... And they were nervous in ways that these men are never nervous. Many would have had to reach back to their college days, or even grade school, to remember a moment when they felt this sort of lump-in-the-throat tension.
>
> As some of the most successful men in the country, they weren't used to being pariahs ... [and] they were indeed *pariahs*. The populist backlash against the financial sector—building steadily since September—was finally beginning to cause grave discomfort on Wall Street. As unemployment ballooned and credit tightened, the country began to look inward, toward the origins of the panic and its disastrous consequences.[37]

The briefly frightened captains of high finance left the meeting pleased to learn that Obama was firmly in their camp. For instead of standing up for those who had been harmed most by the crisis, the people in whose name he had campaigned in 2007 and 2008 (and in whose name he would campaign again in 2011 and 2012)—workers, minorities, and the poor—Obama sided unequivocally with those who had caused the meltdown. "My administration is the only thing between you and the pitchforks," Obama said. "You guys have an acute public relations problem that's turning into a political problem. *And I want to help ... I'm not out there to go after you. I'm protecting you ... I'm going to shield you from congressional and public anger*" (emphasis added). For the banking elite, who had destroyed untold millions of jobs, there was, as Suskind puts it, "Nothing to worry about. Whereas [President Franklin Delano] Roosevelt had [during the Great Depression] pushed for tough, viciously opposed reforms of Wall Street and famously said 'I welcome their hate,' Obama was saying 'How can I help?'"[38] As one leading banker told Suskind, "The sense of everyone after the meeting was relief. The president had us at a moment of real vulnerability. *At that point, he could have ordered us to do just about anything and we would have rolled over. But he didn't—he mostly wanted to help us out, to quell the mob.*"[39]

"When the bankers arrived in the State Dining Room, sitting under a portrait of a glowering Lincoln," Suskind notes, "Obama had them scared and ready to do almost anything he said.... An hour later, they were upbeat, ready to fly home and commence business as usual."[40]

Emboldened and reassured by Obama's expressed desire to "protect" and "shield" them, the nation's leading bankers had little difficulty preventing the president and Congress from making any serious effort to regulate them in response to the disaster they had generated. "Once the [financial] hemorrhaging stopped and Congress sat down to write a new law to prevent a future collapse," notes the veteran national correspondent and Pulitzer Prize–winning author Hedrick Smith in *Who Stole the American Dream?* (2012), "Wall Street was back at lobbying full throttle, resisting almost every regulatory idea.... At the very moment when Wall Street's credibility should have been in tatters" and "the political climate demanded action," the top bankers showed that they "still dominated political Washington despite the dangers [they posed] to the US economy." Endowed with 1,400 lobbyists and following a policy of "obstruct and delay," Wall Street waited for the public to lose track of, and interest in, the complexities of financial reform and the legislative process.

The result was the passage in mid-2010 of a financial regulatory law that was most remarkable for what it failed to contain. Things sought by serious reformers that were not in the bill included a freestanding financial services protection agency headed by a serious consumer advocate, measures to shrink the biggest banks and limit their size to deal with the "too-big-to-[be allowed to]-fail" problem, the revival of Glass-Steagal protections that had separated commercial banking from investment banking between the mid-1930s and the late 1990s, a significant "bank tax" to help meet the expense of future bank failures, a ban on banks marketing risky derivates (including the toxic credit default swaps that had so critically fueled the mortgage meltdown), and a serious and substantive barring of banks from proprietary trading on their own accounts.[41]

Avoiding Obvious Implications of "Too Big to Fail"

The ultimate sign of the great financial institutions' incredible power was that they continued to exist on their giant and indeed significantly growing scale even as they made the argument that they were "too big to fail" and therefore required gargantuan government bailouts after the giant gambles collapse in 2007 and 2008. As Richard Wolff observes,

> The idea seemed to be that letting them collapse or default would have such devastating consequences for the larger economy that the government had to help them "in the national interest." ... However, the banks' arguments had two logical implications that had to be blocked from public discussion, let alone action. The first implication was that such larger enterprises should be broken up into smaller enterprises so that the failure of any one would not effectively blackmail the government into costly support.... The second implication that had to be repressed was this: if big banks and other financial enterprises are too big to fail, then perhaps the solution was to nationalize them. Making their assets and liabilities fully transparent and publicly available would minimize the chance of behaviors that placed society at risk.

Neither of these two solutions indicated by Wall Street's own "too big to fail" arguments were given a remotely serious hearing in the dominant mass media or in the political system. Meanwhile, the "moral hazard" of "too big to fail" (the problem that a guaranteed government bailout of giant financial institutions will encourage those institutions to persist in undertaking excessive risks in the blind pursuit of profit) has only increased since many of the leading US banks are now significantly bigger than they were in 2007.[42]

From Servant to Predatory Master

As the financial sector has exploded quantitatively in the United States it has also been transformed qualitatively, in ways that have fed inequality and related social and economic decline. To be sure, no advanced society has ever survived without the vital services that banks and bankers provide. They enable households and businesses to borrow money; allow commerce to take place across vast spaces without coins, notes, and bills having to change physical hands; channel savings into productive investment; and help businesses and governments raise money by issuing stocks, bonds, and other securities on their behalf. But while big finance has continued to play these roles to some degree in the contemporary American economy, its character changed in important and destructive ways during the New Gilded Age. Its function as servant to the broader economy has given way to a new role as parasitic and even predatory master. As the *New Yorker*'s perceptive economics writer John Cassidy noted in an important November 2010 essay titled "What Good Is Wall Street?," the primary focus of the deregulated financial institutions has shifted from lubricating the wheels of the real economy and financing new productive enterprises to the complex, socially useless extraction of rents from that economy—to taking unproductive and unfair advantage of the economic system for the benefit of a very few. Along the way, the nation's leading banks shifted to risky investing and trading on their own account (what is known as proprietary trading) rather than on behalf of their clients, making giant bets with their depositors' money.

"Most people on Wall Street," Cassidy noted, "aren't finding the next Apple or promoting a green rival to Exxon. They are buying and selling securities that are tied to existing firms and capital projects or to something less concrete, such as the price of a stock or the level of an exchange rate."[43] The leading mechanisms of this derivative and parasitic role included collateralized debt obligations (CDOs)—artificial derivative securities that bundle an often giant pool of similar loans (i.e., mortgage loans, car loans, or credit card debts) into marketable securities. Investors who buy a "tranche" of a CDO are paid a portion of the interest owed by the borrowers in the pool. They face the risk that some borrowers won't pay back their loans. But the risk is supposedly diluted by bundling together a large number (often many thousands) of loans. In fact, bundling only increases the risk of massive defaults as banks seek out poor, unqualified, and debt-heavy loan recipients and as banks incentivize high-risk investing by offering higher rates of return to those who purchase CDO tranches deemed most susceptive to default.[44]

Another related mechanism is the credit default swap (CDS)—an insurance derivative security that insures CDOs and other bonds against default. In the late twentieth and early twenty-first centuries, leading banks and other financial firms bought into the "swaps" market on a purely speculative basis. They tapped it not merely to protect their own business costs but to bet on the failure of loans they had bundled into CDOs. Wall Street traders raked in giant commission incomes drawing up CDS agreements on bonds they didn't own. By the early twenty-first century and prior to the crash, the nation's leading banks issued $20 in swaps for every $1 they issued in bonds. It was no small market. "By late 2007," Cassidy determined, "the notional value of outstanding credit default swaps was about sixty trillion dollars, more than four times the value of the gross domestic product."

To what socially or nationally good end? None, since "wagers on credit default swaps are zero sum games. For every winner, there is a loser. In the aggregate, little or no economic value is created." The main profit goes to traders, who use "superior information" to "charge hefty fees and drive up their own profits at the expense of clients who are induced to take risks they don't understand—a form of rent-seeking." The absence of transparent information and the encouragement of investment and price-setting beyond any rational, evidence-based understanding of real economic value sends incorrect signals for capital allocation, leading to dramatic stock market booms and busts.[45]

In the New postindustrial Gilded "Age of Inequality," the ever more concentrated financial firms derive only a small percentage of their revenues from traditional investment banking—from raising funds for companies and advising businesses on deals. Such service activities accounted for less than 15 percent of Wall Street giant Morgan Stanley's revenues in 2010, and even less at the financial behemoth Goldman Sachs. In the same year, mainly derivative and largely speculative trading accounted for nearly two-thirds of the latter firm's revenues and corporate finance for less than a seventh. "For years," Cassidy notes, "the most profitable industry in America has been one that doesn't design, build, or sell a single tangible thing."

Economists' standard argument for such "financial innovations" as CDSs and CDOs was that they "add ... to the size of the [overall economic] pie. But these types of things don't add to the pie," Cassidy noted. "They redistribute it"—upward, while reinforcing and expanding the economic system's underlying crisis tendencies, which since the 1990s have sparked financial meltdowns on a regular basis, while living standards have languished. For this and other reasons, one leading global financial insider and economist told Cassidy that the "rent-capture" industry of "investment banking, prime broking, mergers and acquisitions, hedge funds, [and] private equity" was "far too large" and should be scaled back to "about a half or third of its current size."[46]

More than merely unproductive, the contemporary financial sector has developed a well-deserved reputation as parasitic, even predatory and criminal. This reputation is reflected in the titles of some leading books focused on Wall Street in the wake of the Great Recession: *The Looting of America: How Wall Street's Game of Fantasy Finance Destroyed Our Jobs, Pensions, and Prosperity* (by Les Leopold, 2008); *Griftopia: A Story of Bankers, Politicians, and the Most Audacious Power Grab in American History* (by Matt Taibbi, 2010); *Greedy Bastards: How We Can Stop Corporate Communists, Banksters, and Other Vampires from Sucking Us Dry* (by Dylan Ratigan, 2012); and *Predator Nation: Corporate Criminals, Political Corruption, and the Hijacking of America* (by Charles Ferguson, 2012). The last book's cover depicts a folded $100 bill in the shape of a hand giving the American people the raised middle finger. Taibbi captures a basic sentiment across these books:

The financial leaders of America and their political servants have seemingly reached the cynical conclusion that our society is not worth saving and have taken on a new mission that involves not creating wealth for all, but simply absconding with whatever wealth remains in our hollowed-out economy.... The same giant military-industrial complex that once dotted the American states with smokestacks and telephone poles as far as the eye could see has now been expertly and painstakingly refitted for a monstrous new mission: sucking up whatever savings remains in the pockets of the actual people living between the coasts, the little hidden nest eggs of the men and women who built the country and fought its wars, plus whatever pennies and nickels their aimless and doomed Gen-X offspring might have managed to accumulate in preparation for the gleaming future implicitly promised them, but already abandoned and rejected as unfeasible in reality by the people who run the country.[47]

By Dylan Ratigan's account, "our banking system, on which every business and every one of us depends," has become the nation's master "Vampire Industry.... Instead of serving its customers," Ratigan observes, "it feeds on them." Continuing the metaphor, "greedy [finance-capitalist] bastards extract the lifeblood of countries, which is capital: the money, resources, and human potential that must flow through the body politic to nourish a nation's health and growth. When our capital is drained away to private bank accounts and foreign investment, the country becomes weak and sick, threatening our investments, our jobs, our homes, and our future." Ratigan's thirteen years of financial reporting at *Bloomberg News*, CNBC, and MSNBC provided him with an education in how what he calls "the greedy bastards" of Wall Street can "tear down a country." John Carpenter's extraterrestrial exploiters in *They Live* are for Ratigan like Bram Stoker's vampire in the original *Dracula*. In that novel, "it took a long time for people to realize that actual vampires walked among them." They were undetected at first as they "move[d] in secret to hypnotize and control their servants, and to drain their victims' blood."[48]

Class Over Country

"More in Common with One Another Than Their Countrymen Back Home"

Part of this apparent indifference to the fate of the nation on the part of "the people who run the country" can be traced to the simple fact that many at the top US economic and managerial levels are now part of what Jeff Faux calls "an international class of people whose economic interests have more in common with each other than with the majority of people who share their nationality." Faux first came to this realization while speaking to a corporate lobbyist in the US Capitol in 1993. The lobbyist was frustrated by Faux's opposition to the North American Free Trade Agreement (NAFTA), a historic cross-national investors' rights treaty that made it easier for multinational corporations to exchange capital and goods across national borders without concern for workers' rights or environmental regulations. It amounted to what Mexico's future foreign affairs secretary Jorge Castañeda called "an accord among magnates and potentates: an agreement for the rich and powerful in the United States, Mexico, and Canada, an agreement effectively excluding ordinary people of three societies."

"Don't you understand?" the lobbyist said to Faux, "We have to help [Mexico's conservative, corporate-friendly president Carlos] Salinas. He's been to Harvard. He's one of us." After a moment of confusion, Faux understood her meaning: "We internationally mobile professionals had a shared interest in freeing transnational corporations from the constraints imposed by government on behalf of people who were, well, 'not like us.' . . . She was appealing to [international] class solidarity. . . . At that moment," Faux recalls, "I realized that globalization was producing not just a borderless market, but a borderless class system to go along with it."[49]

Others have noted the geographical disconnect between the significantly globalized US business elite and the far less mobile American multitude. In the year following NAFTA's passage, liberal historian Christopher Lasch observed in his book *The Revolt of the Elites,*

> The market in which the new elites operate is now international in scope. Their fortunes are tied to enterprises that operate across national boundaries. They are more concerned with the smooth functioning of the system as a whole than with any of its parts. Their loyalties—if the term is not itself anachronistic in this context—are international rather than regional, national, or local. They have more in common with their counterparts in Brussels or Hong Kong than with the masses of Americans not yet plugged into the network of global communication.[50]

"The plutocrats," the global business journalist Chrystia Freeland reports, "are becoming a trans-global community of peers who have more in common with one another than with their countrymen back home. Whether they maintain primary residences in New York or Hong Kong, Moscow, or Mumbai," Freeland finds, "today's super-rich are increasingly *a nation unto themselves*" (emphasis added). Glenn Hutchinson, cofounder of a private equity firm called Silver Lake, frankly told Freeland that "a person in Africa who runs a big African bank and went to Harvard Business School has more in common with me than he does with his neighbors, and I have more in common with him than I do with my neighbors." The circles financial elites moved in, Hutchins told Freeland, are shaped by "interests" and "activities" rather than "geography": "Beijing has a lot in common with New York, London, or Mumbai. You see the same people, you eat in the same restaurants, you stay in the same hotels. But most important, we are engaged as global citizens in crosscutting commercial, political, and social matters of common concern. We are much less place-based than we used to be."[51]

"The rise of the 1 percent," Freeland notes, "is a global phenomenon, and in a globalized world, the plutocrats are the most international of all both in how they live their lives and in how they earn their fortune."[52] Matching culture to economics, this global elite has developed its own transnational gatherings each year: the World Economic Forum in Davos, Switzerland; the Oscars, the Cannes Film Festival, Sun Valley, the TED Conference, Teddy Forstmann's Conference, UN Week, Fashion Week, and Wimbledon Week.[53]

"Superclass"

Former US deputy undersecretary of commerce and international trade policy David Rothkopf concluded in *Superclass: The Global Power Elite and the World They Are Making* (2008) that the growing global connectivity and self-identification of the upper economic elite called for a revision of the great American left sociologist C. Wright Mills's classic text *The Power Elite*. In Mills's famous 1956 analysis, the United States was ruled by a remarkably small and interconnected, overlapping top tier of corporate, political, and military "deciders"—a sort of interlocking national directorate that was "in command of the major hierarchies and organizations of modern society. They rule," Mills wrote, "the big corporations. They run the machinery of the state.... They run the military establishment ... [and] occupy the strategic command posts of the social structure."[54] A half century later, Rothkopf was moved to note "the emergence of a different, global power elite ... unforeseen by Mills." If Mills was shocked by the rise of a national power elite that had transcended and subordinated regional and small-town America, "one could only imagine how he might react to an emerging elite without a country." Were Mills writing in the early twenty-first century, Rothkopf concluded, he would have turned his attention from "the national elite" to a "new and more important phenomenon: the rise of a global power elite, a superclass that plays a similar role in the hierarchy of the global era to the role that the US power elite played in that country's first decade as a superpower."[55]

There had always been national power elites and connections between those elites, termed "foreign relations," Rothkopf observes. What is new, he finds, is a global community of the rich and powerful that has formed as the world economic system spilled across national borders.[56]

"Global Player[s] Out to Succeed in Any Geography"

As numerous media reported after President Obama agreed to extend George W. Bush's deficit-fueling tax cuts for the wealthy few in January 2011, many leading US companies were sitting on giant stores of cash capital and storing up liquidity like never before in the wake of the 2008–2009 financial collapse. Firms that no longer believed they could borrow quickly had decided to keep a lot more cash on hand for precautionary purposes. At the same time, low interest rates produced by the Great Recession had created an incentive for many firms to simply "exploit the spread between a zero funds rate and rates on Treasury bonds." This permitted corporations to "mark profits without selling much or hiring anyone." Some big American firms were showing higher profits because their competition faded. Following the financial collapse of 2008, for example, the financial giants Goldman Sachs and Morgan Chase no longer had to compete with Bear Stearns, Lehman Bros., and Merrill Lynch. Many jobs disappeared with the collapse of the defeated behemoths, of course.[57]

Also important, there was the fact that a large mass of unemployed workers was also a great profits boon to corporate America as it waged its ongoing class war on workers' income and security. As Desmond Lachman, a former managing director at Salomon Smith Barney who served as a "scholar" at the influential right-wing American Enterprise Institute, told *New York Times* business reporter Michael Powell, "Corporations are taking huge advantage of the slack in the labor market—they are in a very strong position and workers are in a very weak position. They are using that bargaining power to cut benefits and wages, and to shorten hours."[58] Lachman spoke not of unemployment as an anomaly for capitalist profits, but rather of joblessness as a source of those profits. His comment was straight out of Karl Marx's notion of the capitalist, wage-suppressing function of the "reserve army of labor." Powell's report bore an instructive if somewhat naïve title: "Profits Are Booming, Why Aren't Jobs?"

There was also the little, equally "Marxist," matter of US capital's global nature. Lachman told the *Times* that capital's wage- and benefit-cutting strategy "serves corporate and shareholder imperatives" but "very much jeopardizes our chances of experiencing a real recovery." But how much did and does big "American" capital really care about America's economic health (or the economic health of any specific nation, for that matter)? Another factor behind the American profits-jobs disconnect is the basic fact that the big US companies are actually global outfits. Insofar as the rise in US corporate profits was creating jobs at all, the Associated Press (AP) reported at the end of 2010, the *employment dividend was being enjoyed primarily abroad.* The EPI found that American firms created 1.4 million jobs outside the United States in 2010, compared to less than 1 million in the United States. Leading "American" firms like Caterpillar (which had twelve manufacturing plants and 8,500 employees in China by the summer of 2011), DuPont (which shrank its US workforce by 9 percent and increased its Asia-Pacific workforce by 54 percent from 2005 to 2009), and Coca Cola (less than 13 percent of its 93,000 global employees are in the United States) were drawn to "emerging middle-class markets" and to an increasingly skilled but low-cost workforce in south and east Asia. Reflecting on such facts, economist Robert Scott told the AP that *"there's a huge difference between what is good for American companies and what is good for the American economy."*[59]

"We are a global player out to succeed in any geography," a leading DuPont official told the AP[60]—an honest statement. For his multinational firm, as for so many others, the comment of a character in John Carpenter's *They Live* seems all too close to the truth: "There ain't no countries anymore."

Nationally bound US taxpayers bailed out big US capital to the tune of more than $14 trillion in 2008 and 2009. They did so thanks to federal policymakers' purported belief that such massive corporate welfare was required to rescue "the American economy." But elite US capital is not nationally bound. Its agents are brazenly "global players" whose only allegiance is their own bottom line, pure and simple. In the early 1990s, Ford Motor Company chief Alex Trotman told then US labor secretary Robert Reich that *"Ford isn't even an American company, strictly speaking. We're global.* We're investing all over the world. Forty percent of our employees already live and work outside the United States, and that's rising. Our managers are multinational. We teach them to think and act globally."[61]

America's elite business class holds no particular attachment to the people, communities, health, or even competitiveness of the United States per se. That is why Reich has advised policymakers to "not be seduced into thinking that the interests of big business are the same as the interests of the American economy, or, for that matter, the interests of American workers," observing that "most Americans just simply are not part of the global economy in terms of American prosperity any longer."[62]

"They've Moved On"

Failure to acknowledge this harsh reality can lead to depressing absurdities. In his January 2011 State of the Union address, the president called for the United States to meet the challenge of foreign competition but never mentioned the multinational nature of the leading "American" business firms and the critical fact that "American" capital invests heavily in overseas labor, raw materials, and consumer markets.[63]

Upper 1%-ers and Richistanis in the corporate and financial world might join politicians in making standard obligatory comments about the bedrock value of America's middle class and why it should be supported. But the cold truth beneath such rhetoric is that "America's ruling class doesn't care.

They've moved on," note the Pulitzer Prize–winning journalists and authors Donald Barlett and James Steele, "having successfully created a world where the middle classes in China and India offer far more opportunities to get rich."[64] Indeed, a US-based CEO of one of the world's largest hedge funds told Chrystia Freeland that, in a recent internal debate at his firm, one of his executive colleagues "argued that the hollowing-out of the American middle class didn't really matter.... If the transformation of the world economy lifts four people in China and India out of poverty and into the middle class," the fellow executive maintained, "and meanwhile means one American drops out of the middle class, that's not such a bad trade."[65]

The chief financial officer of a US Internet firm channeled the same spirit: "We demand a higher paycheck than the rest of the world," he told Freeland. "So if you're going to demand 10 times the paycheck, you need to deliver 10 times the value. It sounds harsh, but maybe people in the middle class need to decide to take a pay cut." At the summer 2010 Aspen Ideas Festival, the CEO of the Silicon Valley firm Applied Materials claimed that if he were to start from scratch, just one-fifth of his workforce would be domestic. "This year," the CEO related, "almost 90 percent of our sales will be outside the US. The pull to be close to the customers—most of them in Asia—is enormous."[66] Speaking at the same conference, Allstate CEO Thomas Wilson was remarkably candid about the way in which globalization creates conflict between working-class and business interests: "I can get [workers] anywhere in the world. It is a problem for America, but it is not necessarily a problem for American business.... American businesses will adapt."[67]

"A Harsh Environment Is a Good Thing"

The seemingly abstract problems of financialization, deindustrialization, and globalization are full of concrete, painfully experienced meaning for ordinary working-class Americans like Mike Borosky. In January 2011, while the media focused on democratic upheaval in Tunisia and Egypt and the *New York Times* reported on the supposed paradox of US corporate profits rising without a concomitant increase in US jobs, Borosky learned that the Coleman pop-up camper trailer factory where he had been employed in Somerset, Pennsylvania, for more than thirty years was shutting its doors. He got the news just as his wife was being carried into an operating room for spinal surgery. "I was numb," Borosky, fifty-three, remembered. "My wife just went in for surgery and I didn't even have a job. I wasn't even thinking at that moment that I didn't have health insurance."[68]

It probably didn't take long for the second terrible thought to register. Thanks to the distinctive power of its corporate and financial sector, the United States is unique among modern industrialized "democracies" in its failure to provide its population with universal health coverage. With its archaic system of employment-based health care, it is a nation where workers fear not merely the loss of their jobs if they dare to question the boss's authority—they also have to worry about losing health insurance for themselves and their families.

Soon Borosky learned that FTCA Inc., which had taken over the Coleman plant years earlier, had failed to pay health premiums, leaving him with more than $63,000 in medical bills. FTCA was owned by Blackstreet Capital, a private equity firm that managed hundreds of millions of dollars in investment capital. Blackstreet claimed there were no more funds left to pay the Coleman plant's 150 employees any of the benefits owed to them under their union contract. FTCA abruptly closed the factory without issuing the sixty-day plant closing notice required under federal law. It canceled workers' health insurance and refused to pay severance and accrued vacation time or to make good on its outstanding 401k retirement contributions.

Borosky's story was told in the winter 2012 issue of the United Steelworkers (AFL-CIO) magazine. That same issue reported that Whirlpool, the world's leading appliance manufacturing corporation, would soon close its large refrigerator plant in Fort Smith, Arkansas, and send much of that plant's production to Rampos Arizpe, Mexico. Whirlpool cited sluggish demand for appliances in its shutdown announcement—the same reason it gave in 2010 for closing a refrigerator factory in Evansville, Indiana, transferring that plant's work to Mexico as well. That move cost the United States 1,000 jobs—a standard item in the broader story of capital's long-standing globalization campaign. The company had nothing to say about its thirst to boost profits by exploiting cheap labor and weaker environmental and other governmental regulations abroad.[69]

It was nothing new. In the long era of global neoliberal capitalism—basically at one with the Second Gilded Age—US capital has gravitated relentlessly toward the cheap and super-exploited labor in places like Foxconn's Longhua factory campus in Shenzhen, China—where "a dutiful army of 300,000 employees eats, sleeps, and churns out iPhones, Sony PlayStations, and Dell computers" (*Bloomberg BusinessWeek*). Employing more than 920,000 workers across twenty mainland Chinese factories, Foxconn "leverag[es] masses of cheap labor, mainly 18-to-25-year-olds from rural areas, to make products like the iPhone at seemingly impossible prices." Foxconn does major business with leading "American" multinationals, including IBM, Cisco, Microsoft, Sony, Hewlett-Packard, and Apple. Foxconn factory workers receive a mere $176 per month in return for performing specialized labor tasks under conditions so alienating that eleven of the company's workers committed suicide in early 2010, most of them by leaping from Foxconn's high-rise worker dormitories. The company subsequently strung "more than 3 million square meters of yellow-mesh netting around its buildings to catch jumpers and set up a 24-hour counseling center staffed by 100 trained workers." The entrance to the Longhua campus "looks like a border crossing, with seven toll-booth-like lanes and uniformed guards."[70]

The "drab and utilitarian" production complex includes "huge LED screens that flash public-service announcements and cartoons, and a bookstore that sells, among other things, the Chinese-language translation of the *Harvard Business Review*." The bookstore prominently displays biographies of Foxconn CEO Terry Gou, the "Henry Ford of China" and the richest man in Taiwan, estimated by *Forbes* to have a personal fortune of $5.9 billion. One of the Gou biographies collects his many pithy aphorisms, including the following Dickensian maxims: "work itself is a type of joy," "hungry people have especially clear minds," and "a harsh environment is a good thing."[71]

The arduous nature of working-class life in Shenzhen, and across the super-exploited peripheries of the world economic system, is a leading factor behind the fact that US workers now make but a small portion of the consumer goods sold in the United States. A harsh environment for "developing country" workers in places like Shenzhen—and for workers in de-developing US communities like Somerset, Pennsylvania—is a good (profitable) thing for globally mobile "American" capital.

Fiscal Martial Law in Michigan

Consider Benton Harbor, Michigan, a stark epitome of America's New Gilded Age. The Whirlpool Corporation's sprawling and plush global headquarters is located on the margins of the city, whose population is 89 percent black. From World War II through the 1960s, Benton Harbor thrived, offering its residents ample good-paying employment opportunities in a variety of factories, including a number owned by Whirlpool. Working-class, middle-class, and even some upper-class residents lived in relatively harmonious proximity to each other in the lakeside industrial town, which also served as a summer destination for middle-class vacationers from Chicago and Detroit.[72]

Decades later, all that was like a distant, lost American dream. The multinational Whirlpool Corporation's predominantly white managers and staff now steered clear of the city proper. Many of its professional and managerial employees preferred to live in Chicago or the Chicago area despite long commutes to and from the company's southwest Michigan headquarters. Site of a riot sparked by white police brutality in the summer of 2003 (the National Guard was called in), Benton Harbor now had a poverty rate of more than 50 percent, a child poverty rate above 60 percent, a deep poverty rate of 26 percent, and a per capita income of around $10,000. It was plagued by the standard ills that accompany poverty at home and abroad: mass unemployment, failing and underfunded schools, crime, drugs, broken government, and endemic despair. For a generation, the once thriving manufacturing town had been *stripped*: of industrial jobs (Whirlpool and other local manufacturers left for cheaper labor elsewhere), of retail stores (it's been hard to find a Whirlpool product in Benton Harbor since Sears and J. C. Penney left town years ago), of environmental health (departing manufacturers left behind hundreds of acres of polluted brown fields and wetlands, including a Superfund site contaminated by radioactive paint), of a favorite local beach (recently appropriated by Whirlpool and pricey developers to create a fancy lakeside golf resort), and even of its last remnants of formal democracy. In April 2011, Benton Harbor's local government was handed over to an emergency fiscal manager (EFM)—a de facto dictator appointed to run the city in accord with business principles under a chilling law passed by Michigan's militantly pro-corporate Republican governor Rick Snyder and state legislature. In what was accurately described as "fiscal martial law," the new czar of Benton Harbor was empowered to sell public assets, revoke labor contracts, dismiss pension boards, and take over pension funds. He simply issued an order removing all powers from the local city council. As the Reverend Jesse Jackson noted in May 2011, "No money can be spent, no taxes raised or lowered, no bonds issued, no regulations changed without his approval."[73]

In early March 2013, Snyder extended the favor of authoritarian state fiscal takeover to another and bigger victim of urban deindustrialization and racial isolation: Detroit, Michigan. It was the second time Snyder—a favorite recipient of campaign, lobbying, and public relations largesse from the monumentally wealthy Tea Party funders Charles and David Koch—put himself in the nation's headlines since the presidential election. The first time came in late December 2012, when he celebrated Obama's union-backed "progressive mandate" by ramming an unpopular anti-union "Right to Work" law (permitting workers receiving union wages and benefits to refuse to pay union dues) through a lame-duck Michigan legislature over mass protests.[74]

Eight months later, in July 2013, Snyder and his handpicked Detroit emergency manager Kevyn Orr made Detroit the largest city in American history to declare bankruptcy. It was reasonably expected by knowledgeable observers that Detroit's historic bankruptcy filing would lead to a significant reduction in the pension and medical benefits received by already retired city workers. As the *Wall Street Journal* explained,

> States aren't allowed to file for bankruptcy protection. But in a few cities—including Central Falls, R.I., and Prichard, Ala., that like Detroit have filed under Chapter 9 of US Bankruptcy Code—bankruptcy has led to big cuts to retired city workers.... Retirees in Central Falls agreed to 50% cuts in pension benefits, in many cases, after the small city filed for bankruptcy in 2011. By contrast, the city's bondholders were paid in full.... Bankruptcy lawyers and pension experts say these cases—and Detroit's filing Thursday—prove it can be less painful for public-sector unions and

city officials to agree on how to curb high pension costs before reaching bankruptcy court.... "The lesson of Detroit is that it is better to take care of this issue before bankruptcy," said James Spiotto, a lawyer at Chapman & Cutler LLP. "Even if you think you have the right to get paid, you are taking a big risk in bankruptcy."

It was understood to be "unlikely that the federal government will intervene in the Detroit bankruptcy to bail out city workers or any other creditors."[75]

In addition to opening the door for an assault on pension benefits, Detroit's Chapter 9 bankruptcy filing would permit an appointed judge to void existing union contracts and impose other cuts on city expenses.

So what if Detroit city retirees had put in years of service on the promise of a decent retirement and could ill afford any such reductions in their senior years? So what if the Michigan Constitution formally protected public pensions in the state ("The accrued financial benefits of each pension plan and retirement system of the state and its political subdivisions shall be a contractual obligation thereof and shall not be diminished or impaired thereby")? So what if the wealthy investors likely to be prioritized for payment-in-full were all part of a financial elite that pulled the plug on domestic US manufacturing and thereby caused the decline of Detroit? And so what if the cost of a federal Detroit city bailout ($18–20 billion) would have been a drop in the multitrillion-dollar bailout bucket transferred by the George W. Bush and Obama administrations to the very same parasitic Wall Street financial institutions that did so much to drive the US and global economy over the cliff in 2007 and 2008?[76]

Goldman Sachs and JPMorgan Chase et al. had been officially designated "too big to fail"—unlike a major US city like Detroit, once called "the Arsenal of Democracy" because of its manufacturing sector's centrality to the defeat of German and Japanese fascism during World War II. The *Wall Street Journal* instructed readers that "the spate of recent municipal bankruptcies are showing that public pensions may lack the basic safety nets that private-sector benefits enjoy. Pensions granted by companies are typically backstopped by the Pension Benefit Guaranty Corp. and regulated by federal law. Public pensions are not."[77] Yet worse, as labor journalist Jane Slaughter noted,

Proponents of making city workers bite the bullet note that bankruptcy judges have wide latitude to break contracts.... A recent law in Rhode Island specifies that in a city bankruptcy, bondholders must be paid first, before pensioners.... Asked if the Michigan legislature could pass a similar law, [Michael] Mulholland [vice president of Detroit's largest AFSCME local] laughed. "If they proposed a law that Detroiters should all be shot," he said, "some of them would get up at midnight to sign that one." ... The Republican-dominated legislature has long been hostile to majority-black Detroit. In November 2012, the state's voters passed a referendum that threw out a previous "emergency manager" law, which had been used almost exclusively to take over majority-black cities and school districts. A few weeks later the legislature simply passed the law again.[78]

Countless other crisis-ravaged US municipalities were looking to Detroit as a model for how to please deep-pockets creditors by slashing city worker pensions. Karol K. Denniston, a bankruptcy lawyer in Stockton, California, told the *New York Times*, "If you end up with precedent that allows the restructuring of retirement benefits in bankruptcy, that will make it an attractive option for cities. Detroit is going to be a *huge test kitchen*."[79] It was a curiously, oddly culinary metaphor for the latest development in capital's long-standing war on working people in the neoliberal era.

A Departure from "True Capitalism"?

To which a good, clear-thinking Marxist or left-anarchist might with some justice say the following: "Welcome to the wonderful world of the profits system." The back cover of Joseph Stiglitz's monumental volume *The Price of Inequality* (which this book has liberally and gratefully quoted and cited) complains that "in recent years well-heeled interests [in the United States] have compounded their wealth by stifling true, dynamic capitalism." The notion that the "vampire" behavior of the New Gilded Age's financial elite marks a departure from the supposedly benevolent historical norm of capitalism also animates much of the angry and critical literature on Wall Street today. Distinguishing between good "capitalists who make" and bad "capitalists who take," Dylan Ratigan claims that the current "vampire" system is "the opposite of capitalism." He calls the new order "extractionism": a system based on "taking money from others without creating anything of value, anything that produces economic growth or improves our lives."[80]

In a similar vein, Matt Taibbi thinks that the difference between understanding and misunderstanding Wall Street's complex financial instruments "is the difference between perceiving how Wall Street made its money in the last decades as normal capitalist business and seeing the truth of what it often was instead, which was simple fraud and crime."[81]

Ratigan and Taibbi have aptly and usefully captured American economic elites' shift away from any commitment to the productive capacity and potential of the United States as such, but how different is the exploitative, rent-taking, parasitic, globalist, and corrupt corporate and financial behavior from the real or "normal" nature of the capitalist system? *Webster's New Twentieth Century Dictionary* (unabridged and second edition, 1979) defines **cap/i-tal-ism, n.** as "the economic system in which all or most of the means of production and distribution as land, factories, railroads, etc., are privately owned and operated *for profit*, originally under fully competitive conditions; it has been generally characterized by a tendency toward concentration of wealth, and, in its later phases, by the growth of great corporations, increased government control, etc."[82]

We should note here the absence of any reference to things routinely identified with capitalism in dominant US political and intellectual discourse—democracy, human freedom, free trade, trade per se, job creation, growth, production, and/or a "free market," characterized by widespread competition and/or little or no government interference. Capitalism is about *profit for the owners of capital, period*, attained through any number of unspecified means, including but not limited to

- the dispossession of others' land and materials
- chattel slavery (the leading source of capital accumulation in the United States prior to its outlawing in 1863–1865)
- the hiring and/or firing, technical displacement, and/or deskilling of workers
- the maintenance of a large "reserve army" of unemployed and marginally employed labor that functions to keep wages low
- the "outsourcing" of work to hyperexploited and low-wage sections of the world economy
- the hiring and super-exploitation of unprotected migrant workers
- the slashing and theft of wages and benefits
- purely speculative investment
- monopoly formation and pricing
- the dismantlement of competing firms, sectors, and industries
- deadly pollution and perversion of the natural environment
- the appropriation of public assets
- deadly military contracting and war production
- the use of various means and methods for shaping the political and intellectual culture and policy in capitalists' favor: funding political campaigns, hiring lobbyists, media ownership and control, public relations and propaganda, investment in the educational system, the offer of lucrative employment offers and other economic opportunities to policymakers and their families, the holding of key policymaking positions, and use of the threat to disinvest in jurisdictions that don't play by capital's rules and/or the promise to invest in jurisdictions that do play by those rules.[83]

"US Steel," that company's former chairman David Roderick once candidly commented in explaining why his firm was laying off workers and closing plants, "is in business to make profits, not to make steel." That is a candid statement of the cold reality of the profits system. "Rarely is the reality put with greater clarity," notes David McNally: "under capitalism, use is irrelevant;

profit is king. Capitalist enterprises have no particular attachment to what they turn out, be it flat-rolled steel, loaves of bread, or pairs of jeans."[84] And, it should be added, capitalism has no attachment to turning out anything material or tangible in any particular country. Purely financial and largely parasitic instruments like credit default swaps and collateralized debt obligations are *normal capitalist productions* no less than a ton of steel produced by a multinational corporation in Gary, Indiana, or central China.

This, too, is less than novel. By turning to the financial and global path and abandoning and dismantling its own formerly formidable domestic productive base, "US capital" in the last quarter of the twentieth century and through the current millennium has "follow[ed] a trajectory analogous to that of British capital a century before, which had also responded to the intensification of [global] competition through financialization" and a related shift of investment outside the home country. As Giovanni Arrighi explains, "When escalating competition reduces the availability of relatively empty, profitable niches in the commodity markets, the leading capitalist organizations have one last refuge, to which they can retreat and shift competitive pressures onto others. This final refuge is [Austrian economist Joseph] Schumpeter's 'headquarters of the capitalist system'—the money market."[85] Before the late nineteenth-century British, in fact, the leading capitalists of sixteenth-century Genoa and eighteenth-century Amsterdam took a similar path when, in the words of the great European and world historian Fernand Braudel, "following a wave of growth ... and the accumulation of capital on a scale beyond the normal channels for investment," investors shifted to "finance capitalism."[86]

The shift was well under way in the United States by "the last years of the [nineteen] seventies," when, the leading American democratic socialist Michael Harrington noted, "the corporate rich *wasted $100 billion in acquiring and reacquiring existing assets without creating a single job.*"[87]

When capitalism is understood for what it is really about (investor profit), there is nothing particularly paradoxical about its failure to serve working people or the common good or the economic development, industrial policy, and employment needs of the United States, China, Ecuador, Bangladesh, or anywhere else. If profits are high for top wealth and capital-holders, then the system is working for its beneficiaries—capitalists. Its great capital-agglomerating and liability-diluting corporations (granted the supreme legal protection of artificial personhood) are working precisely as they are supposed to under US common law, which holds that "managers have a legal duty to put shareholders' interests above all others and no legal authority to serve any other interests."[88] "The focus of businesspeople," Stiglitz offhandedly notes, "is, of course, not to enhance societal well-being broadly understood"[89]—an important point that Marx would certainly have found to be a significant understatement.

Cheap Labor and Eco-Exterminist
Foundations of "Manufacturing Revival"

If manufacturing revives in the United States to any significant degree in coming years, it will not do so because of any particular commitment on the part of investors to American-specific economic or societal development. It will happen because American labor, materials, energy, transportation, and/ or other production costs have fallen to the point where capitalists find it competitively advantageous to make things in the so-called homeland. The jobs created will be relatively few compared to past US manufacturing surges thanks to technological automation and robotics. They will certainly not pay well by comparison with the post-WWII "golden age" of heavily unionized American mass production.

Consistent with this basic understanding of capital's aims, it became possible in early 2013 to talk about a mini-revival of US-based manufacturing.[90] This was thanks in no small part to the facts that mass unemployment, the continuing corporate rollback of private sector unions and the social wage (to be discussed in the next chapter), and pro-management government policy had reduced American manufacturing workers' wages and benefits as the United States increasingly became what the left analyst Joel Geier calls "the cheap labor market of the advanced industrial world."[91] Retired American political economy and philosophy professor Alan Nasser provides a chilling perspective on how this remarkable development—wherein the United States functions as a low-wage periphery for European manufacturing corporations—creates the basic context for why capital might be willing to invest in US manufacturing to an increased degree:

> It is not far-fetched to see a growing resemblance of US and poor-country workers. High-priced economic forecasters and consultants are known to refer to the US as "Europe's Mexico." In the near future, they predict, some US states, mostly in the South but also including California and the Rust Belt, will be not only the cheapest manufacturing locations in the developed world, but also competitive with India and China. Wages are rising in the production- and service-oriented poor countries and falling in the rich ones. And US workers tend to quiescence, while unrest is brewing in the periphery. Costs of production are gradually converging between China and the US: declining-wage US workers are more productive, and fuel prices are expected to continue to rise, making it increasingly expensive to ship goods around the world. Non-union workers contracted by Ford to do inspection and repairs at the Dearborn truck plant make $10 an hour without benefits, which is projected to be less than the Chinese average by 2015.... Companies like Ford, Caterpillar, Wham-O Inc. (Frisbees), Master Lock, Suarez Manufacturing, and General Electric have recently

relocated production from China and Mexico to Georgia, Ohio, Indiana, Wisconsin, California, and Michigan. This may or may not be a growing trend, but the mere fact of some US regions becoming newly competitive with Mexico and China bespeaks the declining fortunes of the US worker.[92]

Along with cheap labor, Geier notes, US industrial competitiveness has recently received a further boost from cheap energy resulting from environmentally disastrous hydraulic fracturing ("fracking") and horizontal drilling inside the United States. "US oil production grew by 779,000 barrels a day in 2012," Geier observes, "more in any one year than at any time since the start of US oil production in 1859.... Within a few years the expectation is that the United States will be the largest world producer of oil.... Oil imports have dropped to a twenty-year low and are now starting to reduce the balance of payments deficit dramatically."[93]

The ecologically deadly way in which this increased domestic oil production has been achieved is a reminder of something else besides national economic dismantlement and de-development that sets the Second Gilded Age apart from earlier periods of spectacular elite wealth accumulation in US history. This time, what passes for development and "the free market" under the rule of capital is quite visibly and unmistakably undertaking the dismantlement of livable ecology and thereby posing a clear and present danger both to the human species and other living things on Earth. Consistent with its global, world-system-wide connections, identity, and investments, it does not seem content just to "tear down a country" (the United States). It also appears to have its sights on tearing down the entire planet and human prospects for a livable future at home or abroad.

CHAPTER 5

How They Rule

The Many Modes of Moneyed Class Power

In the Gettysburg Address, President Abraham Lincoln said that America was fighting a Great Civil War so that "Government of the people, by the people, and for the people shall not perish from this earth." But if what has been happening continues, that dream is in peril.... 1984 is upon us.
—Joseph E. Stiglitz, Nobel laureate, 2012[1]

The Democracy Deficit

It's not for nothing that corporate neoliberal politicians Bill Clinton, Al Gore, and Barack Obama gave significant if carefully hedged voice to progressive, populist-sounding values in 1992, 1996, 2000, 2008, and 2012, even while their campaign teams and the Clinton and Obama administrations were loaded with elite operatives from and for "the 1%." The epic concentration of wealth and the extreme inequality that have taken hold in the United States during its Second Gilded Age—making the United States more comparable to Latin America and Africa than to Western Europe in terms of economic disparity—stand in cold defiance of public opinion on what constitutes a good society. Most US citizens reject corporate and financial dominance, harsh socioeconomic disparity, and the ruination of social and ecological health in service to the rich and powerful. The vast majority do not accept plutonomy and plutocracy. They prefer a roughly egalitarian society where wealth and power are well distributed and the government is run by and for the populace in pursuit of the common good. "Taken literally," the Princeton political scientist Larry Bartels notes in his important book *Unequal Democracy: The Political Economy of the New Gilded Age* (2009), the survey data illustrating these and other progressive majority views imply "an astonishing level of public support for what would have to be a very radical program of social transformation," including the outlawing of inherited wealth and of social and economic advantages based on race, gender, ethnicity, and intelligence.[2]

No such program is remotely entertained by US policymakers and politicians. In fact, even the mildest reforms supported by most US citizens are regularly and routinely vetoed by the "unelected dictatorship of money." The public's progressive policy attitudes are regularly captured by pollsters, but they are not reflected in government behavior, however much they inform the election-time language of corporate-captive politicians. As John Bellamy Foster and leading left media analyst Robert W. McChesney note, "The United States, despite its formally democratic character, is firmly in the hands of a moneyed oligarchy, probably the most powerful ruling class in history."[3]

From Shadow to Dark Enveloping Cloud

None of the US majority's progressive sentiments hold much policy relevance beyond campaign rhetoric. That is a startling fact in "the world's greatest democracy," where the great American philosopher John Dewey once observed that "politics is the shadow cast on society by big business." It would stay that way, Dewey prophesized, as long as power resided in "business for private profit through private control of banking, land, industry, reinforced by command of the press, press agents, and other means of publicity and propaganda."[4] Transcending his prediction, the moneyed elite's control of American politics and government has reached a level that almost defies belief in the New Gilded Age. "Since the 1970s," Noam Chomsky observed in the wake of the elite-manufactured 2011 debt-ceiling crisis, "[Dewey's] shadow has become a dark cloud enveloping society and the political system. Corporate power, by now largely financial capital, has reached the point that both political organizations, which now barely resemble traditional parties, are far to the right of the population on the major issues under debate."[5]

The Health Care "Debate"

The "debate" that took place in the national political and media arena over the 2010 federal health insurance reform as it was reviewed by the Supreme Court in early 2012 is a case in point. In Washington and across the airwaves, the Republican right reprised themes that brought us the corporate-backed "Tea Party" by preposterously accusing Obama and the Democrats of attacking "American liberty and prosperity" with "radical left socialism" in the form of "socialized health care." Republicans and their FOX "news" and talk radio troubadours could hardly contain their fear for the republic, threatened by totalitarian "Obamacare." They did not inform those they egged into dread that the president's measure was based on corporate-friendly prescriptions developed by the right-wing Heritage Foundation in the 1990s and that his notion of "change" left giant insurance and drug companies free to extract massive profits that drove the nation's health care costs to the breaking point.

Nobody on either side of the "debate" bothered to inform Americans that, as economist Dean Baker showed, the United States could eliminate its much-bemoaned fiscal deficit by replacing the nation's highly dysfunctional privatized and largely employment-based health insurance system with a universal public model similar to what exists in other industrial nations—with a system that would cut health costs in half and yet deliver superior outcomes. Also unmentioned in the dominant media discourse was the curious fact that a solid majority of Americans had long favored a Canadian-style single-payer system whereby the government would grant equal coverage to all citizens regardless of wealth, income, and other social distinctions.[6] None of this garnered attention under the doctrinal rules imposed by the plutonomy, where "the financial institutions and Big Pharma are far too powerful for such options even to be considered."[7]

Deficit Reduction vs. Job Creation

Another case in point concerns the priority given to the supposedly urgent necessity of deficit reduction in national politics. The US public repeatedly tells pollsters that government's main priority ought to be job creation, not deficit reduction. As *Demos* magazine noted in December 2012, polls in 2011 and 2012 found that "the public remained focused on jobs and the economy over the deficit by two-to-one margins or more." Surveys undertaken after Obama's reelection found that "49 percent thought the election was a mandate for job creation while only 22 percent said that the President's mandate was for deficit reduction.... NBC's exit poll showed that only 15 percent of voters thought the deficit was the biggest problem facing the country." A majority supports "spending money to invest in infrastructure/public sector hiring, like teachers and firemen, versus cutting to reduce the deficit."[8]

But so what? As *Demos* writer J. Mijin Cha explained, "The 'donor class'—the segment of the population that donates to political campaigns—is disproportionately comprised of affluent Americans." This "donor class" (predominantly from households in the top income quintile) "does not prioritize policies to create jobs and economic growth." Its members are "twice as likely to name the budget deficit as the most important issue in deciding how they would vote than middle- or lower-income respondents." And they strikingly and overwhelmingly reject federal government action to help create jobs. Just 19 percent of the nation's affluent households think the government in Washington should "see to it that everyone who wants to work can find a job"—a statement that is favored by 68 percent in the general US public. A tiny 8 percent of the wealthy think that government "should provide jobs for everyone able and willing to work who cannot find a job in private employment"—something a majority (53 percent) of Americans support. The "donor class" has won the policy argument, in defiance of

The dollar-drenched degeneration of American democracy in the New Gilded Age has reached the point where both major parties resort to auctioning off congressional leadership positions. As political scientist and campaign finance expert Thomas Ferguson explained in the *Financial Times* at the height of the debt-ceiling fiasco,

> A tidal wave of cash has structurally transformed Congress, sweeping away the old seniority system that governed leadership selection and committee assignments. In its place, the major political parties borrowed a practice from big box retailers like Walmart, Best Buy, or Target.... *Uniquely among legislatures in the developed world, US congressional parties now post prices for key slots in the lawmaking process* ... [so that congressional debates] rely on the endless repetition of a handful of slogans that have been battle-tested for their appeal to national investor blocs and interest groups that the leadership relies on for resources.[17]

The motivation behind the "investor blocs" campaign expenditures is crisply summarized by former *Harper's Magazine* editor Roger Hodge: "Politics, we might say, is the continuation of business by other means."[18]

Citizens United: *Frankenstein's Monster Eats His Creator*

The problem has recently been exacerbated by the US Supreme Court. The court's momentous 2010 *Citizens United v. Federal Elections Commission* decision abolished long-standing prohibitions against corporations digging into their regular business coffers to invest in election campaigns. Prior to *Citizens United*, to be sure, corporations already invested massively in American politics and policy. They spent billions on lobbying, "issue ads," political action committees (PACs), and raising PAC money. CEOs, top executives, and corporate board members contributed heavily as individuals to parties and candidates. Still, there "was one crucial thing that CEOs could not do before *Citizens United*: *reach into their corporate treasuries to bankroll campaigns promoting or opposing the election of candidates for Congress or president.* This prohibition," Raskin noted last year, "essentially established a wall of separation—not especially thick or tall, but a wall nonetheless—between corporate treasury wealth and campaigns for federal office" (emphasis added). *Citizens United* blew up the wall by claiming that "the identity of the speaker" is irrelevant and therefore an unconstitutional basis on which to limit the "free speech" rights of campaign contributors.

Never mind that the Court refused to extend elementary free speech protections to "public employees, public school students, whistleblowers, prisoners, and minor-party candidates whose free-speech rights have been crushed by the conservative Court *because of their identity as (disfavored) speakers.*" Or that, as Raskin added, it was unthinkable that the Court could "allow President Obama ... [to] order the Government Printing Office to produce a book advocating his re-election" or let "churches ... or Harvard University bankroll ... political campaigns." The identity of "the speaker" (the campaign contributor in this case) obviously retained high relevance.[19]

Preposterous reasoning aside, *Citizens United* opened the door to spectacular new levels of business election spending. It gave rise to giant new "Super PACs" that funnel tens of millions of shareholder dollars into "independent expenditures" on behalf of candidates with the undoubted purpose of shaping policy in corporate interests. Much of this election funding is difficult if not impossible to trace under *Citizens United*.

They Live, Forever

It is difficult to exaggerate the authoritarian peril in granting such special political weight and invisibility to giant and impersonal economic entities that owe their wealth largely to government. US law bestows awesome benefits on private corporations and their investors. It grants them *limited liability*, making individual investors personally nonliable for harms corporations inflict, no matter how egregious. It also grants corporations *perpetual life* (an existence beyond that of merely mortal investors and managers) and the right to pool and distribute unlimited assets. As Supreme Court Justice Byron White noted in a dissenting 1978 opinion (in *First Nat'l Bank v. Bellott*), a business empowered in these ways is "in a position to control vast amounts of economic power which may, if not regulated, dominate not only the economy but also the very heart of our democracy, the electoral process." Government, White argued, has a compelling interest in "preventing institutions which have been permitted to amass wealth as a result of special advantages extended by the State ... from using that wealth to acquire an unfair advantage in the political process.... *The State*," White said, "*need not permit its own creation to consume it.*"[20] Government, White felt, needed to intercede between a campaign finance–led transition from *They* (the immortal corporations) *Live* to *They Rule*.

The Corporation as Alien, Super-Powered Sociopath

The Frankenstein-inspired language in White's decision seems eerily appropriate. Granted the legal status of artificial "personhood" by the end of the nineteenth century, the modern American corporation is an alien, nonhuman entity granted permanent life and superhuman powers. Its cloak of personhood provides a great shield of invisibility for capitalists who reap benefits from the "economies of scale" and barriers to competition afforded by their freedom to combine assets while avoiding liability beyond their individual investment for the terrible harm their agglomerated entities cause in pursuit of profit over and against any other concerns. "The basis of a corporation," Chomsky casually noted in 2012, "is limited liability, meaning as a participant in a corporation you're not personally liable if it, say, murders tens of thousands in Bhopal."[21]

In 2003 Canadian law professor Joel Bakan published his widely read volume *The Corporation: The Pathological Pursuit of Profit and Power.* Noting that the US judiciary defined corporations (e.g., US Steel and Standard Oil) as legal "persons" by the end of the nineteenth century, Bakan posed an interesting question: What kind of "person" is a modern corporation? His answer: *a sociopath*, consistent with the corporation's judicially certified mandate to pursue relentlessly and without exception its investors' economic self-interest, regardless of—and without any guilt or conscience about—any injury it may cause to others or the common good. Bakan asked the internationally recognized psychologist Dr. Robert Hare to assess the modern corporation in accord with Hare's globally acclaimed diagnostic tool *The Psychopathy Checklist.* The results were instructive:

> Hare found ... a close match. The corporation is *irresponsible*, Dr. Hare said, because "in an attempt to satisfy the corporate goal, everybody else is put at risk." Corporations try to "*manipulate* everything, including public opinion," and they are *grandiose*, always insisting "that we're number one, we're the best." A *lack of empathy* and *asocial tendencies* are also key characteristics of the corporation, says Hare—"their behavior indicates that they don't really concern themselves with their victims"; and corporations often *refuse to accept responsibility for their own actions* and are *unable to feel remorse.* Finally, according to Dr. Hare, corporations *relate to others superficially*: "their whole goal is to present themselves to the public in a way that is appealing to the public [but] in fact may not be representative of what th[e] organization is really like." Human psychopaths are notorious for their ability to use charm as a mask to hide their dangerously self-obsessed personalities. For corporations, [claims of] social responsibility may play the same role.[22]

Granted unlimited investment in American electoral "democracy" by the Supreme Court, the corporation—the 1%'s spectacularly wealthy risk-diluting, capital-pooling, and identity- and responsibility-shielding institution—is a monument to organized sociopathology, consistent with the big business behavior described in earlier chapters. Corporations are like the aliens depicted in John Carpenter's *They Live*—manipulative, artificial, grandiose, devoid of conscience and empathy in accord with ruthlessly selfish, sociopathic inhumanity and attachment (mandated under US legal doctrine, as we have seen) to no higher goal (beneath deceptive talk about "corporate social responsibility") than the profit of invisible investors. The alien and fake "persons" called corporations do not wish to participate in a democratic commonwealth on behalf of the common good. They seek to devour democracy in the interests of investor profit. Seen through the "magic sunglasses" of social and historical criticism, the horrible truth of their monstrous inhumanity becomes visible.

Many-Sided Modes of Control

Chillingly enough, even in the *Citizens Defeated* era, campaign finance is just one among many ways in which the "hidden senate" of corporate and financial money rules. It is a common mistake to reduce the rule of big money in American politics to campaign finance. As William Greider noted in his brilliant volume *Who Will Tell the People? The Betrayal of American Democracy* (1992), "The effects of [campaign] money are real enough," Greider determined, "but the debilitating impact [of corporate wealth and power] on democracy would endure, even if money were magically eliminated from politics."[23]

Consistent with Dewey's prediction, other mechanisms of corporate-plutocratic rule beyond election funding abound. The many-sided methods and modes of elite moneyed-class power include

- The flooding of the nation's capital and the fifty state capitals and an untold number of municipal and county governments with a gigantic army of corporate lobbyists.
- Massive investment in public relations and propaganda to influence the beliefs and values of citizens, politicians, and other "opinion-shapers" on matters of interest to corporations. (Between 2007 and 2012, a major propaganda offensive by the carbon industrial complex reduced the percentage of Americans who believed in climate change from 71 to 41 percent.[24])
- Capture of key positions in government regulatory agencies by pro-business actors who expect to work at significantly increased levels of compensation in the regulated (and not-so-regulated) industries in the future.
- "Cognitive" (ideological) capture of state officials, politicians, media personnel, educators, and nonprofit managers so as to minimize public actions and sentiments that might harm business profits.
- The use by businesses of the threat of disinvestment, capital flight, and "capital strike"—resulting in the loss of jobs and tax revenue—to get what they want (i.e., reduced wages, reduced taxes, reduced environmental regulations, increased public subsidies ... the list goes on) from governments, unions, and communities.

- The systematic destruction and undermining of organizations (i.e., labor unions) that might offer some countervailing power to that of big business. (Thanks to a major and ongoing corporate offensive against organized labor and collective bargaining, the percentage of American workers enrolled in unions has fallen from more than a third at the height of the post-WWII "Great Compression" to roughly a tenth in the 2010s.)
- The offer of jobs, corporate board memberships, internships, and other perks and payments to public officials and their families and to other "influentials" and their families.
- The creation by business elites of fake-populist ("Astroturf") pseudo social movements to provide deceptive "grassroots" cover for the hard right business agenda. (The classic example in recent US history is the Tea Party phenomenon, a right-wing business and Republican invention that was widely and misleadingly discussed by the dominant media as an "independent" and "populist" social and political "movement" during Obama's first term.[25])
- Control of education and publishing in order to (a) filter out, repress, and marginalize "populist" and "radical" (democratic) critiques of the profits system, corporations, and capitalist culture, and (b) identify the public interest and the common good with the business bottom line.
- Ownership, monitoring, and management of mass media (including "entertainment" as well as public affairs news and commentary) for the same purposes.
- Capture of key major party campaign positions by personnel, including public relations firms that represent elite corporate interests seeking to influence policy.[26]

"We've got," President Obama told Democrats in the US Senate in February 2010, "to be the party of business, small business and large business, because they produce jobs. We've got to be in favor of competition and exports and trade. We've got to be non-ideological about our approach to these things. We've got to ... understand that, like it or not, we have to have a financial system that is healthy and functioning, so we can't be demonizing every bank out there."[27] Such statements are bought to some extent with elite campaign contributions. They also reflect the basic structural fact that a first-term president is captive to the investing class when it comes to being able to link his presidency to the labor market in ways that permit him to win enough votes for a second term. In Obama's case, they also reflected a deeply conservative, probusiness, and conciliatory temperament and record that goes back to the beginning of Obama's political career and to his training in the dominant neoliberal ideology at elite educational institutions like Columbia University, Harvard, and the University of Chicago.[28]

Big Brother ALEC

Notorious for their power and influence in Washington, corporate lobbyists probably speak even louder at the state level than they do at the federal level. This is thanks in part to term limits and to the fact that state legislators in most states work part time and lack staffs to assist them in their work. State legislators' limited resources open a door that corporate lobbyists—including the giant national right-wing Republican network called ALEC (the American Legislative Exchange Council)—eagerly walk through to cultivate pro-business policymakers and even to draft state-level legislation. As John C. Harrington, a leader of the socially responsible investment movement, noted in *The Challenge to Power* (2005),

> Guess who shows these part-time legislators, with little or no staff, the ropes? Guess who writes their legislation? Guess who hosts lunches, receptions, educational seminars, and special outings in exotic places? ALEC, that's who…. ALEC sponsors ongoing state legislations to weaken environmental laws, build privatized prisons, deregulate energy, limit gun control, and support the tobacco industry. Members include the NRA, Chevron, Arthur Anderson, Archer Daniels Midland, R. J. Reynolds Tobacco, Exxon, DuPont, Phillip Morris, GTE, and on and on. You get the picture.[29]

ALEC presents itself as a "nonpartisan public-private partnership" interested in "grassroots activism" for a better democracy. Beneath that good guy cloak, however, the truth is very different. It is a potent national syndicate of "conservative" (radically regressive) state politicians and powerful corporations dedicated in Bill Moyers's words to "the increase [of] corporate profits at public expense without public knowledge…. In state houses around the country," Moyers notes, "hundreds of pieces of boilerplate ALEC legislation are proposed or enacted that would, among other things, dilute collective bargaining rights, make it harder for some Americans to vote, and limit corporate liability for harm caused to consumers—each accomplished without the public ever knowing who's behind it."

The organization's reach is remarkable. Its more than fifty full-time staffers had by 2011 worked up "850 boilerplate laws that ALEC legislators could introduce as their own in any state in the union."[30]

The Real Polarization

According to a dominant media narrative that rose to the fore during the debt-ceiling crisis of 2011, the "fiscal cliff" drama of late 2012, and the federal government shutdown (and potential second debt-ceiling crisis) of October 2013, Washington and the nation's politics are crippled by partisan polarization and a related inability of the nation's elected officials to compromise. While there should be little doubt about the very real and tightly gerrymandered cultural, geographic, and demographic divisions between "red" (Republican) and "blue" (Democratic) America, this narrative misses two key things. The first thing left out is the fact that the right-leaning Democrats under Obama as under Bill Clinton have been highly flexible and far more willing than Republicans to makes deals with the other dominant political organization. It's the rightmost of the two great state-capitalist parties—the "stand your ground" Republican Party—that is by far and away most responsible for gridlock in Washington. Standing to the right of Republican presidents of the long New Deal era (Nixon and Eisenhower), the Democratic administrations (Carter, Clinton, and Obama) and party of the neoliberal era have shifted ever more rightward on key political and socioeconomic matters like "entitlements" (Social Security and Medicare), "free trade," labor rights, taxes, regulation, the environment, and more. Along the way they have remained no less committed than top Republicans to the maintenance of a giant military empire that accounts for half the world's military spending and maintains more than 1,000 US military installations across more than 100 "sovereign" nations.

A second and related thing missing from the dominant narrative is the deeper and more significant polarization between the US party and policy system ("Democracy Incorporated") on one hand and the majority working-class US citizenry on the other. In the current New Gilded Age of extreme inequality, a flood of elite corporate and financial political money meant to keep the 1%'s ever more astonishing fortunes safe from popular envy and public redistribution has pushed both of the nation's reigning parties and the government well to the right of the populace, whose progressive views are ever more irrelevant to the conduct of politics and policy.[31]

Ideology aside, *New York Times Magazine* chief national correspondent Mark Leibovich notes in his recent best-selling book *This Town: Two Parties and a Funeral Plus Plenty of Valet Parking in America's Gilded Capital*[32] that Washington, DC, has become a richly bipartisan "Gold Rush" wherein office-holders, lobbyists, and staff of the two dominant parties are part of the same "permanent feudal class of insiders." The nation's capital "becomes a determinedly bipartisan team when there is money to be made"—an "inbred company town where party differences are easily subsumed by membership in the club." As Leibovich told Bill Moyers on PBS in August 2013,

> Self-perpetuation is a key point in all of this.... The original notion of the founders [was] that a ... public servant would serve a term [and] return to their communities, return to farm. Now the organizing principle of life in Washington is "how are you going to keep it going?" Whether it's how you're going to stay in office by pleasing your leadership so that you get money, by raising enough money so that you can get reelected, by getting a

gig after you're done with Congress, after you're done in the White House, by getting the next gig.... Cowardice is rewarded at every step.... The true mavericks are punished ... if you want to build a career outside of office when you're done, when you're voted out as a lobbyist, as a consultant, as many of them do, you are encouraged not to anger too many people. Not to take a big stand. No truth is going to be told. There are many ways in which the money, the system is financed, the politics are financed. The way the media works, that will not under any circumstances reward someone who takes a stand.[33]

Much the same could certainly be said about most if not all the nation's fifty state capitals.

The Culture of Neoliberalism

Why isn't there more mass and popular rebellion against all of this, which led to *more than 700,000 federal employees being thrown out of work* for an indeterminate period of time in early October 2013? The cultural and related media dimensions of domestic ruling-class power in the United States are critical. In 1958 Aldous Huxley wrote *Brave New World Revisited*, penned nearly three decades after the publication of his famous dystopian novel *Brave New World*. The original work had imagined a future society divided between haves and have-nots, with a vast lower class doing all the work for a corporate and governmental elite. The subjects of this regime were lulled into complacent acceptance of their lot by a steady diet of electronic distraction, intoxicating narcotics, propagandistic mass media, advertisements, and consumerism.

Looking at mass-consumerist Cold War America nearly a generation later, Huxley was struck by how relevant his stark projection from the interwar years seemed. He noted how "Big Business" ruled America's "capitalist democracy," which was "controlled by what Professor C. Wright Mills has called the Power Elite." This "Power Elite," Huxley observed in *Brave New World Revisited*, "directly employs several millions of the country's working force in its factories, offices, and stores, controls many millions more by lending them the money to buy its products, and, *through its ownership of mass communication, influences the thoughts, the feelings, and the actions of virtually everybody*."[34]

Fifty-three years later, long after most of the nation's once burgeoning factory sector had been dismantled, left broadcast journalist Amy Goodman found a copy of *Brave New World Revisited* in the rubble of the original Occupy campsite, after OWS had been razed by the NYPD. In the America of the twenty-first century, Huxley would certainly have recognized even more of what he warned about in the 1950s: a harsh division between haves and have-nots; the domination of every major industry and economic sector—including ever more powerful thought- and emotion-influencing mass media—by an ever-shrinking handful of giant multinational corporations; the ubiquitous presence in private and public space of glowing telescreens blaring round-the-clock entertainment, diversion, spectacle, pleasure/pseudo-pleasure, mass consumerism, materialism, and nationalist military propaganda; the media's constant presentation of news and history in accord with the needs and views of the wealthy elite; the rampant control of schools and universities by Big Business institutions and values; the capture of local, state, and federal government structures by corporate and financial agents, organizations, and beliefs; the rampant medical prescription and mass epidemic-level use of highly profitable, heavily advertised, and corporate-manufactured psychosomatic drugs to alleviate the widespread depression and anxiety that result from nerve-racking levels of inequality, insecurity, and corporatism; and millions absorbed in private electronic discussions and seemingly endless information-, entertainment-, and community-seeking on the Internet, via cell phones, and through such atomized and often superficial, narcissism-nurturing avenues as Facebook and Twitter. Much of this was foreseen in different ways by other dystopian postwar writers like George Orwell (*1984*), Kurt Vonnegut (*Player Piano*), and, above all perhaps, Ray Bradbury (*Fahrenheit 451*).[35]

Solidarity and Empathy Imperiled

Huxley might also have noted the viciously selfish and specifically capitalist nature of the messages that are ubiquitous across mass media and culture. In the current era and for at least three decades now, the 1%'s mass media and the nation's broader propaganda and public relations system have worked to keep "the thoughts, the feelings, and the actions of virtually everybody" sealed within the narrow parameters of neoliberalism—the profits system's reigning ideology in the Second Gilded Age. Beyond merely a set of corporate-friendly "free market" policies (including deregulation of businesses and markets, the cutting of taxes on the rich and their corporations, the slashing of union power, corporate privatization of public programs and wealth, the cutting of social welfare and uplift programs, and more), neoliberalism is an ideology. This ideology resurrects and repackages the older "laissez-faire" liberalism of the nineteenth century—the classic industrial-bourgeois "free market" doctrine that was so badly discredited by the Great Depression and supplanted by Keynesianism through "the Golden Age of Western capitalism" and the Great Compression. Nicely encapsulated in onetime British prime minister Margaret Thatcher's proclamation that "there is no such thing as society, there are only individual men and women and there are families," neoliberalism's core precept was summarized by the celebrated Marxist theorist David Harvey as follows: "There shall be no serious challenge to the absolute power of money to rule absolutely.... Those possessed of money power shall not only be privileged to accumulate wealth endlessly at will, but they shall have the right to inherit the earth, taking either direct or indirect dominion therein, but also assume absolute command, directly or indirectly, over the labor and creative potentialities of all those others it needs. The rest of humanity shall be deemed disposable."[36]

The basic principle, political scientist Gary Olson notes, is "that the market rules." Other key components of the neoliberal creed are elegantly summarized by Olson in his powerful study *Empathy Imperiled: Capitalism, Culture, and the Brain*:

> If left alone, robust competition in the market will effectively allocate soci-ety's resources in a manner that ensures that everyone rightfully obtains what is coming to her or him; deregulation in all areas where profits might be enhanced, particularly state regulations on the flow of capital; greatly reduc-ing or eliminating public expenditures for the poor; privatization of public enterprises to private domains on behalf of "efficiency"; ... discredit[ing] and destroy[ing] labor organizations, and ... eliminat[ing] any notions of community or the collective good while fostering the belief that one must advance in society through rugged self reliance.[37]

Basic egalitarian instincts and sentiments of human solidarity, empathy, and social justice have no place in this doctrinal system. Neoliberalism, the left educational theorist and cultural critic Henry A. Giroux notes, "can imagine public issues only as private concerns." It sees "human agency as simply a mat-ter of individualized choices, the only obstacle to effective citizenship being the lack of principled self-help and moral responsibility" on the part of those victimized by structural oppression and the amoral agency of those who stand atop the nation's steep and interrelated hierarchies of class, gender, race, and empire. In the vapid, capitalist culture of neoliberalism, "human misery is largely defined as a function of personal choices," consistent with "the central neoliberal tenet that *all problems are private rather than social in nature*."[38]

To those who cry out against mistreatment and the ruination of society and ecology by system masters, neoliberalism offers a malicious rejoinder: "Be quiet, your situation is entirely of your own making. Do not expect help from, or offer help to, others beyond your own family. There is no other way, for this is the end point of history, the final unfolding of human nature." As Olson notes, "Those left behind not only merit no sympathy but deserve to be caricatured, sneered at, and accused of personal defects including a 'poverty of ambition.'"[39]

The long-standing Wall Street campaign to weaken and privatize Social Security is based on more than the billions of dollars in profits the leading financial institutions expect to result from destroying the nation's success-ful and popular public old-age retirement system. Also relevant to Social

Security's deep pockets enemies is the fact that the retirement system and other welfare state programs are rooted in the notion that society cares about those who experience social and economic *insecurity*, on the margins of the "free market." As Chomsky notes, "The preferred doctrines are *just to care about yourself; don't care about anyone else*[40].... You have," Chomsky has told the Canadian law professor Joel Bakan, "*to drive out of people's heads natural sentiments like care about others.* ... The ideal is to have individuals who are totally disassociated from one another ... whose ... sense of value is 'Just how many created wants can I satisfy?'"[41]

Government and other collective efforts to meaningfully address and ame-liorate (not to mention abolish) societal disparities and injuries are deemed alternately futile, counterproductive, and inappropriate. As the social State is liquidated in the name of "the market," government's functions are progres-sively concentrated on "making war," "enhancing opportunities for the inves-tor class," "suppressing wages for everyone else," and "suppressing dissent."[42]

Consistent with Thatcher's insistence that "there is no such thing as col-lective conscience [or] collective kindness," neoliberalism militantly attacks the bonds that connect humans to each other—and to their shared natural environment and other sentient beings. It might be termed "the political economy of narcissism. Once people are brought around to the belief that society is a chimera," Olson observes, "a perverse 'rational pursuit of self-interest' favors the commodification of the self as a survival strategy," leading to "a commodification of morals" and "an incapacity for empathy" as "people are increasingly valued only for their utility, their market value." To "survive under this arrangement," Olson adds, "many otherwise selfless, ethically disposed people ... are forced into uncaring behavior, a daily denial of their better selves."[43]

This is the vapid and sickening culture that is portrayed in withering terms in *They Live*, written and produced as neoliberalism flexed its muscles under Ronald Reagan. As John Carpenter sensed, a democratic political culture cannot last or take root in a society whose members are led to pursue only their own narrowly defined self-interest. It cannot flourish where people have been turned into "disconnected, apolitical individuals," as Latin American-ist Cathy Schneider has described the shell-shocked people of Chile after a US-sponsored military coup overthrew their nation's democratically elected government on September 11, 1973 ("Latin America's 9/11," which ushered in a proto-fascistic dictatorship that instituted neoliberal economic policies designed by academics flown in from the University of Chicago's "free market" economics department). Under the reigning authoritarian-neoliberal doctrine of what we might call the post-Allende era, the populace must be "taught," in British activist Susan George's words, "to believe that we are not citizens or members of a social body but discrete, individual consumers. We are entirely responsible for our own destinies and if we fall by the wayside for whatever reason—illness, job loss, accident, failure, whatever—it's our own fault.... We have no responsibility for other people either. Solidarity is a banished word.... That's the essence of the neo-liberal spirit: 'You're on your own.' ... If you are well-schooled in neo-liberalism," George adds, "you will never join a social movement, never engage in a struggle against an unjust action of the government, never contribute to an effort to protect the natural world."[44]

There's not much novel about these quintessentially bourgeois ideas. As Chomsky noted as the neoliberal triumph reached its apex after the collapse of the "Marxist" Soviet Union, "As in the early nineteenth century, we are now once more to understand that it is a violation of natural liberty and even science to deceive people into thinking that they might have some rights beyond what they can gain from selling their labor power."[45]

It should be added that the "rule of the market" since the early twentieth century means *the rule of that great sociopathic entity the modern corporation*, at once creature and master of the market as well as the state.[46]

Starve the Left Hand, Feed the Right

Neoliberalism is linked to "antigovernment" sentiment, but the connection is deceptive. Despite the ideological claim that "government is the problem" (one of President Reagan's favorite phrases), the neoliberal state eagerly retains ample capacity to carry out key objectives when it comes to subsidizing, protecting, and otherwise serving the rich, corporate (top-down) globalization, and military empire (itself a great form of corporate subsidy, as we shall see). Neoliberalism isn't about tearing down government, it's about the rich deepening their grip on state power and wielding it more decisively than before on behalf of the few. Increasingly stripped of social and democratic functions created partly through past popular struggles, neoliberal government is inadequate and cash-poor primarily when it comes to meeting the needs of the nonaffluent majority and especially of the disproportionately black, urban, concentrated, and demonized poor. Its relationship to the working and lower classes and especially to the nonwhite poor is increasingly weighted toward policing and repressive functions, which have expanded dramatically in ways that are more than just coincidentally related to the assault on social supports and programs. Neoliberalism starves the "left"—social, egalitarian, democratic, and peaceful—but feeds the "right"—regressive, repressive, militaristic, and authoritarian—"hand of the state."[47] This, too, is less than novel.

Like the Air We Breathe ...

Neoliberalism's core precepts may be less than original, but the delivery system whereby these ideas assault public consciousness today is certainly unprecedented in reach and power. Developed and spread across elite policy formation and political venues like the Business Roundtable, the US Chamber of Commerce, the American Enterprise Institute, the corporate lobbying and public relations industries, leading academic departments (especially economics and business departments), and elite think tanks, neoliberal ideology has filtered down to become ubiquitous across the corporate-crafted mass culture. The above description of the culture of neoliberalism captures much of the essence of what one can see on American television. Self is God and purely individual life strategies reign in the corporate-crafted mass culture that have in the Second Gilded Age brought us *Survivor*, *American Idol*, Dr. Phil, Suzie Orman, Dr. Laura, NBC's vapid *Today Show* (where small bits of packaged news and weather reporting that never mentions climate change or its anthropogenic causes are surrounded by longer segments on how to "reverse the effects of aging," shop for clothes more efficiently, and manage one's personal stock portfolio), and the highly advertised state lottery systems, which teach their disproportionately working- and lower-class customers a number of false and reactionary lessons, including the following:

- Great wealth is a matter of pure chance, not a product of structural inequality.
- "Anyone can play" and "anyone can win" in the "level playing field" that is the American "land of opportunity."
- Acquiring great individual wealth is the central purpose of human experience and the best thing that could happen to someone.
- People don't need to join together and fight for social justice but should focus their hopes instead on individual advancement and luck.
- The best response to alienation in the (tyrannical capitalist) workplace is to escape it, not to organize with your fellow workers to create more equitable, participatory, and sustainable work environments.[48]

Neoliberalism's update and repackaging of bourgeois-individualist ideas for the corporate and mass consumerist/mass media era is so omnipresent and repetitive across dominant corporate news, commercial, and entertainment media[49] and the broader ideological and intellectual culture that it has become almost like the cultural air many millions of Americans breathe. Its messages have become so seemingly universal, natural, and commonsensical that they have become practically invisible to the naked political eye, requiring a good pair of John Carpenter's sunglasses to be decoded and exposed for what they really are: vicious and historically specific capitalism-generated notions and sensibilities fed to the citizenry through potent, corporate-dominated means and modes of thought- and feeling-control.

People and Mice: *Who Moved My Cheese?*

An especially graphic example of neoliberal propaganda in the New Gilded Age is *Who Moved My Cheese?*, a short pamphlet and parable that became a best-selling "self-help" phenomenon after it was released in 1998. A deeply authoritarian response of sorts to growing liberal and progressive criticism of the nation's deepening class inequalities and related economic insecurities in the New Gilded Age's version of the "Roaring Nineties," *Who Moved My Cheese?* depicted two pairs of miniature beings who responded in two different ways—one functional and the other dysfunctional in author "Dr. Spencer Johnson's" view—to the disappearance of "Cheese Stations" (the author's not-very-subtle metaphor for the corporate dismantling and outsourcing/ offshoring of workplaces with good jobs) that had formerly provided them with sustenance and the bases of community in the great "maze" (Johnson's equally obvious metaphor for the market) of life. An unhappy antiheroic pair was made up of "Hem" and "Haw," two "little people, with complicated mind and thinking processes." They foolishly felt *entitled* to receiving "cheese" (jobs, benefits, and community) where they had obtained it for many years. They spent inordinate energy being agitated about "who moved [their old] cheese," feeling ripped off and sorry for themselves. Hem and Haw were set in their old ways, a cardinal sin for the neoliberal mindset, which puts a premium on flexible response to the ever-changing mandates of the market. The angry little humans did not adjust and move with the times (with the moving cheese) because of their silly concern with the irrelevant and dysfunctional John Carpenter-esque question of *who* rules the market ("maze") and abuses wealth and power to the detriment of others. This was a reflection of their overattachment to thinking and complexity in "Dr. Johnson's" tale.

Things were very different with "Sniff" and "Scurry," a functional, forward-looking pair of "mice with simple mind and thinking processes." Sniff and Scurry were unburdened by any pointless and self-defeating sense of entitlement to stability, comfort, community, and predictability. They had no concern for why their old source of sustenance and community had been taken away and who might have profited from the closing and moving of the lost Cheese Stations (of reliable workplaces and communities). Properly devoid of unproductive and "complicated" reflections on immaterial problems of social power and justice and on who owns and runs and profits from the maze (the investors behind corporations who rule in the name of "the free market," that is), Sniff and Scurry simply let go of the Keynesian New Deal past and embraced the neoliberal present. They just rushed back out into the great mice-person maze (market) to sniff out and scurry over to whatever new "cheese" might be found.[50]

Who Moved My Cheese? spoke to working Americans suffering the traumas of the Second Gilded Age as if they were small children. The pamphlet's dehumanizing, properly anthropomorphized lesson was clear: working people were entitled to nothing from their superiors and needed to think and feel less and scamper around more, like hungry little rodents. "Dr. Johnson's" juvenile tale instructed everyday working people to abandon and disown elementary human concerns for justice, community, and elite accountability, and to purge any "complicated" notions that economic and political elites owe society and its working- and middle-class majority anything at all. It was an apt message on behalf of corporate and financial chieftains in the 1990s. They and their many cheerleaders spoke in glorious terms of the "fabulous" Clinton economy even as they closed down factories, moved jobs overseas, slashed wages, cut job benefits, attacked the social safety net, and badly polluted and overheated the environment (an ecological variant of Hem and Haw might have been depicted asking "Who Poisoned Our Cheese and Planet?"). No wonder the book's back cover included an enthusiastic blurb from a leading finance titan and an imposing list of corporate endorsers (including Apple, Citibank, Chase Manhattan, General Motors, IBM, Morgan Stanley, Merck, and the New York Stock Exchange), along with the US Army, Navy, and Air Force.

"Can Do": Hope and Depression as Tools of 1% Power

Beyond their inherently counterproductive (by the rules of neoliberal ideology) sense of entitlement to decent jobs and lives and their dangerous and un-American attachment to identifying the ruling class (the "who" behind the elimination and offshoring of good jobs), Hem and Haw committed the related cardinal American sins of pessimism and negativity. "Americans," international relations professor Stephen Kinzer notes, "are brought up on a 'can-do' mentality. It tells them that if one wants something badly enough, and works hard enough, for long enough, it will be won."[51] This mindset goes back a long way in the national character.

In the neoliberal Second Gilded Age, positive thinking has become an industry that has "gone," Jeff Faux notes, "from publishing self-improvement books and training salesmen to smile even when they don't feel like it to a loosely constructed system of social engineering that distracts and discourages Americans from dealing with what is happening to their society." Jobless Americans are "instructed to look to themselves for survival" by motivational speakers hired by corporations to instruct laid-off workers "to not waste energy on anger at the company, the economy, or the country's leaders" but instead to "concentrate on the more practical task of beating the hundreds of others who are lined up to apply for a handful of jobs." The basic message is that "you can succeed if you just try harder and stay positive."[52] Battered by this message, which resonates with older traits in the national culture, many Americans exhibit a disturbing and unrealistic "gap between [their] perception of the nation's economic fate and their own." They tend to significantly exaggerate both their own current socioeconomic status—58 percent of Americans identified themselves to Gallup as "haves" rather than "have-nots" at the end of November 2011, and a June 2010 poll found that 71 percent of Americans reported they were "doing better than average"—and to exaggerate their own chances of economic advance in a nation that is regularly and falsely described as the land of unmatched upward mobility and opportunity. As numerous polls show, most Americans seem to think that they and their children will do well but that their fellow citizens are in for a rough time. These beliefs are pleasing to the economic elite and governing class, whose basic message is to keep their heads down, stay positive, work hard, and have patience and—the campaign keywords of both Bill Clinton and Barack Obama—"hope" since "markets will eventually recover, and nudged on by a few marginal changes in policy or a change in the party in control of Congress and the White House, you and your family will soon be on your rightful track to perpetual prosperity."[53]

Many cannot play the game and keep smiling, given the harsh realities of the Second Gilded Age, which include a "profound and historical decline in their economic and political bargaining power" and a ruling elite that is "constitutionally unwilling to make the necessary concessions to restore that bargaining power." Thus, as Faux notes, "millions of [Americans] suffer clinical depression and [the United States is] by far the largest consumer of antidepressants. Every week or so, another one of us goes berserk and murders coworkers, family members, or perfect strangers"[54]—all too often with automatic repeat-fire weapons that are all too freely available on the American "free market" thanks to the powerful gun industry and its lobbying arm, the National Rifle Association. According to the leading New York City–based psychotherapist Richard O'Connor, writing at the height of the most recent economic crisis,

> We are living in an epidemic of depression. Every indication suggests that more people are depressed, more of the time, and starting earlier in their lives, than ever before.... Researchers estimate that almost 20 percent of the population meet the criteria for some form of depression at any given time.... Depression is second only to cancer in terms of economic impact, and approximately the same as the cost of heart disease and AIDS. The number of deaths from suicide in the United States each year (33,000) is approximately twice the number of deaths from AIDS and shows no signs

of declining.... If current trends continue, children today will develop depression at the average age of twenty, instead of the thirty-plus we are used to.[55]

But this, too, is not unwelcome to the ruling class. Alienated, depressed, medically drugged, and gun-toting/gun-fearing citizens are unlikely recruits for engaged and active collective participation in grassroots movements for social justice and democratic transformation. The exhaustion, financial worries, interpersonal tensions, divorce, disaffection, substance abuse, domestic abuse, cruelty, and depression that so endemically result from the profits system in its neoliberal phase are no small parts of how that system grinds on without serious organized popular resistance. Beyond economic impact, O'Connor might consider the authoritarian consequences. Depression undermines its victims' capacity to participate meaningfully in social and political movements and organization, feeding plutocracy's democracy deficit by stealing the willpower and confidence of citizens, draining their shared and personal senses of effectiveness and purpose. Millions of Americans are simply too depressed and demoralized to resist "the greedy bastards'" assault on the common good.

Hearts and Minds for Capitalism

All of this and more function in accord with top corporate attorney Lewis Powell's semi-legendary August 1971 memo to the director of the US Chamber of Commerce. Written two months before Richard Nixon appointed Powell to the Supreme Court, the memo detailed what Powell considered to be an unprecedented and "broadly based" assault on "the American economic system" (capitalism) emanating not just from the radical margins but even from "perfectly respectable elements of society: the college campus, the pulpit, the media, the intellectual and literary journals, the arts and sciences, and from politicians." By Powell's reckoning, a dangerous antibusiness uprising led by such "charismatic" critics as Ralph Nader and the radical 1960s professor Herbert Marcuse meant that corporations should undertake a concerted and many-sided public relations and media counteroffensive—a veritable capitalist cultural counterrevolution. "It is time," Powell proclaimed, "for American business—which has demonstrated the greatest capacity in history to produce and influence consumer decisions—to apply their great talents vigorously to the *preservation of the system itself*" (emphasis added). Powell felt that the struggle to win back hearts and minds for capitalism should target the universities, the publishing world, and the mass media, including an effort to place the television networks "under constant surveillance."[56] According to the distinguished political scientist Edward P. Morgan, Powell's "urgent appeal helped set in motion forces that subsequently transformed public discourse in the United States for decades to come."[57]

Consistent with Powell's call, the "business community" mobilized to shape public opinion in response to perceived threats to its profits and freedom posed by the upsurge of democratic social movements (civil rights, women's rights, environmentalism, and consumer and worker protection) of the 1960s and early 1970s. Threatened by the regulations these movements won, and by a related rising spirit of rank-and-file worker militancy in a time when American business faced growing foreign competition, the corporate sector undertook a concerted public relations and "education" campaign to influence everyday Americans' world views in a "pro-business" direction.[58]

It is fitting that Powell appealed to the American business class's historic advertising prowess in connection with the project of more properly aligning popular sentiments with the needs of the profits system, the mass acceptance or rejection of which he revealingly described as a *"consumer decision"*—not a *citizen choice*. A brilliant and pioneering propaganda critic, Alex Carey rightly attributed corporate propaganda's remarkable power in the United States to the American business class's distinctive and long-standing skill at reaching popular hearts and minds through mass advertising. As Carey noted in his wonderfully titled volume *Taking the Risk Out of Democracy*, "Commercial advertising and public relations are the forms of propaganda activity common in a democracy. In the United States over a very long time now these methods have been honed by incomparably more skill and research than in any other country."[59]

"That's Politics": Electoral Spectacle and Tyranny, American-Style

"These Personalized Quadrennial Extravaganzas": *Elections as Brand Marketing*

Speaking of advertising, the heavily marketed, candidate-centered spectacles of carefully managed popular "voice" that are staged for the *citizenry qua electorate* every four years are themselves critical and fundamentally propagandistic mechanisms of 1% rule. Chomsky's acerbic description of the US presidential election in the fall of 2004 applies well to all of the nation's once-every-four-years presidential contests:

> Americans are encouraged to vote, but not to participate more meaningfully in the political arena. Essentially the election is another method of

marginalizing the population. A huge propaganda campaign is mounted to get people to focus on these personalized quadrennial extravaganzas to think, "That's politics." But it isn't. It's only a small part of politics.... Bush and Kerry can run because they're funded by similar concentrations of private power. Both candidates understand that the election is supposed to stay away from issues. They are creatures of the public relations industry, which keeps the public out of the election process. Their task is to focus attention on the candidates' "qualities," not policies. Is he a leader? A nice guy? Voters end up endorsing an image, not a platform.

In 1985 the clever antitelevision writer Neil Postman dissected the authoritarian nightmare that is modern US political advertising. The television commercial, Postman noted, is the antithesis of the rational popular consideration that leading early philosophers of Western economic life took to be the enlightened essence of capitalism. The television commercial makes "hash" out of the capitalist assumption of intelligent and informed consumer sovereignty. It undercuts the notion of rational claims based on serious propositions and evidence. In the place of cogent language and logical discourse, it substitutes evocative imagery and suggestive emotionalism. When political success came to revolve largely around the same manipulative anti-enlightened methods prevalent in commodity advertising, Postman observed, the same sorry fate fell to "capitalist democracy's" assumption of rational and informed voters. Like the bamboozled commodity purchasers propagandized by relentless television ads, voters are subjects of persuasion through deception instead of respectful and sensible communication.[60]

That is why we didn't hear Obama's liberal supporters say much about the interesting fact that Obama was selected by the Association of National Advertisers (ANA) as the "Marketer of the Year" on the eve of the 2008 presidential election. Or about how the ANA's trade journal *Advertising Age*[61] heralded "Brand Obama" as a "case study in audacious marketing," praising the President Elect's "understanding of ground-level marketing strategies and tactics ... everything from audience segmentation and database management to the creation and maintenance of online communities."[62]

The marketing practiced by politicians and their brand makers relies heavily on a standard technique in commercial advertising—the pretense of empathy. Just as the nation's great sociopathic corporations commonly wrap the products and services they advertise in the counterfeit clothing of concern for others and the earth,[63] American politicians generally claim to be motivated by a deep concern for ordinary people, democracy, and the common good—this even as they follow their ambitions in accord with the selfish interests of the nation's deep-pockets money dictatorship.

"America's Signature Exclusion"

The depressing fact that many voters—enough to make the difference in a closely divided electorate—make candidate choices that have little to do with policy and much to do with marketing and imagery reflects in part the narrow nature of the policy differences between the two reigning business parties. If American elections were primarily about the serious popular consideration of policy platforms, not the marginalization and manipulation of the citizenry qua "electorate," they would be won or at least seriously contested on at least some occasions by candidates from third and fourth parties like the Green Party, whose platforms match majority progressive policy opinion and values to a far greater degree than those of the reigning parties. But thanks to the wealth primary, the heavily gerrymandered "winner-take-all" nature of the nation's elections and representation system, the collaboration of the major parties in creating giant procedural roadblocks to third-party viability, the dominant media's instinctive framing of US politics in terms of two and only two parties, and the US Supreme Court's long-standing support of existing steep state and federal barriers to substantive third-party formation, few candidates with opinions to the left of the ever more right-leaning major party duopoly have any serious chance of making viable runs for significant electoral office. In what Raskin calls "America's signature exclusion," third (and fourth and fifth) parties are essentially prohibited from competing on a free and equal basis. That itself is a major form of undemocratic policy since majority US opinion has long and consistently supported the existence of a third political party that would run candidates for president, Congress, and state offices against the dominant major party candidates.[64]

Differences That Matter, Sadly Enough

Still, some US voters certainly choose corporate-backed Democrats over corporate-backed Republicans for rational reasons that relate to partisan differences of socioeconomic policy, not just imagery and advertising. Better situated and more inclined than their GOP counterparts to artfully practice the "manipulation of populism by elitism" that has long been central to US political culture, Democratic politicians promise to do progressive-sounding things that most of the populace supports: stimulate the economy, tax the rich, protect "the middle class" (the lower and working classes do not seem to exist in the nation's official political culture) and the environment, and generally make government "work on behalf of the many and not just the few" (in the words of Barack Obama's 2013 State of the Union address). And while they do all too little along these lines, Democrats in office tend to temper the business class's assault on middle- and working-class security and what remains of the social welfare state, if only to a slight degree. They also have a record of more reliably acting to stimulate the economy through deficit spending.[65] The Republicans wage top-down class war with savage zeal, seeking to shred what remains of labor power, livable ecology, minority rights, and the welfare state in service to a militantly authoritarian variant of right-wing state-capitalist doctrine, falsely sold as "free market" ideology.

The differences are not wholly irrelevant, especially to vulnerable people who depend on what's left of the social welfare state that is targeted for liquidation by the radical Republicans, falsely labeled "conservative" in the dominant political culture. As Faux reminds us,

> Even within the confines of this plutocracy, it *does matter* who becomes president and who runs Congress. More economic distress is on the way. Under Democrats, it will come at a slower pace and hurt the working class less than under Republicans. Under Democrats, there will be less shredding of the social safety nets than under Republicans.... Under Democrats, Supreme Court appointments will tend to be economic centrists; under Republicans they will be economic reactionaries.... *These distinctions are not unimportant. For people who struggle every day to pay their rent or mortgage, to buy food and clothes for their kids, to squeeze out a health insurance premium*, there is a world of difference between having a smaller Social Security or unemployment compensation check and not having one, between having access to a threadbare Medicare program and having no program at all.[66]

Identity over Class Politics

Yet to a remarkable degree despite these distinctions, the US electorate is polarized between the two dominant parties not on the basis of class but rather in accord with differences of racial, ethnic, religious, cultural, gender, moral, and regional identity. In the neoliberal era of the New Gilded Age, "identity politics" has come to "replace what was once [during the long New Deal era of 1932–1976] something like class politics ... as the basis of coalition formation and electoral mobilization. In the process," the eminent Marxist historian Perry Anderson notes, "traditional income determinations [of voting behavior] have been losing their salience, or warping into their opposite." Thus, in 2008 Republican presidential candidate John McCain won the majority of white voters living on less than $50,000 a year and the Democratic victor Obama got a majority of those receiving over $200,000 a year. Four years later, eight of the nation's ten richest counties backed Obama. "In every one of these cradles of plutocracy," Anderson adds, the president's "margin of victory was greater than the national average."[67]

Obama's two presidential election victories depended not on labor and working-class support so much as on the rising female vote and the votes of unmarried professionals, single parents, gays, and racial and ethnic minorities. The 2008 Democratic presidential primaries produced what Anderson calls "the perfect candidate for the [new multicultural and identity-politicized] hour: not only younger, cooler, and more eloquent [than the Caucasian Hillary Clinton] but magnetic for the minorities on which victory depended." As Anderson explains,

> Image, which in a politics of spectacle always matters more than reality, normally requires projection. But here, in the perception of color, it was literal, allowing edifying legend (an autobiography under contract before even graduation) to develop around reality with unusual speed. . . . Personification of national triumph over race prejudice, vindication of the American dream of success for all, devout yet moderate reconciler of divisions, bearer of hope to the disregarded and afflicted, Obama could serve as a hold for any number of uplifting popular identifications.[68]

So what if Obama's 2012 platform consisted, in the words of one of his strong backers, "of Mitt Romney's health-care bill, Newt Gingrich's environmental policies, John McCain's deficit-financed payroll tax-cuts, George W. Bush's bailouts of failing banks and corporations, and a mixture of Bush and Clinton's tax code"?[69] Democrats hold the upper hand in national elections, winning the popular vote in five of the last six presidential contests, largely because the ethnic, racial, and social demographics of the electorate have changed in their favor.

This does not mean that US citizens necessarily or inherently privilege social identity over economic class in terms of what they think matters most in public affairs. It reflects the significant extent to which the plutocratic US elections system tends to privilege and prioritize nonclass social identity politics over class politics when it comes to forming coalitions and mobilizing voters.[70] Both of the reigning political organizations play the game so that for all their current "populist" utterances, even Democratic politicians and their "niche marketing" consultants and pollsters focus on social identity, reflecting their party's "long-term trend away from economic class issues" in deference to wealthy corporate campaign funders.[71] Reduced to the status of a "managed electorate,"[72] the citizenry is relentlessly and electorally played by a moneyed political elite that pulls the strings behind a political culture that pumps out highly partisan dramas over largely identity-based issues while keeping itself invisible. As Chris Hedges noted in July 2013 on the Real News Network,

> Both sides of the political spectrum are manipulated by the same forces. If you're some right-wing Christian zealot in Georgia, then it's homosexuals and abortion and all these, you know, wedge issues that are used to whip you up emotionally. If you are a liberal in Manhattan, it's—you know, they'll

all be teaching creationism in your schools or whatever.... Yet in fact it's just a game, because whether it's Bush or whether it's Obama, Goldman Sachs wins always. There is no way to vote against the interests of Goldman Sachs.[73]

Public "Input Every Four Years"

For what it's worth, most Americans reject the viciously elitist notion that they are granted adequate popular input into federal policy through the big money, big media, narrow-spectrum, major party, candidate-centered electoral extravaganzas and political passion plays that are played for (and on) them once every four years. When asked in 2008 by the Program on International Policy Attitudes if they believed that "elections are the only time when the views of the people should have influence," a remarkable 94 percent of Americans disagreed, saying "government leaders should pay attention to the views of the public between elections." The same survey indicated that the public knew very well that its desires were not honored in that regard: 80 percent "sa[id] that this country is run by a few big interests looking out for themselves" and not "for the benefit of all the people."[74]

Some in the power elite do not agree with the notion that public opinion matters between electoral extravaganzas. In the spring of 2008, ABC News correspondent Martha Raddatz asked then vice president Dick Cheney about opinion surveys showing that the vast majority of Americans opposed the US war in Iraq. Cheney had an interesting response: "So?"

"So—you don't care what the American people think?" the correspondent asked.

"No," Cheney elaborated, "I think you cannot be blown off course by the fluctuations in public opinion polls."

Justifying Cheney's blunt remarks, White House spokesperson Dana Perino was later asked if the public should have "input" on US policy. "You had your input," Perino replied. "The American people have input every four years, and that's the way our system is set up." Chomsky aptly summarizes the core sentiment behind this remark: "Every four years the American people can choose between candidates whose views they reject, and then they should shut up."[75]

Time as a Democracy Issue

The fact that many "ordinary" Americans tend to focus on election funding alone when talking about how and why the nation's political system is unduly controlled by concentrated wealth does not mean that they are stupid. The campaign finance dimension *is* critical, after all. And going deeper into the often exasperating complexity of the various many-sided mechanisms and veritable simultaneous equations system of business-class rule in the New Gilded Age requires research and reflections that relatively few Americans have time, energy, and inclination to undertake.

Time, it is worth noting, is a core requirement of democracy. What use, early nineteenth-century labor activists and workers asked, were the American Revolution and the extension of voting rights to property-less citizens if they lacked the time and energy to inform and educate themselves on the issues of the day and to meaningfully participate in civil life? As these union pioneers knew, formal democracy was an empty gift without enough leisure time for the populace to enjoy and utilize its benefits. The struggles for the ten- and later the eight-hour work day expressed among other things everyday citizen-workers' desire to meaningfully participate in the purported age of democracy.[76]

That forgotten history provides interesting context for a disdainful remark made by a veteran Wall Street financial executive in mid-October 2011, when the Occupy Movement was in its short-lived heyday. "It's not a middle-class uprising," the banker told the *New York Times*. "It's fringe groups. It's *people who have the time to do this.*"[77] Beyond the facts that most of the Occupiers came from middle- and working-class backgrounds, that Wall Street had created (often unwanted) free time for millions of Americans by collapsing the job market, and that Occupy's core grievances (the excessive wealth and power of the super-rich and the corrosive impact of America's shockingly high levels of economic inequality) were shared by most Americans, the most remarkable thing about the banker's complaint was the scorn it conveyed for the notion that part of the citizenry might actually *possess enough time to participate in a protest movement*. In a better America, the financial master seemed to think, the populace would be so busy, so occupied, so yoked to what nineteenth-century labor activists routinely called "wage-slavery" (and/or to salary-slavery, debt-slavery, student-hood, private business and home tasks, or other individual pursuits) that nobody would have enough hours, minutes, and days to fight back against concentrated wealth and power.[78*]

Consistent with the banker's implicit wish, the United States surpassed Japan to become the nation with the longest working hours and hence the worst "time-squeeze" in the industrialized world during its Second Gilded Age. As economist Juliet Schor showed in her widely read book *The Overworked American* (1992), this overwork takes three key forms: (i) the extensive hours experienced by salaried employees, whose annualized (per year instead of per

---

* I advanced a different take on Occupy activists' free time on the left website *ZNet*: "Movements for justice and democracy require (and at their best sustain activists with) time and energy to learn, reflect, organize, and struggle. Thank God that thousands of Occupy activists across the country have time and energy to put some real egalitarian and populist risk back into the free speech and other democracy rights that corporations and the hired servants of the wealthy masters work *around the clock* to subvert, channel, co-opt, and otherwise control."

hour) compensation mode incentivizes employers to push their employees into long workdays and workweeks; (ii) the holding of multiple hourly paid jobs by working-class Americans who cannot get by on one job in a period when employers have rolled back wages and union power; and (iii) the distinctive overwork of women, who continue to be saddled with a disproportionate amount of domestic work even as more and more married females enter the full-time job market. The successful employer offensive against unions in the New Gilded Age is a critical factor behind the expansion of working hours, for organized labor has long been the leading force behind the attainment of a shorter work day and more vacation time in the United States as across the industrialized world.[79]

One solution to the overwork problem would be to introduce work-sharing, combining reduced hours for overextended employees with employment at decent work schedules for jobless and underemployed Americans. This obvious fix is not remotely considered by corporate employers and politicians, however, for it would dry up the nation's reserve army of labor, undermining the labor market disciplining of the employed. At the same time, work-sharing/ -spreading would mean a large number of new hires becoming eligible for medical and pension benefits, something that few employers are willing to tolerate.[80]

Reducing overwork would also mean considerably more free time for popular participation in the much-ballyhooed democracy American workers and citizens are supposed to enjoy. That is perhaps the unspoken fear behind a remarkable statement made by marketing professor Phillip Kotler (of elite Northwestern University's prestigious Kellogg School of Management) in the leading business paper *Financial Times* in the spring of 2003. "If there are no more needs," Kotler argued on behalf of the virtues of mass advertising, "then we have to invent new needs"—a remarkable statement in a time when almost half the species (nearly 3 billion people) lived on less than $2.50 a day. "Capitalism," Kotler elaborated, "is a system where we've got to motivate people to want things so they'll work for those things. If there's no more things they want they won't work as hard: they'll want 35-hour work weeks, 30-hour weeks and so on."[81]

What exactly would be so terrible about thirty-hour work weeks? From an elite 1% perspective, the downsides include increased wage and benefits costs along with more time for citizens to understand and challenge the plutocracy and profits system's environmentally disastrous attachment to the generation of endless artificial needs in blind pursuit of endless growth and accumulation.[82]

Complexity

Time becomes especially essential for democracy when society and the policies regulating it become so complicated that unraveling their inner workings requires significant investigation and reflection. "Our world isn't about ideology anymore," Matt Taibbi writes. "It's about complexity. We live in a complex bureaucratic state with complex laws and complex business practices, and the few organizations with the corporate willpower to master these complexities will inevitably own the political power."[83]

Taibbi is wrong about the irrelevance of ideology, but he is correct to note the daunting complexity of contemporary society for most ordinary citizens. Even highly educated professionals and academics struggle to master the intricacies of the Affordable Health Care Act, the national debt/fiscal deficit, financial regulation, national and/or international monetary policy, campaign finance law, "free trade" agreements, the Federal Reserve, trade law, tax law, labor law, currency policy, health care law, voting rights law, antitrust and merger law, corporate ownership structure and concentration, intellectual property rights, environmental change and regulation, and much, much more, including the maddening obscurity of Wall Street's favorite financial instruments: credit default swaps, synthetic collateralized debt obligations, interest rate swaps, and the like. All this and more takes time and in many cases specialized training to disentangle and demystify. Much of it is made highly opaque and complicated on purpose, precisely with the intent of marginalizing the "unqualified" citizenry.

A classic example is provided by the nation's legendarily exasperating tax code. Untold millions of ordinary Americans struggle to understand and properly fill out their elaborate tax forms each year. Meanwhile, accountants employed by the 1% work through byzantine tax laws to make sure their wealthy clients continue to enjoy the benefits of complex and regressive tax breaks and loopholes that cost the US Treasury more than $1.1 trillion per year—a sum greater than Medicare and Medicaid combined, greater than Social Security, and greater than both "defense" and nondiscretionary defense spending.[84] Most Americans' eyes glaze over quickly when learning about the intricate workings of such policies. Many in the economic superelite probably experience the same, no doubt. They do so with a critical difference, however: they retain highly paid legal professionals who understand contemporary tax law and its complex loopholes very, very well.

It doesn't help, of course, that corporate interests invest in obscuring popular understanding of current events and policy issues. A classic example is climate change, where the oil and coal industries have launched a massive public relations (propaganda) campaign to discredit basic science on greenhouse gases and their planet-warming consequences. Corporate America has long invested heavily in the deliberate obfuscation of popular economics understanding, regularly feeding schools, universities, and mass media reams of misleading, pseudo-social scientific, and self-serving nonsense about the alleged "trickle down" benefits of letting "the market" (the corporations and their wealthy investors) have their way and the supposedly dysfunctional nature of efforts to regulate the economy in the public interest.

Mass confusion is only worsened by the standard political talk show method of treating controversial social and policy issues. An "expert" is invited from what passes for the left (typically a Democratic Party–friendly think tank like the Center for Budget and Policy Priorities) to briefly debate the matter in question with an "expert" from what passes for the "conservative" right (typically a fellow at the radical-right Heritage Foundation or the equally arch-reactionary American Enterprise Institute). These representatives of what passes for a broad ideological spectrum typically come to an obscure and unenlightening stalemate, leaving many viewers less knowledgeable on the issue than they were before.[85]

The Tragic Farce of Corporate Media News and Commentary

The interrelated problems of time, complexity, and citizen confusion highlight the critical role of corporate news media and journalism in how the rich rule America. Democracy, McChesney notes, "works best" when "three basic criteria are met": (1) no significant inequalities in wealth and property exist across society; (2) there is a strong "sense of community" with the widespread notion that "an individual's well-being is determined to no small extent by the community's well-being"; (3) there is "an effective system of political communication, broadly construed, that informs and engages the citizenry, drawing people into the polity. This becomes especially important," Robert McChesney notes, "as societies grow larger and more complex,"[86] making citizens more dependent on information from beyond their direct observation.

McChesney's three-legged table of democracy's requirements has been wobbling badly, to say the least, in the Second Gilded Age. His first criterion is obviously nonexistent, as we have seen. His second is regularly assaulted by the ideology and culture of neoliberalism. His second and third criteria are undercut by the nation's highly and ever more concentrated and commercialized corporate mass communications system (fewer than ten multinational corporations currently control more than half the nation's print and electronic media), whose owners, advertisers, and top managers have little interest in accurately informing, inspiring, engaging, and otherwise equipping the working-class majority of Americans for democratic and collective engagement and self-governance. Media elites prefer complacent, culturally privatized consumers who leave the handling of public affairs and the management of society to their supposedly superior, benevolent, and far-seeing betters in the business and professional classes. Journalists and commentators who think differently and who act to meaningfully inform and activate citizens for democratic participation and social justice do not tend to do well in such a media, to say the least. Those who wish to keep their increasingly insecure positions in the ever-consolidating corporate communications empire learn to fashion their reports and opinions in accord with reigning neoliberals and to keep the 1% as cloaked and unaccountable as possible in their treatment of current events.[87]

Like a Company Paper

The US corporate media is *not simply or merely beholden to the capitalist establishment* through advertising. It is itself a key market-driven and profit-seeking *component of that establishment*. As Chomsky once observed, expecting NBC News (owned by the leading "defense" contractor General Electric) to give an objective, unbiased account of domestic and world affairs would be *like expecting General Motors' company newspaper to give a truthful and detached account of working conditions in its automobile plants*. GM's company paper is a form of propaganda meant to sell that corporation's values and agenda to its employees. It is a mechanism for "manufacturing consent" within and to the firm.[88] In a similar vein, news, commentary, and documentaries broadcast at NBC (General Electric), ABC (Disney), CBS (Westinghouse), FOX (News Corporation), and other corporate media holdings seek to sell the broader American business elite's agenda and values on a society-wide basis, along with a vast array of consumer goods and services and a way of life that fits mass consumerist imperatives. It is naïve to expect them to tell anything like the full story on current affairs and developments of critical relevance to democratic, human, and ecological prospects at home and abroad.[89]

An especially chilling example of this dominant corporate media's unreliability and irresponsibility was given in 2012, when viewers of the Discovery Channel (Disney) saw a remarkable seven-part series on global warming that contained graphic high-definition images of vast swaths of melting ice breaking off in Antarctica. Titled *The Frozen Planet*, the documentary presented similarly dramatic pictures of imperiled polar bears, penguins, and seals, all dealing with the consequences of climate change. There was something important left out of the series, however. By their own admission, *The Frozen Planet*'s producers steered clear of the inconvenient truth of *why* the planet is warming. Addressing causation would have upset powerful petrochemical corporate interests and other parts of the carbon industrial complex and its financial backers, who could be counted on to withhold advertising dollars and retaliate in other ways, so the documentary's makers chose to play it safe. As Bill McKibben observed, "It was like doing a powerful documentary about lung cancer and leaving out the part about cigarettes."[90]

Manufacturing Mass Ignorance

"A popular government without popular information, or the means of acquiring it," James Madison once noted, "is but a prologue to a farce or a tragedy, or perhaps both."[91] How are the people supposed to act to make "their" government behave decently and in accord with public opinion when they are fed a diet of "news" and commentary strictly crafted and systematically filtered to fit the 1%'s narrow interests and doctrine? The individual body cannot respond adequately to a threat of injury—an incoming punch or projectile, for example—if its mind does not transmit the information of impending harm. In a similar way, the body politic and its popular majority cannot respond adequately to threats to democracy and collective survival if society's information and cultural centers do not adequately communicate the dangers.

Popular perceptions about American wealth distribution are a good case in point. As business professor Michael Norton and psychologist Dan Ariely have shown, most Americans think that the ideal distribution would be one in which the top 20 percent owned between 30 and 40 percent of the privately held wealth and the bottom 40 percent had between 25 and 30 percent. "Americans prefer [social democratic] Sweden," Norton and Ariely observe, reflecting on how 5,552 US citizens they surveyed responded to three unlabeled pie charts of wealth distribution. One chart depicted a perfectly equal distribution of wealth. Unbeknownst to survey participants, a second chart reflected the real wealth distribution in the United States, with the top quintile owning 84 percent of the nation's wealth and the bottom two quintiles together owning 0.3 percent. A third chart depicted the income distribution of unnamed Sweden, with the top quintile getting 38 percent and the bottom two together 30 percent. An overwhelming majority, fully 92 percent, of Americans surveyed preferred the Swedish distribution to the United States. An also large majority (77 percent) preferred the totally equal distribution over the United States.

Given most Americans' clear preference for a more egalitarian distribution of wealth, Norton and Ariely ask, why is there not a mass popular uprising against the extreme inequality of New Gilded Age America? Part of the answer, the researchers determine, is that most Americans are woefully ignorant of how unequal their country is. When shown three pie charts representing possible wealth distributions, more than 90 percent of the survey respondents—regardless of gender, age, income level, or party affiliation—thought US wealth distribution most resembled one in which the top 20 percent possesses 60 percent of the wealth. Most people in the survey guessed that the bottom 40 percent had between 8 and 10 percent.[92] In a similar vein, just 42 percent of Americans believe that inequality has grown in the United States in recent years, when, as Joseph Stiglitz notes, "the increase has been tectonic."[93]

It's hard to be angry about a problem you don't know exists. Here we confront a viciously circular fact of ruling-class power. The top 1 percent owns the major media that millions rely on for information about the world they inhabit. And the wealthy few are hardly eager to see the citizenry accurately informed about the distribution of wealth and, hence, power in the United States. As a result, the problem of extreme wealth concentration and its negative consequences does not receive serious and sustained treatment in the dominant mass media that ordinary Americans depend on for the accurate and relevant public information that popular governance requires.

The terrible evidence of mass public ignorance discovered by Norton and Ariely and numerous other opinion researchers[94] is not simply the consequence of national "can-do" culture or mass stupidity or laziness. The tragic farce of a "company paper" mass media is no small part of why, as Stiglitz laments, "Americans … believe that there is less inequality than there is, … underestimate its adverse economic effects,… [and] underestimate the ability of government to do anything about it."[95] It is also part of how the "skills gap" narrative has become so ubiquitous in American discussions of unemployment and inequality. The owners of the nation's leading perception-shaping communications institutions (the corporate media) have a rich economic and political stake in the suppression of the real story on the degree, and the causes, of class inequality in the United States today.

Marginalizing Protest

Of critical significance and for the same basic reason, the dominant mass media chronically underreport and disparage popular protest. When tens of thousands of workers and activists marched against the corporate-neoliberal model of globalization in Seattle in the fall of 1999, the dominant communications authorities gave the remarkable events there sparse live coverage. The same was true when 40,000 marched against American and European militarism at the meetings of the North Atlantic Treaty Organization (NATO) in May 2012.[96] And after 50,000 citizens gathered in the nation's capital in a historic march on Sunday, February 17, 2013, to urge President Obama not to approve the environmentally disastrous Keystone XL pipeline (designed to carry "dirty" tar sands oil from the Canadian province of Alberta to refineries in the US Gulf Coast), the nation's "newspaper of record" the *New York Times* did not see the rally as part of "All the News That's Fit to Print" in its first section the following day. Here are some of the news topics the *Times* did include in that section: The tech industry's growing interest in the gambling industry (page 1); a car, van, truck, and motorbike police pound (humorously called "the car Guantanamo") in Kabul, Afghanistan (page 1); Irish assistance to an Irish-American neighborhood in Queens (Breezy Point) that was particularly devastated by Hurricane Sandy (page 1); the fraud prosecution of a former Israeli foreign minister; and Catholics' confusion about "what to call a retired Pope."

The Monday, February 18 *Times* did mention the previous day's historic climate demonstration, to be sure. The reference came in the paper's business section, alongside an article on the Facebook marketing strategies of Universal Studio's *Fast and Furious* car-racing film series and a report on the rising use of cheaper parts in the manufacture of virtual reality game sets. It failed to seriously or substantively address the severe ecological risks posed by the Keystone pipeline and badly underreported the protest's turnout, saying only that "thousands rallied." By placing their reportage on the historic climate rally in the business section, the *Times*'s editors suggested that the pipeline was mainly a corporate and marketing matter, not an issue of vital public and political concern. This is just one among countless examples that might be given of corporate media's tendency to downplay and disrespect mass demonstrations with a progressive flavor.[97]

The protest coverage that does take place in dominant media typically overfocuses on emotionally potent, threatening images of disruption and isolated incidents of protestor violence (the occasional smashed window or overturned car) and other displays of anger and militancy at the expense of protestors' political demands. There is disproportionate attention to some protestors' appearance (typically "dirty" and "ragged") and "rage" but little if any serious attention to the protest's specific issues, concerns, recommendations, and vision. The protestors appear as little more than nay-sayers, nattering negativists who have no positive, forward-looking ideas and advance no alternatives. Thus, the global justice movement has been routinely misrepresented in dominant media coverage as alienated "antiglobalization" Luddites, not committed citizens and activists with serious ideas on how to manage economic globalization in more socially equitable and democratic ways that are very different from the dominant neoliberal model of corporate globalization. This media method for undermining mass popular support for democratic resistance to elite policies and power was honed during the late 1960s and early 1970s, when ominous and frightening media portrayals of anti–Vietnam War protestors helped make antiwar activists unpopular among a citizenry that had turned against the war itself. Spectacular and often fear-mongering coverage of protestors and the chaos and violence they supposedly engendered and portended fed a right-wing backlash that helped usher in the neoliberal era.[98]

Some of this method for marginalizing protest was reenacted with the Occupy Movement. The dominant media's coverage of Occupy paid disproportionate attention to the Occupiers, their campsites, and their tussles with police and other authorities, pushing Occupy's fundamental issue of economic inequality and ruling class more and more into the background as the Occupy Movement reached its conclusion. The more police and other state authorities attacked protestors, the more the protestors and violence, not the protestors' grievances and ideas, became the dominant news story. Like the Vietnam War protestors who lost popularity even as popular opposition to that war mounted, the Occupiers lost favor even as most Americans registered agreement with their fundamental issue—economic inequality and its consequences—and as that issue came to play a central role in Obama and other Democrats' 2012 campaign rhetoric.

Neoliberal Education

Functioning democracy's prospects are further challenged by the fact that public education—what we might consider a fourth and missing leg of McChesney's shaky democracy table—has been under relentless corporate-neoliberal assault during the Second Gilded Age. One wing of the attack is economic, involving the systematic underfunding of public schools and a related, business-led campaign for the privatization of schools and corporate control of public educational programs. Another wing of the assault is more directly ideological, involving a dedicated business effort to yoke teachers and students to an authoritarian, mind- and soul-deadening theory and practice of pedagogy. The standardized test–obsessed "skill-and-grill" pedagogy that big business and business-backed education foundations and think tanks, politicians, and policymakers advance with special insistence on inner city schools attacks critical and independent thinking with the goal of turning students into what the legendary left education author and children's advocate Jonathan Kozol calls "examination soldiers—unquestioning and docile followers of proto-military regulations." As Giroux notes, "Behaviorism becomes the preferred model of pedagogy and substitutes a mind-numbing emphasis on methods that are critical, moral, and political in substance. Learning facts and skills . . . becomes more important than genuine understanding." The facts and methods forced into students' minds by the neoliberal educational model are selected to fit the broader ideological system that makes solidarity a banished word, materialism a virtue, "the market" (the corporation) the legitimate master of society, the renting out of one's labor power to an employer the sole purpose of study, and narcissistic self-interest the only reasonable purpose of work and life.[99]

This is precisely the opposite of how the nation's foremost educational philosopher John Dewey conceptualized the ideal purpose of American K–12 education—as the production not of commodities and employees but "free human beings." Believing that workers should be "the masters of their own industrial fate" and not merely tools of their "superiors," Dewey considered it "immoral" to train children to work "not freely and intelligently but for the wage-earned." The point of worthwhile schools for him was to cultivate critically engaged citizens capable of full and active participation in a true democracy.[100]

It is a sorry testament to the success of the neoliberal education project that calling for such schooling today "sounds," as Chomsky notes, "exotic and extreme, perhaps even anti-American."[101] That success is essential to the power of the broader neoliberal ideological project in other areas. It undermines the schools' capacity to equip youth and young adults with cultural antidotes and decoders—with a civic version of John Carpenter's magical sunglasses—to resist the corporate, imperial, consumerist propaganda that is so ubiquitous across the mass media landscape in the Brave New World of twenty-first-century America. This is distressing since that landscape grants the prevailing "me first" and "you're on your own" doctrine a daunting array of delivery systems, from the "surround sound" multiplex movie theater to the iPhone, the personal computer, the ever-enlarging flat screen television, and the video game console to the billboards that are so ubiquitous alongside our freeways.

The problem continues into the ever more difficult-to-afford preserves of "higher education," where business values and corporations reign as supreme as in the rest of the nation's ideological institutions. A fading marginal cadre of seriously engaged progressive and critical thinkers holds down a small number of tenured positions in the nation's highly pacified colleges and universities, which have in the New Gilded Age reverted to their long-standing role—briefly disturbed by the New Left campus rebellion of the 1960s and early 1970s—of serving the reigning nation's power centers. A disproportionately progressive mass of proletarianized college and university subprofessors now toils in the militantly corporate-neoliberalized adjunct teaching market, receiving marginal pay without benefits and hope for future advancement.

From Welfare to Prison State

"The Greased Chute to Destitution"

The slashing of social programs and the distinctive weakness of the welfare state in Second Gilded Age America are an additional aspect of how the unelected dictatorship of money rules. As many formerly middle-class Americans discovered with the onset of the 1%-generated Great Recession, the "downward plunge into poverty [can] occur with dizzying speed" in the United States. Americans are "particularly vulnerable to economic dislocation" since, as Barbara Ehrenreich and John Ehrenreich explain,

> We have little in the way of a welfare state to stop a family or an individual in free-fall. Unemployment benefits do not last more than six months or a year, though in a recession they are sometimes extended by Congress. At present, even with such an extension, they reach only about half the jobless. Welfare was all but abolished 15 years ago, and health insurance has traditionally been linked to employment.... Where other once-wealthy nations have a safety net, America offers a greased chute, leading down to destitution with alarming speed.[102]

Terrible in and of itself, this kind of vulnerability has broad authoritarian implications. People who lack a social safety net outside the labor market are less likely to challenge the authority of their bosses or other elites than those who know that they and their families will be able to maintain a minimally decent standard of living in the event of job loss. In the absence of suitable social protections beyond the job market, millions see long hours of low-wage work and/or job searching as their only option—something that leaves them with little time or energy for meaningful participation in America's vaunted "democracy." In this and other ways, the neoliberal assault on public assistance and other forms of the social welfare state is part of the broader capitalist war on workers and democracy.

Ordinary working Americans' democracy-deadening insecurity and dependence on the capitalist job market are furthered by the nation's distinctively employment-based system of health insurance for working-age Americans. The American employee "fortunate" enough to receive health coverage on the job often has to fear not just the loss of her income but also the loss of her and her family's health insurance if she dares to question the boss's authority or engage in any other activities that might threaten her employment status. At the same time, since employers' considerable fringe benefit (pensions, health and life insurance, paid vacations and more) expenditures (equivalent to as much as 60 percent of total employee compensation in many firms) are paid per worker, not per hour worked, employment-based health care provides employers with a deep structural incentive to extend their employees' working hours in order to get as much work out of as few employees as possible.[103] It's a deadly mix for democracy within and beyond the workplace.

Shame on the Job

In the late 1990s, at the peak of the "Clinton boom," the progressive author and essayist Barbara Ehrenreich began the participant-observatory research for what became her best-selling 2001 book, *Nickel and Dimed: On (Not) Getting By in America*—a harrowing account of her attempts to pay her bills and maintain her dignity while working at the bottom of the American occupational structure. Her book offered a bracing wake-up call to those who hoped that Clinton-era "welfare reform" (welfare elimination) might help the situation of poor people by moving them out of the shamed category of the "welfare poor" and into the supposedly more dignified zone of working poverty. How, Ehrenreich wanted to know, could anyone make it on $6 an hour without benefits as a hotel maid, house cleaner, waitress, or Wal-Mart sales "associate," working in the precarious zone between fading public benefits eligibility and good jobs? She soon learned that the nation's lowest-status jobs were both physically and mentally exhausting and that one such job was not enough to pay for decent food, clothing, and shelter. But what most particularly struck Ehrenreich about life at the low-wage end of the "fabulous" 1990s was the remarkable extent to which working people were "required to surrender . . . basic civil rights . . . and self-respect" thanks to employer practices and policies that helped "mak[e] ours not just an economy but a culture of extreme inequality." The humiliations she witnessed and experienced included routine mandatory drug testing, intrusive pre-employment tests full of demeaning questions, rules against "talking" and "gossip" (really against organizing, often enough), restrictions on trips to the bathroom, abusive rants by overbearing supervisors, petty disciplinary measures, stolen labor time, the constant threat of being fired for "stepping out of line," and learning as a waitress that management had the right to search her purse at any time.

Connecting economic oppression to psychological mistreatment, Ehrenreich "guess[ed] that the indignities imposed on so many low-wage workers—the drug tests, the constant surveillance, being 'reamed out' by managers—are part of what keep wages low. If you're made to feel unworthy enough, you may come to think that what you're paid is what you're worth."[104] Debilitating shame and the related psychological battering of working people in the all-too unprotected, deunionized, and hidden abode of the workplace is part of how the ruling class rules in "the land of freedom."

Prison Nation

Where the discipline of the labor market does not suffice, the mass incarcerationist discipline of the nation's unmatched penal state steps in with special viciousness toward largely nonwhite lower-class Americans stuck in communities that have been almost completely abandoned by employers in the New Gilded Age. Strange as it may seem, the nation that proclaims itself the homeland and headquarters of world freedom comprises 5 percent of the world's population but houses more than 25 percent of the world's prisoners. By the turn of the current millennium, the rate of incarceration in the United States reached 699 per 100,000. The next highest rate in the world was Russia, at 644, and the American rate was six times higher than that of Britain, Canada, or France. As University of Chicago law professor Norval Morris, an academic colleague of Barack Obama, noted, "No other Western democratic country has ever imprisoned this portion of its population." He might have added that the US incarceration rate was higher than the incarceration rates of more openly authoritarian states like China, Russia, and Saudi Arabia.[105]

In harmony with the emergence of the neoliberal era, the American imprisonment rate began a dramatic upward rise in the mid-1970s. By the early twenty-first century, public investment in incarceration was so extensive that several US states spent as much or more money to imprison adults as they did to provide their citizens with college educations. States spent 60 cents on prisons for every dollar they spent on higher education, up from 28 cents in 1980. Illinois, for example, built twenty adult prisons, an average of one per year, between 1980 and 2000. By June 2001 there were nearly 20,000 more black males in the Illinois prison system than in the state's public universities.[106]

Gilded Age America's outlay of taxpayer dollars on mass arrest and imprisonment has been so extensive as to significantly distort the nation's unemployment rates. Princeton sociologist Bruce Western has shown that an American rate properly adjusted for incarceration would rise by two points and that counting prisoners as jobless would have pushed the official black unemployment rate to nearly 40 percent during the Clinton boom. By artificially reducing official unemployment through a "large and coercive intervention into the labor market," American mass arrest and incarceration help the 1% and its media and politicians cloak the terrible jobs performance of their profits system.[107]

At the same time, it removes millions of Americans from the chance of functional participation in American "democracy," or what's left of it. It does so not just through incarceration itself but also through a racialized epidemic of criminal marking so extensive that one in three black adult males carries the crippling lifelong stigma of a felony record, which makes its carriers ineligible for numerous benefits and rights—including even the right to vote in elections in more than a dozen states.[108] The denial of voting rights to felons in Florida (and the related scrubbing of black voting rolls under the pretext of seeking out illegal felon voters) was a critical factor in George W. Bush's 2000 presidential victory,[109] which brought us (through Bush's appointment power) the Supreme Court that made the *Citizens United* decision—a court that has signed off on a slew of executive branch assaults on civil liberties in this century.

The Pentagon System and the Permanent War Economy

Another part of the equation of how the US ruling class rules is the ongoing division of the citizenry and workforce along sharp and highly segregated lines of race, ethnicity, and nationality. Economic elites have long enjoyed a special ability to exploit popular fragmentation in the United States, where the working class has been significantly more ethno-culturally divided than in other rich industrialized states.

Also critical to 1% power is the nation's giant Pentagon system, source of nearly half the world's military spending and keeper of more than 1,000 military bases across more than 100 nations. This vast empire, unmatched in world history, functions on behalf of the US 1% in seven basic ways. First, its many foreign provocations and entanglements afford many opportunities for the elite to deflect popular attention from the nation's internal disparities and domestic injustices, directing citizen anger away from "the homeland's" plutocracy and onto an ever-changing parade of officially designated enemies abroad.

Second, global deployment of troops on the American scale both reflects and nurtures an inherently authoritarian, obedience-related culture of militarism, something that is directly opposed to the egalitarian and democratic spirit that popular social movements cultivate and require to fight the business elite.

Third, the wars and "blowback" (terrorist attacks on US forces and citizens, including assaults on and in "the homeland" like 9/11) that empire on the American scale creates and invites provide pretexts for political authorities and their business sponsors and allies to sacrifice civil liberties and foster a culture of "national unity" that shames dissent and protest as selfish and "unpatriotic," even as its cloaks the profit seeking of the business elite in the flag of nationalism.

Fourth, the sprawling Pentagon system is itself a gigantic and unmatched public subsidy for "American" corporations like Boeing, General Electric, and Raytheon, just three firms that are part of the high-tech corporate sector that owes its profits and commercial viability to cost-plus "defense" (war and empire) contracts and other Pentagon connections.

Fifth, the US Air Force, Navy, Army, and Marines have long worked to protect, expand, and otherwise serve American corporate investments—and corporate access to markets, labor supplies, and raw materials abroad (Middle Eastern petroleum above all, and of primary significance since the 1940s).

Sixth, the American military's vast experience fighting military enemies, popular rebellions, and national and other independence movements has provided numerous lessons, methods, technologies, and other tools of population control that have proved useful in the suppression of domestic protest in what has been given the revealingly imperial name "the homeland"—the United States itself. (The lessons and tools of internal repression are generally applied by domestic police, but the imperial military remains at hand to put down US citizens when deemed necessary in the self-declared headquarters of global freedom.)

Seventh, massive spending on empire, war, and the preparation for war provides a useful way for government to stimulate demand and sustain the corporate political economy without threatening business-class power and the unequal distribution of wealth. *Business Week* explained in February 1949 the economic elite's preference for guns over butter when it comes to government stimulus. It observed,

> There's a tremendous social and economic difference between welfare pump-priming and military pump-priming.... Military spending doesn't really alter the structure of the economy. It goes through the regular channels. As far as a businessman is concerned, a munitions order from the government is much like an order from a private customer. But the kind of welfare and public works spending that [liberals and leftists favor] ... does alter the

economy. It makes new channels of its own. It creates new institutions. It redistributes wealth.... It changes the whole economic pattern.[110]

The point holds more than six decades later. As Chomsky noted in the early 1990s, elaborating on *Business Week*'s post-WWII reflections in explaining why there would be no "peace dividend" (no major shift of resources from military to social spending) in the United States ever after the demise of the Soviet bloc, the Cold War enemy,

> Business leaders recognized that social spending could stimulate the econ-omy, but much preferred the military Keynesian alternative—for reasons having to do with privilege and power, not "economic rationality." ... The Pentagon system['s] ... form of industrial policy does not have the undesir-able side-effects of social spending directed at human needs. Apart from unwelcome redistributive effects, the latter policies tend to interfere with managerial prerogatives; useful production may undercut private gain, while state-subsidized waste production (arms, Man-on-the-Moon extravaganzas, etc.) is a gift to the owner and managers, to whom any marketable spin-offs will be promptly delivered. Social spending may also arouse public interest and participation, thus enhancing the threat of democracy; the public cares about hospitals, roads, neighborhoods, but has no opinions about the choice of missile and high-tech fighter planes.

It was with these sorts of considerations in mind, perhaps, that former and future General Electric president and serving War Production Board execu-tive Charles Edward Wilson warned in 1944 about what later became known as "the Vietnam syndrome"—the reluctance of ordinary citizens to support the open-ended commitment of American troops and resources to military conflict abroad. "The revulsion against war not too long hence," Wilson cautioned fellow US industrialists and policymakers in an internal memo, "will be an almost insuperable obstacle for us to overcome. For that reason, I am convinced that we must now begin to set the machinery in motion for *a permanent war economy*."[111]

Reflecting the long reach of military Keynesianism's triumph, US "defense" (military) spending nearly doubled and rose to a fifth of the federal budget and fully 57 percent of all federal discretionary spending between 2001 and 2012. US military spending rose by 35 percent between 2002 and 2012—and by 48 percent if war costs are included. Domestic discretionary spending rose by only 8 percent during the same period,[112] a telling disparity given the significant increases in joblessness and poverty that came with the Great Recession. As Ronald Reagan's former assistant secretary of defense Lawrence Korb noted in early 2011, American military spending, adjusted for inflation, was "higher than at any time since the end of World War II. Over the past decade," Korb acknowledged, "the US share of global military spending has risen from one third to one half. The United States now spends six times as much as China, the country with the next biggest budget."[113]

"Defense" spending increased significantly under Obama, who was advised and who agreed before the 2008 election that (in the words of researchers at the leading financial bailout recipient firm Morgan Stanley) "there is no peace dividend."[114]

The government could have attained the $4 trillion in spending cuts over ten years that Obama proposed early in the 2011 "debt-ceiling crisis" simply by returning to the enormous military budgets of the Clinton era. But such a move was off the table of serious policy discussion. Claiming to be nervous about "the business impact of the winding down of wars in Iraq and Afghanistan" and Defense Secretary Robert Gates's call for modest reductions in "security spending," the Aerospace Industries Association, anchored by war masters Boeing, Lockheed Martin, and Raytheon, launched a major lobbying push to "defend their interests on Capitol Hill."[115] But the high-tech "defense" firms had little to worry about in Washington, where the Pentagon never has to worry about fiscal solvency even as Wall Street interests claim regularly and falsely that Social Security is nearing bankruptcy and thus requires privatization.[116] The military system enjoys an open-ended entitlement to tap the treasury of a government that has spent decades raiding the Social Security trust fund to offset deficits caused by the war budget and tax cuts and loopholes for the rich.[117]

"War is a racket." So wrote Smedley D. Butler, a decorated Marine general who recalled functioning in essence as "a high class muscle man for Big Business, for Wall Street and the bankers" during numerous early twentieth-century deployments in Central America and the Caribbean. The militarism that he coordinated enriched a select few wealthy Americans, Butler reflected, not the mostly working-class soldiers on the front lines. "How many of the war millionaires shouldered a rifle? How many of them dug a trench?"[118] Butler's reflections have if anything grown in relevance since World War II, when the United States became home to the greatest empire the world has ever seen—a vast military-industrial complex whose direct prices (including death and injury in a long line of neocolonial wars of invasion and occupation from Korea through Vietnam, Iraq, and Afghanistan) and more indirect costs (including social welfare opportunity costs) have been borne by society as a whole (not to mention the many millions of non-Americans killed, injured, or displaced by the US military and its military client states) even as the benefits have flowed especially to wealthy Americans. Today, as during the Cold War and before, Ralph Nader notes, war and the apparently permanent preparation for war are sources of corporate mega-profits as they provide a cloak of national unity behind which elites concentrate wealth and power, shaming those who question that upward redistribution as unpatriotic carpers seeking to "divide rather than unite America."[119]

It is true that "defense" was included on an even basis in the across-the-board federal budget "sequestration"—the $85 billion in automatic spending cuts that took effect on March 1, 2013, as a result of the government's failure to make a "deficit reduction deal" earlier in the year. But while the austerity measure had a devastating impact on many domestic social programs, the Pentagon was well-positioned to absorb the cuts thanks to the significant and disproportionate increase in military spending that had occurred over the previous decade. Meanwhile, the Pentagon continued to "waste billions of [taxpayer] dollars developing and purchasing Cold War legacy weapons" (examples include the F-34 fighter, the V-22 Osprey aircraft, and the SSN-774 Virginia attack submarine) that bear little relation to real "national security" threats in the twenty-first century.[120]

Degraded Civil Liberties

The pretexts for the permanent war economy and the Pentagon system have shifted—from the alleged global and domestic threat posed by Soviet-backed communism (through the late 1980s) to the alleged global and domestic threat posed by Islamo-terrorism since September 11, 2001—but the basic core functions of militarism for the business class remain the same. So do the dangers to popular governance, well understood by many among the nation's founders. "Of all the enemies of public liberty," James Madison wrote in 1795, "war is perhaps the most to be dreaded, because it comprises and develops the seeds of every other.... No nation could preserve its freedom in the midst of continual warfare."[121]

"The fetters imposed on liberty at home," Madison added four years later, "have ever been forged out of the weapons provided for defense against real, pretended, or imaginary dangers abroad."[122]

It's interesting to imagine what Madison would say today, looking at an America where "our twenty-first-century presidents have openly touted the state of permanent war on every square inch of the planet"[123] and where those presidents are routinely and inappropriately described by ordinary citizens—not just soldiers (for whom alone the term is constitutionally correct)—as "our commander-in-chief."[124] The George W. Bush and Obama administrations have used 9/11 and the US "Global War on [and of] Terror" as justification for a draconian assault on basic civil liberties. As Nader observes, "The dictatorial side of American politics emerges most obviously when the president begins to beat the drums of war.... Dissenting Americans may hold rallies in the streets, but a flag-draped, dictatorial president promoting fear from the bully pulpit to induce obedience from Congress and the people easily drowns their voices out."[125]

The corporate sector has few problems with that "dictatorial side," especially when leading high-tech corporations cash in on lucrative Pentagon contracts while the "fog of war" provides cover for other government favors to big business and feeds a climate of fear and self-censorship among those who might otherwise question elite authority. Meanwhile, core rights have "fallen by the wayside," thanks to a number of policies and practices introduced and expanded by the George W. Bush administration and then embraced and often expanded upon by Obama (clearly one of the most militantly anti–civil libertarian presidents in US history[126]). Among the policies and practices introduced and enhanced in the years since the jetliner attacks of September 11, 2001:

- Government asset seizures inflicted against Muslim and other charities and civic organizations merely suspected of hostility toward US foreign policy.
- Watch lists and no-fly lists for many thousands of citizens suspected of the same.
- Invasive airport and border body searches and scans.
- Regular racial, ethnic, and national profiling within the country and at its borders.
- Subjection of arrestees to judgment by military commissions instead of regular civilian courts, with a drastic reduction in protections against summary and arbitrary justice for the accused.
- Assassination ("targeted killing") even of US citizens off battlefields and without due process at the order of the president.
- Warrantless surveillance of citizen phone calls, e-mails, and web-surfing behavior.
- Widespread secret data-mining to gather intelligence on citizens.
- Infiltration of peaceful protest and solidarity groups by federal, state, and local police.
- Prosecution of whistleblowers (e.g., Bradley Manning) who seek to reveal vital information to the public from within government and corporate bureaucracies.
- FBI searches of public library and business records without probable cause or judicial review.
- Covert "sneak and peek black bag job" invasions and searches of private homes.
- "Extraordinary rendition": the susceptibility of any American citizen suspected of terrorist affiliation to being secretly kidnapped by the CIA and transported to a foreign country to be interrogated and tortured without due process.
- Indefinite detention: the US military's freedom to detain US citizens indefinitely without charge or trial for mere suspicion of ties to terrorism.
- The significantly increased militarization of domestic policing and intelligence gathering, "seen in such developments," former State Department official William Miller notes, "as the formation of the Pentagon's

Northern Command, the Joint Special Operations Command (JSOC) involvement in domestic intelligence and counter-terror efforts, Pentagon involvement in infiltration of domestic peace and anti-war groups ... and the surveillance, biometric, and other equipment and weapons that defense contractors have imported from Iraq and Afghanistan into America ... all in great tension with our Constitutional regime and historic bias against domestic deployment of military forces."[127]

On January 3, 2013, President Obama signed into law Section 1021(b)(2) of the National Defense Authorization Act (NDAA). This law, Chris Hedges notes,

permits the military to detain anyone, including US citizens, who "substantially support"—an undefined legal term—al Qaida, the Taliban, or "associated forces," again a term that is legally undefined. Those detained can be imprisoned indefinitely by the military and denied due process until "the end of the hostilities." In an age of permanent war this is probably a lifetime. Anyone detained under the NDAA can be sent ... to any "foreign country or entity" ... [something that] ... empowers the government to ship detainees to the jails of some of the most repressive regimes on earth.[128]

The NDAA also codifies into law the participation of the military in domestic policing, violating a libertarian principle that goes back to the nineteenth century. But it is difficult to know what real protections the 1875 *Posse Comitatus* law provides American citizens against domestic military policing in a time when metropolitan US police departments have for all intents and purposes become militarized and when high-tech private "security" companies loaded (at all levels) with military veterans proliferate across "the homeland." As the British urban geographer Stephen Graham has shown in his chilling 2010 book *Cities under Siege: The New Military Urbanism*,

There's been a longstanding shift in North America and Europe towards paramilitarized policing, using helicopter-style systems, ... infrared sensing, ... really, really heavy militarized weaponry. That's been longstanding, fuelled by the war on drugs and other sorts of explicit campaigns. But more recently, there's been a big push since the end of the Cold War by the big defense and security and IT companies to sell things like geographic mapping systems, and even more recently, drone systems, that have been used in the assassination raids in Afghanistan and in Pakistan, as a sort of domestic policing technology.[129]

Among the many weapons of this "new military urbanism" is the long-range acoustic device (LRAD)—a type of high-tech "sonic cannon" developed by "defense" corporations in league with the military and local law enforcement. It emits a focused beam of sound or ultrasound that "incapacitates enemies" by disrupting and potentially destroying eardrums, causing severe pain and disorientation. First developed to help the military defeat adversaries abroad, it has proven irresistible as a weapon of crowd dispersal in the imperial homeland, where elites face the daunting task of imposing neoliberal austerity on the many while the wealthy few ("the 1%") enjoy fantastic profits and opulence. After initial homeland deployments by the NYPD in 2004 (during that year's Republican National Convention) and the Louisiana National Guard in 2005 (in New Orleans after Hurricane Katrina), the LRAD's democracy-deterring scream was unleashed for the first time in the United States at the G20 summit in Pittsburgh in June 2009. Paramilitary local and state police also and bizarrely used the LRAD against Western Illinois University students during an annual college beer party in May 2011. The LRAD was on hand during metropolitan crackdowns on Occupy Oakland and the original Occupy Wall Street encampment in New York City in the fall of 2011 and during mass demonstrations against NATO in Chicago in the spring of 2012.[130]

The LRAD is just one part of a new publicly financed, privately developed arsenal of proto-totalitarian "non-lethal crowd control technologies" designed for use within and beyond the United States—a chilling new authoritarian munitions store that could prove fatal to free assembly. One day, not so far in the future, we may see domestic deployment of a technology known as "the microwave" and "the pain ray." Developed by the US "defense" contractor Raytheon, this new tool of population control (given the name "Silent Guardian") is what the Pentagon has called a "revolutionary heat-ray weapon to repel enemies *or disperse hostile crowds.*" It projects an invisible high-energy beam that "produces a sudden burning feeling" so intense that according to British reporter Michael Hanlon, "even the most hardened Marines flee after a few seconds of exposure."[131]

Some day *sooner* miniature drones will likely be deployed against protestors in an American city. In February 2012, Obama signed into law a Federal Aviation Administration (FAA) funding bill that will significantly expand the use of drones in the United States, "opening the skies to hundreds—likely thousands—of unmanned aircraft piloted by companies and public agencies."[132] The legislation directs the FAA to "integrate unmanned aircraft into the civilian airspace" by 2015 and will enable the police state to fly small drones to track and spy on suspects without special approval. After reviewing recent legislation, police practice, and the drone industry's own promotional materials and shareholder reports, the prolific civil libertarian author and essayist Glen Greenwald has concluded, "The belief that weaponized drones won't be used on US soil is patently irrational. Of course they will be. It's not just likely but inevitable." As Greenwald explains, "Police departments are already speaking openly about how their drones 'could be equipped to carry nonlethal weapons such as Tasers or a bean-bag gun.' The drone industry has already developed and is now aggressively marketing precisely such weaponized drones for domestic law enforcement use."[133] The airborne surveillance technology is already in use in some jurisdictions, feeding the dark suspicions of doomsayers like Hedges, who writes,

> The global corporatists—who have created a new species of totalitarianism—demand, during our decay, total power to extract the last vestiges of profit from a degraded ecosystem and disempowered citizenry. The looming dystopia is visible in the skies of blighted postindustrial cities such as Flint, Michigan, where drones circle like mechanical vultures. And in an era where the executive branch can draw up secret kill lists that include US citizens, it would be naïve to believe these domestic drones will remain unarmed.[134]

We should not expect much help from the Supreme Court. In *Holder v. Humanitarian Law* (2010), the nation's high court upheld the Obama administration's chilling claim that one offers "material assistance to terrorists" merely by having conversations—even conversations in which one advocates nonviolence—with any group on the federal government's wide-ranging list of terrorist organizations.[135] Also alarming is the court's openly Kafkaesque February 2013 ruling that US citizens cannot challenge the federal government's warrantless domestic surveillance program since they can't prove they are targets of it. As cartoonist Tom Tomorrow put it in his popular *This Modern World* comic strip, "So the Supreme Court has ruled that Americans can't sue the government over secret domestic spying—because it is *too secret to prove any damages!*"[136]

Plato posed the eternal question of who should guard our guardians. The high court that brought us *Citizens United* (which rendered vast swaths of the corporations' campaign finance largesse/bribery *untraceable*) has spoken on the matter: *nobody*.

Rulers Unseen and Unknown

Meanwhile, the "homeland's" 1% masters prosper in remarkable anonymity, largely unknown and undetected. In March 2008 a young US military veteran named Mike Prysner gave a remarkable speech that channeled the venerable radical and antiplutocratic spirit of past Left orators like Mary Ellen Lease and Eugene Debs at an antiwar "Winter Soldier" gathering in New York City. Prysner had initially joined the US Army as a John Kerry supporter who believed in America's right to invade and occupy Iraq. Deployed to northern Iraq in March 2003, he emerged from twelve months on the front lines a changed person. Denouncing army officers who used racism to justify the oppression of the Iraqi people and bearing witness to the many crimes of the occupation, he was struck by the realization that the most significant threat to Americans' freedom and security lay not in faraway nations but rather inside their own country. The real danger, Prysner had discovered, was posed by the rich and powerful elite that lined its own deep pockets while it shipped ordinary Americans out to kill fellow working-class people in foreign countries. It was "the ruling class, the billionaires who profit from human suffering, who care only about expanding their wealth and controlling the world economy" and "who send us to war." Prysner's audience rose to its feet as he came to an eloquent crescendo that linked the dialectically inseparable problems of empire and inequality at home and abroad:

> I threw families onto the street in Iraq only to come home and find families thrown onto the street in this country and this tragic, tragic and unnecessary foreclosure crisis. We need to wake up and realize that our real enemies are not in some distant land and *not people whose names we don't know and cultures we don't understand. The enemy is people we know very well and people we can identify.* The enemy is a system that wages war when it's profitable. The enemy is the CEOs who lay us off our jobs when it's profitable, it's the insurance companies who deny us health care when it's profitable, it's the banks who take away our homes when it's profitable. Our enemy is not five thousand miles away, they are right here at home.[137]

Many progressives, especially those who call themselves leftists and radicals (including this author), would agree that Prysner's oration spoke volumes about where the greatest threat to American justice and democracy lay—in the profits system and the superwealthy elite that sits atop it. Prysner nicely captured the complete indifference of much of America's ruling class to the lives of ordinary Americans below them.

But how true is it that the American elite is known and unmysterious to the mass of Americans? Given the remarkable wealth and destructive power of the American rich, it might seem reasonable to expect that many Americans could name a significant number of the nation's economic elite. In reality, Richistan and its inhabitants are in fact something of a great and largely invisible secret to most of us. Most Americans would be hard pressed to actually name more than a very few members of the economic elite. Beyond high-profile uber-capitalists like software giant Bill Gates, super-financiers Warren Buffett and George Soros (mentioned quite frequently on right-wing talk radio), and perhaps the stupendously wealthy right-wing political funder Sheldon Adelson and the notorious far-right-wing billionaire Koch brothers (Charles and David), the short list of 1% members that many everyday Americans could name is disproportionately comprised of people whose fortunes and/ or notoriety are the result of their status as entertainment, sports, and media celebrities. (The two names that I most commonly hear when I ask friends and acquaintances to mention a member of the elite are Donald Trump and Oprah Winfrey, both giant media personalities.) Ask ordinary US citizens to name any of the nation's leading financial CEOs or corporate executives or corporate lobbyists or campaign funders and you can expect blank stares. Expect much the same response if you ask about the leading global gatherings of the super-rich or about where exactly the rich tend to live and gather, how the rich live and think, what the rich buy, and so on. You will not learn much if you ask ordinary, nonaffluent Americans to relate much of substance about the lives and culture of their opulent masters beyond the simple fact that the wealthy have the attribute Ernest Hemingway is reputed to have given when F. Scott Fitzgerald told him that "the rich are different from the rest of us"—more money (and more of the stuff that money buys).

The 1%'s Bubble

Much of this ignorance is a simple and predictable outcome of segregation—sheer separation reinforced by what leading wealth and power analyst Kevin Phillips has called "an increasingly Latin American array of gates, walls, and distance."[138] It is no small matter in this connection that, as John Ehrenreich and Barbara Ehrenreich noted in the fall of 2011, "the 1 percent are, for the most part, sealed off in their own bubble of private planes, gated communities, and walled estates"[139]—and, the Ehrenreichs might have added, exclusive academies.[140] Separated and protected by money and an ever more paramilitarized and high-tech security regime, the rich speak their own different language and live according to their own cultural norms in an almost *literally separate* world or nation—Robert Frank's "Richistan"—very much of their own. It is a nation and world significantly beyond national borders and not accessible to the rest of us, who lack the cash, clothes, lawyers, travel resources, global connections, accountants, and limited liability (and much more) required for entry. Penetrating that "Nation Apart" requires sociological, even anthropological, inquiry on a scale that is impossible for most Americans, who lack the time, energy, and predisposition to pore through the Forbes 400 lists, the *New York Times* society page, and *Vanity Fair*'s coverage of the rich and famous, or to hunt down and go through the small bibliography of commercial books and essays produced by those (Robert Frank, David Rothkopf, and Freeland, for example) who infiltrate or reside in and research and report on the world of the wealthy few.

Even those with time, inclination, and energy to seek out serious investigations of the rich and powerful will find that the nation's ruling class is woefully understudied. The poor are "studied to death" by government agencies and liberal foundations seeking to inform policymakers on how to change the behavior of "the underclass." The middle class is also heavily researched, thanks to the interest of corporate managers, politicians, and other elites in capturing its consumer dollars, votes, and campaign contributions. By "contrast," Jeff

Faux notes, "there is comparatively little serious research on the composition and behavior of the American elite," something Faux attributes to the fact that "academic departments of sociology, political science, and economics are parts of the university system run by people of or near the governing class."[141] The liberal post-WWII economist John Kenneth Galbraith's observation half a century ago apparently still holds relevance: "Of all the classes, the wealthy are the most noticed and the least studied."[142]*

Meanwhile, ordinary Americans aren't going to get a serious portrait of the rich from American television or movies. The media tend to portray almost everyone as upper-middle class, if not upper class, and to focus on eccentric, fleeting, and over-leveraged members of the elite (i.e., *Real Housewives of New Jersey*) when it does purport to present the rich. A clever cartoon by the liberal activist Ted Rall is titled "The Invisible Majority." Its four successive captions read as follows:

> To read the newspaper, you'd think everyone drove $30,000 cars, summered in France, and replaced their wardrobes twice a year.

> To watch TV, you'd think everyone lived in enormous suburban houses, dated models, and worked at cool jobs.

> To listen to politicians, you'd think everyone paid capital gains taxes.

> It's almost like the overwhelming majority of people, who are struggling just to get by, don't exist.[143]

The Managerial and Professional Class Buffer

Another part of Richistan's ironic invisibility and relative absence from popular awareness is experiential in a different way. Barbara Ehrenreich and John Ehrenreich overstated their case when they called the top income hundredth "the actual, Wall Street–based elite" and referred to professionals and managers

---

* In an earlier life as a civil rights and social policy researcher at a leading nonprofit agency in Chicago, I grew tired of the elite-funded foundation world's seeming obsession with the experience, behavior, culture, and values of the often welfare-reliant poor "underclass" and with the costs the poor imposed on government and society. Reflecting on Galbraith's observation, I drafted a half-satirical Letter of Inquiry to the Chicago-based John D. and Catherine T. MacArthur Foundation seeking funding for a study that would examine the experience, behavior, culture, and values of the very rich and the costs that plutocracy and inequality imposed on America. The letter's punch line came at the end when I estimated that my study would require at least $10 million for me to gain proper access for a comprehensive participant-observatory study of the wealthy classes' world over the course of two years in the Chicago, Washington, DC, San Francisco, and New York areas, including travel to such elite venues as the World Economic Forum in Davos, Switzerland.

as merely "annoying pikers" in comparison to "the 1 percent."[144] Leaving aside the facts that the top hundredth income percentile includes no small number of professionals and that the real "Wall Street–based elite" is more accurately placed in the 0.1 and .01 percentiles, what the Ehrenreichs failed to grasp above all was that the power, income, and wealth of the coordinator or professional and managerial class is no less "true," "real," substantive, or vital to the contemporary hierarchy than that of the financial elite. The power of the latter depends heavily on the coordinating and other system-sustaining and -justifying roles of the former. Without the managers and professionals, what the late working-class journalist Joe Bageant called "the catering classes," the 1%'s system could not work, which is "why," Bageant noted in *Deer Hunting with Jesus: Dispatches from America's Class War* (2008), "they must be purchased at a higher rate than the proles [workers]." At the same time, "the catering classes" are considerably more numerous than the financial elite, something that Bageant thought made the former "more to blame" than the latter for contemporary inequality.[145] It's not for nothing that Carpenter included many professionals alongside wealthy capitalists among the alien invaders and their human collaborators depicted in *They Live*.

Most relevant of all to the 1%'s invisibility, the upper-middling professional and managerial class provides what the Ehrenreichs call "the authority figures most people are likely to encounter in their daily lives." Examples included "teachers, doctors, social workers, and professors. These groups (along with middle managers and other white-collar employees)" might, as the Ehrenreichs say, "occupy a much lower position in the class hierarchy" than the true capitalist elite, but they are very real, comparatively ubiquitous, and indispensable (to the most elite of the elite classes) and they are the elite that most ordinary working-, lower-, and lower-middle-class Americans come into contact with in the workplace, school, and local community. That makes them among other things a potent buffeting force, keeping the most fortunate and powerful members of the privileged classes—the "genuine elite" (the Ehrenreichs' term)—off the popular radar screen except in extraordinary circumstances.

The Occupy Movement itself came up against this problem of separation and buffering. In mid-November 2011, after the movement had been cleared by force, the original cultural subversives who sparked the rise of Occupy Wall Street went to the op-ed pages of the *Washington Post* with an interesting grievance. "Why," Kalle Lasn and Micah White of *Adbusters* asked, "didn't Bloomberg come down to talk to us? Or Goldman Sachs' chief executive Lloyd Blankfein? Why didn't President Obama acknowledge the protestors—largely the people who elected him—and mingle in the open-air town halls?... Why can't the American power elite engage with the nation's young?"[146] Reflecting on this curiously naïve complaint, Faux notes the movement's failure to overcome the vast distance between "well protected" Richistan and the rest of us:

The occupiers' 99-percent-versus-the-1-percent formulation was appealing. But *the visible confrontations were with the police* whom most Americans see as workers doing their job of keeping order and with the clerks and lower middle managers walking to their jobs—*not with the superrich, who are well protected from personal contact with even ordinary people* and who were out of reach of the OWS activists. What was important to the governing class— the financial markets—was unimpeded. After all, the money was not in bank vaults or safes in Wall Street offices, nor was it in offices in London or Zurich. It was in cyberspace.[147]

"Stealth Wealth"

Another factor contributing to the relatively invisible and "unseeable"[148] nature of the wealthy "true elite" is the reluctance of many rich people to flaunt their wealth and the determination of many elites to cloak that wealth in more plebian or at least middle-class wrappings. Following four decades during which grand wealth exhibition fell out of favor, the "get-rich" 1980s brought a comeback for conspicuous consumption on the part of the economic superelite. Embodying the spirit of the Hollywood character Gordon Gecko's maxim (expounded in the movie *Wall Street*) that "greed is good," wealth culture reverted to a "flaunt-it-if-you-have-it" mindset after a historic explosion of stock market values in 1982. It was "a period in which it was never easier to quickly make a fortune and then lose it just as fast with blowing some of that fortune on any number of things—houses, toys, art or blow itself—now a major pastime for the wealthy," and "watching the lifestyles of the rich and famous became a popular sport for those on the sidelines."[149] Indeed, *Lifestyles of the Rich and Famous* quickly became the nation's most widely viewed syndicated television show during the early 1980s. It offered viewers a tantalizing look at the private lives of the wealthy few in a "shameless celebration of pure, unadulterated materialism."[150]

But elites fell back from showing off after the market collapsed in 1987. By the early 1990s, Larry Samuel notes, the rich, as in the 1930s, "seemed to be taking a duck-and-cover tack, keeping a low profile." Even as the rich got richer and more numerous than ever during the 1990s, the backlash against Reagan-era excess meant that conspicuous consumption went "underground" and leading Wall Street firms placed new restrictions on the public release of information about their traders' and executives' salaries. *Forbes* magazine's portrayal of the nation's richest 400 inhabitants in 1999 noted that "there is still plenty of lavish consumption and display on the part of today's over-class, only it's kept, as much as possible, hidden from public view."[151] The "hunger for more extravagant goods," journalists Peter Bernstein and Annalynn Swan note, "was counterbalanced by a desire in many quarters to hold back from display."[152] The trick now was to enjoy "stealth wealth," trading four-wheel-drive vehicles for Rolls Royces and "industrial-grade diamonds for ostentatious sparklers." The camouflaging project was abetted by the author and wealth-profiler Thomas J. Stanley's best-selling late-1990s book *The Millionaire Next Door*, which told approving stories of the many low-grade millionaires who—according to Stanley—lived distinctly middle-class lifestyles.[153]

The trend has continued into the current millennium. While certain super-rich elites still glory in parading their wealth (Donald Trump is a classic if laughable example), Bernstein and Swan note that "a substantial number of the Forbes 400 would rather do just the opposite." Most of the nation's officially richest 400 people "wish to remain anonymous." Despite the remarkable and sumptuous 1% wealth-holdings and lifestyles discussed earlier in this book, extravagant self-display has fallen predominantly out of favor with the American upper class. The 1% prefers on the whole to keep its opulence behind private walls and gates, making it less likely to provoke popular ire in the supposed "land of equality."

"You Need to Be Able to See Them"

And so it is that the US ruling class remains largely unnamed, unknown, and mysterious to the populace of the "the world's most celebrated democracy."[154] Is this a problem? For right-wing sociologist Charles Murray, the answer is "no." He is concerned in his own way about the separation dividing the rich from the rest of us. "As the new upper class increasingly consists of people who were born into upper-middle-class families and have never lived outside the upper-middle-class bubble," Murray writes, "the danger increases that the people who have so much influence on the nation have little direct experience with the lives of ordinary Americans, and make their judgments about what's good for other people based on their own highly atypical lives[155] [and] ... with little idea of what life is like in an ordinary working-class or middle-class neighborhood is like."[156]

Murray has no concomitant concern about the reverse ignorance—that of ordinary Americans about the nation's ruling class. He is explicit about this, arguing that the "upper class['s] ... balkanized ... *ignorance about other Americans is more problematic than the ignorance of other Americans about them.* It is not a problem if truck drivers cannot empathize with the priorities of Yale professors," Murray writes. But "it is," Murray proclaims, "a problem if Yale professors, or producers of network news programs, or CEOs of great corporations, or presidential advisers cannot empathize with the priorities of truck drivers."[157]

A self-described libertarian fan of the profits system, Murray cannot imagine a good society in which a superior class is not in charge of basic social, political, and economic decisions. For him, a decent society that respects community values requires a smart, informed, and benevolent elite that knows a lot about the lower orders—the rest of us. Ordinary working people do not need to know all that much about their betters because they don't really have the qualifications or the capacity to shape policy and influence the nation.

Progressive democrats, populists, and leftists hold a different perspective. Refusing to depend for progress on the supposed superior wisdom and kindness of elites, they want the "other Americans" to know as much as possible about their masters. They desire "we the people" to know those Prysner calls "our real enemies" as well as possible so as to more effectively fight and overthrow them.

"If you have an infestation of greedy bastards," Dylan Ratigan writes, "you need to be able to see them."[158] John Carpenter agreed. In *They Live*, the people's struggle against the corporate and financial elite was first of all a struggle to render the ruling class visible.

Millionaires' March

That is at least part of why a coalition of labor and community activists affiliated with Occupy Wall Street led a "Millionaires' March" that wound its way around the Upper East Side of Manhattan on October 10, 2011. Under the watchful gaze of police, the marchers made "house calls" outside the Park Avenue homes of media mogul Rupert Murdoch, JP Morgan Stanley CEO Jamie Dimon, billionaire industrialist David Koch, real estate developer Howard Milstein, and billionaire hedge fund manager John Paulson.[159] Beyond protesting the extreme wealth and power of such super-titans, the OWS action told the citizenry that "this is where you can find them (at least sometimes)." It also made a threatening statement to the few: "We know where and how well you live. We've crossed into your privileged space to let you know that we find your wealth and power offensive." The Millionaires' March was an act of border-crossing and decloaking Carpenter would have appreciated.

CHAPTER 6

No Crystal Ball

On What Might and Must Be Done

Wrecked

"No country," the American international relations expert Stephen Kinzer notes, "hectors other countries about their shortcomings more actively and regularly than the United States. The State Department," he says, "keeps a host of lists cataloguing the guilt of others. There are countries judged to violate human rights, restrict religious freedom, enable the drug trade, or tolerate human trafficking. Some senior American diplomats seem to spend almost as much time denouncing other countries as they do engaging and trying to understand them."

Beneath this arrogant, nationally narcissistic habit lay the doctrine or perhaps more accurately the conceit of "American exceptionalism," what Kinzer calls "the founding credo of the United States. Its meaning has changed a bit over four centuries but its essence is the same. Americans ... believe that the United States has discovered the best way for a nation to live and be governed" and that "refusing to share this wonderful discovery with others ... would be unpardonably selfish."[1]

Leaving aside Kinzer's questionable sense that this belief is what pushes the United States into repeated disastrous military interventions abroad, US diplomats and other Americans who share this in fact widespread national credo might want to take a closer look in the societal "homeland" mirror. As Noam Chomsky darkly observes,

> The truncated democracy that [John] Dewey condemned has been left in tatters in recent years. By now control of government is narrowly concentrated at the peak of the income scale, while the large majority "down below" are virtually disenfranchised. The current political-economic system is *a form of plutocracy that diverges sharply from democracy, if by that concept we mean political arrangements in which policy is significantly influenced by public will....*

There have been serious debates over the years about whether capitalism is, in principle, compatible with democracy. If we keep to really existing capitalist democracy—RECD for short (pronounced "wrecked")—the question is effectively answered: they are radically incompatible.[2]

The article in which this passage occurs bears a bracing title: "Can Civilization Survive Really Existing Capitalism?" The article is concerned primarily not with the profits system's threat to—or eclipse of—democracy but with the related yet even more dire and immediate threat that system poses to livable ecology, in by-now-standard defiance of majority US public opinion's support for government regulation of greenhouse emissions.[3]

Aristotle's Choice

In seeking to understand the changing forms of ruling-class power in the United States since the end of World War II, we might consult the ancient Athenian philosopher Aristotle. In *Politics*, a foundational text in modern political theory, Aristotle reflected on conflicts arising from class inequality and private ownership of property in ways that hold relevance to the present day. Democracy and economic inequality, he observed, were in conflict with each other. In a democracy marked by extremes of rich and poor, Aristotle reasoned, the poor would use their democratic rights to initiate land reform and confiscate property from the rich. He considered that outcome abhorrent, arguing that if one considered this just, then "all the acts of a tyrant must of necessity be just; for he only coerces other men by superior power, just as the multitude coerce the rich."

In democratic states, Aristotle envisioned two ways of handling the contradiction. The first method was to *reduce inequality* so that the poor would be less inclined to undertake redistribution. The second was to *reduce democracy* so that the property-less mass would lack the power to equalize economic resources.[4]

Aristotle's dichotomy roughly applies to the shifting dynamics of US business-class rule since 1945. During the Golden Age and Great Compression, from the end of World War II through the pivotal 1970s, America moved to an unprecedented degree in the direction of greater relative equality. At the same time, popular democratic energies enjoyed remarkable expansion in the 1960s and early 1970s, with a significant expansion of social and political movements stretching from the Civil Rights Movement to the Free Speech Movement, the rise of the New Left, the peace movement, the women's movement, and more.[5] Since the mid-1970s, by contrast, American inequality has fallen back to 1920s ("long Gilded Age") levels. Not just wealth but also power have been concentrated in fewer and less accountable hands, with no small help from the top-down dissemination of a cancerous ideology that attacks the social solidarities and the very sense of a common good that functional democracy requires.

This historical dichotomy can easily be overdrawn. Never fully extracting itself from the paranoid "us and them" mindset of the Cold War, whose embers burned through the Reagan era, Golden Age/Great Compression America witnessed terrible assaults on domestic democracy. The period's many authoritarian outrages included the "McCarthyite" repression of Communist Party members and numerous other dissenters during the late 1940s and 1950s and the continuing infiltration, surveillance, and harassment of social and peace movement "subversives" (Civil Rights, Free Speech, antiwar, women's rights, Black Power, and other activists) by the FBI, military intelligence, and other, more local wings of the Cold War police state. Regressive military Keynesianism trumped social democratic trends even at the mid-1960s "Great Society" height of New Deal liberalism, when the briefly declared "War on Poverty" was undermined by the expensive and mass-murderous US war on Indochina—the protest of which elicited no small degree of coordinated state repression (COINTELPRO and more).

Still, by any reasonable comparative standard, popular social movements and citizen engagement flourished during the 1960s and early 1970s. Reaching their apex at the same time that big US business was facing serious new competition from abroad, the many-sided popular upsurge led the nation's establishment to proclaim a "crisis of [American] democracy" (according to right-wing Harvard political scientist Samuel P. Huntington), meaning (with proper Orwellian translation) *too much democracy*—too much popular excitement and activism for the owning and directing class.[6]

The "crisis" of excessive democracy sparked a four-decades-long ruling-class assault on basic institutions and values of democratic association, popular self-defense, and social justice. Much of the assault has been undertaken with "soft power"—cultural, ideological, and mass-consumerist, all heavily tied to the mass media. But "hard," coercive, and repressive state power remains highly relevant and ever more technologically potent, as can be attested by anyone who has observed the awesome and multijurisdictional array of high-tech quasi-military police state forces and tools on display at major US protests in recent years. Sheldon Wolin is correct when he describes the current US variant of incipient corporate-managerial totalitarianism as distinct from its German and Italian fascist predecessors in that it rests on mass individualized demobilization. Contemporary American authoritarianism—what Wolin calls "Democracy, Incorporated"[7] and what Chris Hedges considers "a new species of totalitarianism"[8]—does not put masses of angry, modern-day brown-shirts in the streets to smash liberal and left demonstrations, meetings, and organizations. It's about keeping folks separate, private, self-absorbed, and individualized rather than mobilized and collectively active on either the left (of course) or (even) the right. Still, the high-tech police state, drawing heavily on the tools, lessons, culture, and mindset of the global military empire, remains on hand to respond with brute force to moments and movements that might break a significant part of the populace out of atomization and expose the unelected class dictatorship that rules behind the façade of democracy. Just ask the Occupy activists of New York City, Oakland, and numerous other Occupy camps dismantled by militarized police-state force in the fall of 2011 to make way for the next quadrennial electoral extravaganza as the dominant domestic news story for the next year. Among their many sins, the Occupiers had challenged the dominant definition of "the only politics that matters" as being about the limited choice between two ruling-class–backed candidates. Their brief moment of favor passed as state and media worked hand in hand to push them down Orwell's "memory hole"—this even as the Obama team employed "99 percent values" rhetoric against Mitt "Mr. 1%" Romney. The iron hand of repression was part of the process.

The "No Solution"/Unfocused Carper Charge

What might and should be done in the interest of restoring or introducing democracy to the United States and saving civilization from catastrophe? In the fall of 2011 and since, the standard critique of the Occupy Movement heard in the mass media and establishment venues has held that the protestors developed and advanced no concrete proposals or demands. Occupy, this unflattering appraisal held, was all about "no." It was clear on what it was against but aimless when it came to alternatives, offering no reasonable or coherent idea of what precisely it was for. Thus it was that *New York Times* financial columnist Andrew Ross Sorkin claimed that OWS would "be an asterisk in the history books, if it gets a mention at all" because "its mission was always intentionally vague."[9]

To a degree that might strike some observers (though not this author) as surprising, this disdainful take on Occupy was common not only among pro-corporate/banking commentators but also among many left observers. Thus, for example, *Harper's* columnist Thomas Frank accused the movement of "pointless antihierarchical posturing" while Doug Henwood used his venerable Marxian publication *Left Business Observer* to complain about OWS's unwillingness "to say clearly and succinctly why they're there."[10]

It's an old and generally false charge hurled at those who resist concentrated wealth and power. "One commonly hears that carping critics complain about what is wrong, but do not present solutions," Chomsky noted in 2006, adding that "there is an accurate translation for that charge: 'they present solutions and I don't like them.'"[11]

Chomsky's translation applies well to the dominant culture's take on Occupy. Occupiers were hardly devoid of practical short-term proposals, as was clear to anyone who visited their campsites and engaged them during their wide-ranging General Assemblies and beyond. I discussed numerous such proposals with a large number of Occupiers in Zuccotti Park, in Chicago, and in Iowa City in October 2011.

"We all know broadly where [the Occupy Movement] will aim" in the short term, the left anarchist activist and author Michael Albert wrote at Occupy's height: "for a future of good jobs, fair distribution, increased social justice and security, greater democracy, reduced imperial expense and a peace dividend, enhanced housing, infrastructure, and education.... The details will emerge from the participants, as consciousness and solidarity climb."[12]

Beyond reforms, there was nothing unclear or aimless about Occupy's longer-term goal of ultimately overturning the profits system. A young New York City Occupy activist named Yotam Marom responded eloquently on *AlterNet* to the charge of unfocused directionless-ness, leaving little doubt about the movement's advocacy of both reformist and revolutionary objectives:

> It's not that we don't have demands, it's that we speak them in a different language. We speak them with our struggle. Our movement is made up of people fighting for jobs, for schools, for debt relief, equitable housing, and healthcare. We are resisting ecological destruction, imperialism, racism, patriarchy, and capitalism. We are doing it all in a way that is participatory, democratic, fierce, and unwavering. There is nothing vague about that.
>
> We want a political and economic system that we all actually control together, one that is equitable and humane, one that allows for people to self-manage but act in solidarity, one that is participatory and democratic to its core.... We want a world with institutions that take care of our youth, our elderly, and our families in ways that are nurturing, liberating, and consensual. We want a world in which community is not a hamper on individual freedom, but rather an expression of its fullest potential.... If that's not a clear enough statement of demands for you, CNN, I don't know what to tell you.[13]

It is true that Occupy was reluctant to hitch its star to any one demand or set of demands. This reluctance reflected activists' well-founded desire to avoid public overidentification with one, two, or a few policy ideas for the dominant parties and media to bandy about, dilute, co-opt, and marginalize. As many leading Occupy activists knew, moreover, what's most lacking on the left is not so much good policy and an alternative societal vision as the power to put its ideas into practice and indeed to effectively "demand" anything. The biggest thing required to develop that capacity is an organized and independent social movement with the strength and determination to challenge the standard top-down corporate-managed game of politics and policy by capturing and chan-neling popular resolve. Opinion polls are useful and important when it comes to capturing and registering privately held public sentiments, demonstrating the telling gap between popular beliefs and plutocratic policy enacted in the people's name. But there's a world of difference between (1) everyday people telling pollsters they support progressive values and policies in the privacy of their homes, and (2) those people joining together in a durable and powerful social and political movement.

Reforms

"At this point," Richard Wilkinson and Kate Pickett argue in *The Spirit Level*, "creating the political will to make society more equal is more important than pinning our colours to a particular set of policies to reduce inequality."[14] There is, it is true, no shortage of good progressive policy ideas to check and roll back the plutocratic reach of the corporate and financial elite. A short list of well-known proposals includes the "Tobin" financial transactions tax; the Employee Free Choice Act (which would relegalize union organizing in this county); regular raising of the minimum wage; increased regulation, downsizing, and even nationalization of the leading financial institutions; full employment as a matter of federal policy; a significantly reduced work week; the removal of private money from public elections and the full public financing of those elections; seriously progressive taxation; single-payer health insurance; renegotiation of NAFTA and other "free trade" deals to include significant new labor and environmental protections; national and international measures to control carbon emissions; green jobs public works programs; an expanded social safety net; a shift from mass incarceration, the "War on Drugs," and military empire to investing in public schools, antipoverty programs, and the broader advance of human welfare; and the restoration of American civil liberties through the repeal of NDAA, the Patriot Act, and numerous other repressive measures.

No "demand" is more urgent and necessary than the call for large-scale public green jobs programs, connected to a wider program for the conversion of the American (and global) economy to environmental sustainability—something that likely takes us beyond the profits system, for reasons suggested in Chapters 2 and 4. We will return to this topic later in this chapter.

Popular Sovereignty through Constitutional Amendment

Left progressives have long advocated amendments to the US Constitution meant to more properly align US politics and policy with public opinion. Among the changes proposed through the constitutional amendment route:

abolition of the anti-majoritarian Electoral College system for the election of the US president and the introduction of direct national popular election and majority choice either in a first multiparty round or (if no candidate attains a majority in the first round) a runoff race between the top two presidential candidates; reversal of the Supreme Court's equation of political money and "free speech"; the full public financing of campaigns; undoing the special legal "personhood" protections enjoyed by corporations; the introduction of proportional representation (whereby seats are awarded to parties in accord with their share of a popular party vote, opening the possibility for significant third, fourth, and more parties) into congressional elections; the elimination of partisan gerrymandering in the drawing of electoral districts; introduction of statehood for the District of Columbia; and the Equal Rights Amendment, establishing equal civil and political rights for women and people of nontraditional sexual orientation.

The established process for amending the US Constitution is absurdly difficult. The left Constitution critic Daniel Lazare argues that *the people are not actually sovereign under that practically sacred founding document*. This is thanks in no small part, Lazare believes, to the Constitution's Article V, which makes it practically impossible for the populace to alter the government—in defiance of the Declaration of Independence's announcement that "whenever any form of government becomes destructive ... it is the right of the people to alter or to abolish it" and of the Constitution's opening statement that "We the People of the United States ... ordain and establish this Constitution for the United States of America." As Lazare observes,

> Moments after establishing the people as the omnipotent makers and breakers of constitutions, [the 1787 US Constitution] announced that they would henceforth be subject to the severest of constraints. Changing so much as a comma in the Constitution would require the approval of two-thirds of each house of Congress plus three-fourths of the states. At the time, Article V meant that just four of the 13 states representing as little as 9.7 percent of the total population would be able to veto any change sought by the remainder. Today, it means that thirteen out of the 50 states can do the same even though their share of the population stands at as little as 4.2 percent. (In a couple of decades, it will be down to just 3.9 percent.) Over the course of a few thousand words, the people had gone from being all-powerful to virtually powerless.... It is important to keep in mind that the people did not assert their sovereignty in Philadelphia in 1787. Rather, the founders invoked it. Once they uttered the magic incantation, moreover, they hastened to put the genie back in the bottle by declaring the people all but powerless to alter their own plan of government.... Democratic politics are crippled as a consequence.... *The question is how much longer this absurd state of affairs can continue.*[15]

More optimistically, the constitutional scholar Akhil Reed Amar finds that "Article V nowhere prevents the People themselves, acting apart from ordinary government, from exercising their legal right to alter or abolish government.... Article V presupposes this background right of the People, and does nothing to interfere with it. It merely specifies how ordinary government can amend the Constitution without recurring to the People themselves, the true and sovereign source of all lawful power." Seattle-based progressive constitutional change activist Kelly Gerling advocates a "mass movement for amending by popular sovereignty." He proposes a national popular referendum to alter the Constitution (beginning with its restrictive amendment process) outside and beyond the "minoritarian" constraints of Article V, in accord with what Amar claims to be the broader majoritarian, popular-sovereignty leanings of the Constitution.[16]

America beyond Capitalism

"Political will," Wilkinson and Pickett note, "is dependent on the development of a vision of a better society which is both achievable and inspiring."[17] Here again, beyond reform, there is no lack of first-rate thinking on how to construct a radically transformed and democratized *America beyond Capitalism*—the title of an important book by the University of Maryland economist Gar Alperovitz. He proposes that America provide workers and communities stakes and self-management through the expansion and support of significantly empowered employee stock ownership programs (ESOPs) and other programs and policies (including highly progressive tax rates, political decentralization, and a twenty-five-hour work week) designed to replace the current top-down plutocracy with a bottom-up "pluralist commonwealth."

Alperovitz is a founder of the University of Maryland's Democracy Collaborative (DC), which focuses on community wealth-building through the creation of worker co-ops and worker-owned companies that build structures that reflect communities' stakes as well as workers' stake in the design and purpose of economic enterprises. The Evergreen Cooperatives in Cleveland, Ohio, embody the DC's worker-community model. It makes reference to the more well-known Mondragon Cooperative Corporation in Spain, a successful conglomerate of worker-owned cooperatives that employs 85,500 workers in areas ranging from medical technology to the manufacture of home appliances and running a credit union with more than 21 billion Euros' worth of assets. Formerly opposed to worker-ownership, the United Steelworkers union has become "a strong advocate of worker ownership, and is actively working to develop new models based on the Mondragon Cooperative," with which it has recently undertaken a joint initiative. Alperovitz and others believe that Mondragon-like experiments could become seeds of a future postcapitalist economy within the current profits regime.[18]

Another "utopian" proposal is MIT engineering professor Seymour Melman's call—developed in his 2001 book *After Capitalism* and other works—for a nonmarket system of workers' self-management. Also meriting mention: Marxist economist Rick Wolff's *Democracy at Work: A Cure for Capitalism*, combining a Marxian analysis of the current economic crisis with a call for "worker self-directed enterprises"; philosopher David Schweikert's *After Capitalism*, calling for worker self-management combined with national ownership of underlying capital; Michael Liebowitz's *The Socialist Alternative*, taking his cue from Latin America's leftward politics to develop a division of participatory and democratic socialism; Joel Kovel's *The Enemy of Nature* (which argues that environmental crisis requires a shift away from private and corporate control of the planet's resources); and Michael Albert's prolific writing and speaking on behalf of *Parecon*, inspired to some degree by the "council communism" once advocated by the early twentieth-century libertarian Marxist Anton Pannekeok. Albert calls for a highly but flexibly structured model of radically democratic economics that organizes society around workers' and consumers' councils—richly participatory institutions that involve workers and the entire community on an egalitarian basis in decisions as to how resources are to be allocated, what should be produced and how, and how income shall be distributed.[19]

A recent Occupy-inspired volume published by a major US publishing house, HarperCollins, is titled *Imagine: Living in a Socialist America*. It includes essays from leading American intellectuals and activists (including Frances Fox Piven, Mumia Abu Jamal, Rick Wolff, and Michael Moore) and provides eminently practical reflections on how numerous spheres of American life and policy—environmental policy and practice, workplace relations, finance/investment, criminal justice, gender relations, sexuality, immigration, welfare/public assistance, food, housing, health care/medicine, education, art, science, media/the news, religion and spirituality—might be experienced and organized under an American, democratic, and participatory version of socialism, and on how to get from the current rule of the 1% to this desirable future.*

Freedom Budget 2.0

In the fall of 1966 the civil rights and social justice champions Martin Luther King Jr., A. Phillip Randolph, and Bayard Rustin, and more than 200 prominent academics, religious leaders, trade unionists, and civil rights figures put forth an ambitious Freedom Budget for All Americans.[20] Their people's budget

---

* Full disclosure: I am author of the book's first part, dedicated to describing the horrors of the currently existing profits system.

built on Franklin Delano Roosevelt's calls (in 1941) for "freedom from want" (the third of Roosevelt's "four freedoms") and (in 1944) for an Economic Bill of Rights, including the rights to "a useful and remunerative job," to "earn enough to provide adequate food and clothing and recreation," to "decent homes," to "adequate health care," to "a good education," and to "protection from the economic fears of old age, sickness, accidents, and unemployment."[21]

The Freedom Budget projected the eradication of US poverty within a decade, along with the attainment of full employment, universal decent health care, housing, and economic and social security. Its liberal architects (chiefly the Keynesian economist Leon Keyserling) claimed in the document that this could be achieved without any reduction in either military spending or in the power of the private sector. There would be adequate funding to meet its objectives, by culling a socially minded "growth dividend" off the expanding American capitalist economy. "The 'Freedom Budget,'" its makers wrote, "does not contemplate that this 'growth dividend' be achieved by revolutionary nor even drastic changes in the division of responsibility between private enterprise and government under our free institutions."[22]

If the Freedom Budget had been successfully adopted and implemented in its time, "a majority of voters would not have responded positively to candidate Ronald Reagan's challenge to Democratic incumbent Jimmy Carter when the conservative hopeful asked the American people … 'Are you better off than you were four years ago?'"[23] As the socialist scholars Paul Le Blanc and Michael Yates argue in their book *A Freedom Budget for All Americans: Recapturing the Promise of the Civil Rights Movement in the Struggle for Economic Justice Today*,

> The history of the United States and the world would have been qualitatively different from the way things have turned out from the 1980s until now … poverty in the United States would have been abolished. Everyone who wanted a job would have had a job. Instead of economic inequality dramatically increasing over the past several decades, all people would be better off as the wealth gap narrowed and human needs were not sacrificed to amass super-profits for the top one percent. The very young, the elderly, and everyone in-between would enjoy greater care, greater security, greater dignity.… There would be universal health care as a matter of right … quality education … available to all as a matter of right, without students amassing exorbitant debt in the process … decent housing for all … no slums. Our social and economic infrastructure … would have been improved … environmental and ecological concerns would have been incorporated into the re-building of our economy and society.… Crime would have diminished.… The immense power of the big business corporations over our economic, political, social, and cultural life would be diminished, while the power of the great majority of the people (the 99 percent) over these things

would be greatly enhanced (that is, there would be greater democracy)....
Institutional racism would be gone.[24]

The Freedom Budget was defeated and pushed to the margins of historical memory by the end of the 1960s. The main culprits behind its failure were the Vietnam War, which diverted massive federal resources and national energy away from potentially attacking poverty to fighting an imperial war, and the accommodationist position of many of the Freedom Budget's key champions, including Rustin, Tom Kahn, and Michael Harrington. These and other key social democrats of the time "concluded that the Democratic Party was the pathway to political relevance" and "identified the working class and organized labor movement with the person of the relatively bureaucratic and conservative AFL-CIO President George Meany. And they went along with (or at least didn't organize opposition to) the Vietnam War, which was promoted by the Democratic Party leadership and fully supported by Meany."[25] This was a tragic calculation. As Le Blanc explains, "Most Democrats saw the Freedom Budget as too radical, especially given the spending priorities associated with the Vietnam War. Meany himself never endorsed the Freedom Budget, and the bulk of those around him were not inclined to mobilize the ranks of labor on its behalf—only the more radical elements in the unions were inclined to go in that direction."[26]

Dr. King took a different stand, linking opposition to the war to the struggle for economic justice because of moral opposition to the nation's mass-murderous assault on Southeast Asia and from an understanding that the Freedom Budget was economically impossible while the war was fought and as the nation "continues year after year to spend more money on military defense than on programs of social uplift."[27]

When the high-growth Golden Age of post–World War II Western and US capitalism came to its Vietnam War–assisted conclusion in the 1970s, giving way to the neoliberal era, the Freedom Budget's "growth dividend" hopes were swept into the dustbin of history. So was its faith in the benevolence or at least neutrality of "private enterprise," whose corporate and financial captains proceeded to attack basic welfare protections, labor rights, and democracy itself in their campaign to dramatically reconcentrate wealth and to remake American politics and policy in accord with their interests over the past four decades (as we have seen in this book).

It is doubtful that the Freedom Budget could have been achieved even if all of its leading advocates had taken King's left position, however. It could not in all likelihood be won under capitalism, as King appears to have sensed, given that system's underlying incompatibility with democratic social planning and the common good. If a new Freedom Budget for All Americans is going to be crafted and fought for today (Le Blanc and Yates advocate this and draft some principles toward that end in the last chapter of their book), it seems best to understand a Freedom Budget 2.0 as "what some revolutionary Marxists call a transitional demand ... a proposal for social-economic improvement that makes sense to a majority of people, which consequently could mobilize massive and militant support in the here and how, but which the capitalist system of the here and now cannot provide."[28]

Contemporary left Freedom Budget–fighters would also be well advised to reject the original Freedom Budget's architects' refusal to challenge the nation's gigantic Pentagon budget and their equally misguided attachment to endless economic growth. "Defense" (empire) spending steals hundreds of billions of dollars each year from the potential meeting of social needs at home and abroad, something that is regularly demonstrated in relation to domestic needs by the publications of the National Priorities Project.[29] Besides being incompatible with ecological sustainability in an age of accelerating environmental catastrophe, "growth" (as I have argued in Chapter 2) has long been the profits system's false "solution" for the inequality that it creates.

The inequality that creates mass poverty must no longer be evaded through a growth ideology that fuels an environmental collapse that will render everything else progressives talk about irrelevant if it is not averted. Fortunately enough, environmental catastrophe can be averted or at least significantly contained through large-scale public investment in the ecological reconversion of economy and society, something that would put many millions of Americans to work in "useful and remunerative jobs"—the "Green New Deal" advocated by the Green Party and discussed in Chapter 1.

Besides reckoning with militarism, capitalism, and potential ecocide, a contemporary Freedom Budget that wants to succeed must reject the "dependence on the Democratic Party that was built into the strategic orientation of [the original Freedom Budget's] architects."[30] If the deep systemic change required to end poverty to Democrats at the corporate-liberal height of the long New Deal era, it is certainly pointless to pursue that objective through alliance with Democrats in the current neoliberal New Gilded Age, when both of the two dominant business parties have moved well to the right of the populace.[31]

Mental Slavery

The greatest obstacle to the development of mass political will around these and other progressive and radical ideas (reformist and revolutionary) is the widespread sense of powerlessness and isolation shared by countless citizens and workers struggling to get by and stay sane in Brave New Gilded Age

America. It's the pervasive sense, drummed into millions of Americans for decades by the top-down many-sided (at once economic, political, ideological, cultural, and highly personal) neoliberal assault, that we are all on our own and the intimately related idea that there's no serious or viable alternative to, and nothing really that can be done about, the dominant order. "We live," Wilkinson and Pickett note, "in a pessimistic period."[32]

This "no alternative" sense is the "mental slavery" of our time. It is buttressed to no small extent by the failure of Stalinist-supposed Marxism in Russia and Eastern Europe, not to mention the egregious ongoing misery and repression imposed on tens of millions in the archauthoritarian so-called Marxist People's Republic of China. As Wilkinson and Pickett note, the failures and crimes of state command economies in the former Soviet Union and Eastern Europe "[seem] to have made us feel that there are no workable alternatives to the standard capitalist model and prevented us thinking creatively about more democratic and egalitarian methods."[33] This "feeling" has been encouraged and cultivated by the reigning US ideological institutions, which seized on the faults and collapse of the official Cold War enemy to spread the notion that the so-called free market system is the only viable model of a decent and democratic society—and (in elite intellectual circles) that it marks the benevolent endpoint (what political scientist Francis Fukuyama famously called "The End of History") to the great historical contest over the question of how to structure society.

Occupy's Achievements

For all its many departures from the mission of the national-developmental US founders, the parasitic nationally de-developmental contemporary US money and power elite agrees with American founder John Jay's belief that "the people who own the country ought to govern it." It stands with the late eighteenth-century New England minister Jeremy Belknap's apt summary of the wealthy founders' dominant, proto-Orwellian notion of what "popular government" really boiled down to at the end of the day: "Let it stand as a principle that government originates from the people; but *let the people be taught ... that they are not able to govern themselves.*"[34] Along the way, the owning and governing elites know very well that, as Chomsky noted in the spring of 2011, "if [the] people are made to feel helpless, isolated, atomized, then power will win."[35]

The Occupy Movement's greatest achievement was to at least momentarily change the nation's class-free political discourse, pushing the submerged question of economic inequality and ruling-class wealth and power—the 1% versus the 99%—into the forefront of the political culture. The hopeful new salience of the issue of economic inequality in America (it dominated the rhetoric of the 2012 "quadrennial extravaganza" like no presidential election since 1936) was to no small extent a consequence of the Occupy Movement, whose clever juxtaposition of the 1% and the 99% became what historian Judith Stein in late November 2011 called "part of our vocabulary now."[36]

"For the first time since the 1930s," former US labor secretary Robert Reich wrote in early 2012, "a broad cross section of the American public is talking about the concentration of income, wealth, and political power at the top. Score one for the Occupiers."[37]

Jeff Madrick agreed more than a year later, noting that "Occupy achieved more than its critics allow. True, the movement failed to realize specific legislative victories, but it did achieve its broader purpose: to raise awareness of the injustice of inequality in this nation. 'We are the 99 percent' will remain with us as a political slogan every bit as galvanizing for the moment as 'Hell no, we won't go' was for the draft protestors of the 1960s." Madrick also notes that "offshoots of Occupy remain active in many areas"—resisting foreclosures, challenging the *Citizens United* ruling, and providing relief to victims of Hurricane Sandy ("Occupy Sandy"), among other things.[38]

Occupy's next most significant success was to at least briefly overcome mass atomization "to bring people together to form functioning, supportive, free, democratic communities—everything from kitchens to libraries to health centers to free general assemblies, where people talk freely and debate. It's created bonds and associations," Chomsky observed in January 2012, "that, if they last and they expand, could make a big difference."[39] The campsites were, however briefly, noble experiments in and demonstrations of *the people's ability to govern themselves.*

Repression: "The Real Cause of Occupy's Decline"

The Occupy Movement/moment bears some responsibility for its collapse. It was attached to an often cumbersome and alienating consensus decisionmaking process (embedded in the movement's famously prolonged "General Assemblies") and to the ultimately nonviable tactic of maintaining urban physical encampments that invited police assault and attracted homeless people. Relatively few ordinary and busy working- and middle-class Americans could be expected to come and spend hours in all-too-commonly tedious deliberation or to join a group living under embattled, family-unfriendly circumstances in cold downtown parks.

Still, there is no telling how Occupy might have developed further but for the state repression it faced. Dedicated to the proto-totalitarian goal of "strategic incapacitation," state authorities used a number of by-now-standard "command and control" tactics to manage and marginalize the anticorporate/antiplutocracy protestors: "frequent and often mass arrests, surveillance, the use of barricades and kettling, and infiltration." As Madrick argued in *Harper's Magazine* last year,

It has become increasingly clear that OWS didn't fizzle because its objectives were muddled or its talk too abstract or its organization too chaotic. In fact, the movement was undone by a concerted [multijurisdictional] government effort to undo it.... Taken together, the coordinated and disproportionate actions of the NYPD, the FBI, and Homeland Security represent a campaign of suppression without which Occupy might well have evolved into something more formidable, even in the cold of New York City's winter.[40]

Government repression, Madrick notes, was "the real cause of Occupy's decline."

"There Is No Real Left Now"

What good is political will—and how are serious dissenters and progressives supposed to survive elite opposition and repression—without serious movement organization? A key task going forward has been and remains to carry the Occupy spirit beyond the inherently short-lived campsite tactic and into the broader society, into schools, nonprofits, community organizations, organized labor, and other sectors where that spirit might inform a popular movement with the power to make demands that actually have to be addressed by those in power. Another and equally significant task is to form a durable Left organization and a continuously entrenched Left cadre ready to spark and lead popular struggles through thick and thin and over a long period of time. The dominant media and many mainstream politicians, particularly Republicans, are strongly attached to the notion that something called "the Left" (a term that preposterously ranges in application from the anarchists and Marxists who sparked Occupy to Oprah Winfrey, the *New York Times*, and Barack Obama) is a powerful force in the United States today. The news and commentary media speak constantly about the supposedly sharp "polarization" of US politics between "left" (meaning the corporate- and Wall Street–captive Democrats) and "right" (the deeply reactionary, arguably radical Republicans). But, as Chomsky pointed out in an April 2010 interview with David Barsamian, there is an abject silliness to at least one aspect of this terminology:

Barsamian: The Left seems to have nothing to say.
Chomsky: The Democratic Party and even the Democratic left are not going to tell people, "Look, your problem is that, back in the 1970s, we took part in a major process of financialization of the economy and the hollowing out of the productive system. So your wages and income have stagnated

for thirty years, while what wealth is produced is in a very few pockets. Those are our policies." No, there is no real left now. If you are just counting heads, there are probably more people involved than in the 1960s, but they are atomized, committed to different special interests—gay rights, environmental rights, this, that. They don't coalesce into a movement that can really do things.[41]

Ever since the decline of the "Old Left," primarily the Communist Party (itself crushed by state repression in the age of McCarthyism), progressive forces have been plagued by the absence of organizational and cadre continuity. "We're not supposed to say it," Chomsky told Barsamian in 2010,

> but the Communist Party was an organized and persistent element. It didn't show up for a demonstration and then scatter so somebody else had to start something new. It was always there and it was there for the long haul.... That's why the old Communist Party was so significant. There was always somebody around to turn the mimeograph machine.... They didn't expect quick victories. Maybe you win something, maybe you don't, but then you lay the basis for something else. That mentality is basically missing [now]. And it was during the 1960s, too.[42]

In John Carpenter's *They Live*, for what it's worth, the extraterrestrial capitalists and their co-opted human collaborators are challenged by a dedicated cadre of rebels and revolutionaries. The aliens' occupation is resisted by a tight-knit underground of democracy-fighters who are there "for the long haul," through thick and thin, at no small personal risk. Over and against the dominant culture's media, politics, and police state, this cadre distributes the tools and weapons of popular-democratic resistance, including the aforementioned magical sunglasses—Carpenter's metaphor for the demystifying vision of left social criticism and its alternative vision. Tellingly enough, the Old Left, Occupy, and Carpenter's cadre share the same basic enemies: the capitalist superelite, the plutocrats, and their servants—those the latest incarnation of genuine American antiplutocratic populism has so famously labeled "the 1%."

If a new "real left" can come into being, it will not lack a clear near-term objective that unites immediate demands (particularly the demand for socially necessary and useful work) with the longer-term goal of societal transformation and the related aim of saving human beings and other living things from environmental catastrophe: the conversion of America's giant and inherently political economy from its current deadly imperatives of private profit, waste, and ecocide to democratic alternatives of real participatory politics, equality, sustainability, and serving the common good.

Socialism in the American Zeitgeist

There appears to be a real constituency for such a left in the United States. According to *Merriam Webster*, one of the world's leading dictionaries, the most looked-up words in 2012 were *capitalism* and *socialism*. The number of times each word was searched on the company's website doubled over the previous year, something the dictionary's editor-at-large saw as a "no-brainer" since "they're words that sort of encapsulate the zeitgeist" in the wake of the Great Recession and the Occupy rebellion.[43]

Besides stirring new interest, the word *socialism* is now viewed in positive terms to a remarkable degree. In two recent polls by the right-leaning survey group Rasmussen Reports, Americans younger than thirty were almost evenly divided on whether capitalism or socialism was preferable. A December 2011 Pew survey discovered that 49 percent of young Americans aged eighteen to twenty-nine positively viewed the term *socialism*, compared to 46 percent who reacted negatively to the term. By contrast, more of those young people viewed capitalism negatively (47 percent) than saw it positively (46 percent).[44]

Alperovitz finds these polling data unsurprising thanks to the stark economic failures, harsh inequality, austerity, and plutocratic authoritarianism imposed by the contemporary US profits system and the fading capacity of liberal and progressive policy and institutions to mitigate capitalism's negative impact on society, popular governance, and livable ecology:

> As economic failure continues to create massive social and economic pain and a stalemated Washington dickers, search for some alternative to the current "system" is likely to continue to grow. It is clearly time to get serious about a different vision of the future....
>
> Classically, the central idea undergirding various forms of socialism ... is democratic ownership of "the means of production," or "capital," or, more simply, "productive wealth." ... The core idea is simple and straightforward: those who own wealth—and the corporations who control it—have far more power to control any system than those who don't.
>
> In a nation in which 400 people own more wealth than the bottom 180 million together, the point should be obvious. What is new in our time in history is that the traditional compromise position—namely progressive, or social democratic or liberal politics—has lost its capacity to offset such power even in the modest (compared, for instance to many European states) ways the American welfare state once represented. Indeed, the emerging direction is to cut back previous gains in many areas—not to sustain or enlarge them. Even Social Security is now on the table for cuts.... Union membership has steadily decreased from roughly 35 percent of the workforce in 1954, to 11.3 percent now—a mere 6.6 percent in the private sector.

Along with the decay, and give or take an exception here and there, major trends in income and wealth, in civil liberties, in ecological devastation ... in poverty and many other important indicators have been "going South" for several decades.[45]

It helps "socialism's" favorability rating, no doubt, that we are now more than two decades past the collapse of the Soviet Union and its satellite regimes and the end of the Cold War. This makes it more difficult for the US capitalist elite and its supporters to automatically identify the democratic and egalitarian project of socialism—workers' control and "people over profits"—with the archauthoritarian state-capitalist and/or bureaucratic-collectivist nightmare of Stalinist Russia, the Soviet bloc, and the so-called People's Republic of China.

Green-Red New Deal: No Space Invasion Required

Socialism's polling numbers aside, I cannot agree with Wilkinson and Pickett's refusal to embrace any particular set of demands. The Green New Deal mentioned in Chapter 1 is clearly emerging as the ineluctable core contemporary policy demand in the contemporary age of simultaneous and interrelated economic, jobs, and ecological crises. It is precisely the policy demand to which any real next left worth emerging in the United States should and indeed must "pin its colours."

And here we confront some droll and disappointing musings by the leading liberal economist Paul Krugman, who has half-jokingly proposed an interesting idea for pulling the US economy out of stagnation: *prepare for an alien invasion*. "If you actually look at what took us out of the Great Depression," Krugman told MSNBC last year, "it was Europe's entry into World War II and the US buildup that began in advance.... So if we could get something that could cause the government to say, 'Oh, never mind those budget things; let's just spend and do a bunch of stuff.' ... My fake threat from space aliens is the other route," Krugman said before a laughing crowd. A longtime fan of science fiction, Krugman had advanced his space alien proposal before. In 2011 he told CNN about a *Twilight Zone* episode in which "scientists fake an alien threat in order to achieve world peace," adding that "this time ... we need it in order to get some fiscal stimulus."[46]

It was curious that Krugman felt compelled to humorously concoct the fantastic and futuristic imagery of an alien space invasion to make the case for replicating the governmental stimulus that World War II military spending provided to end the Great Depression. Home- and human-made existential threats to survival seem sufficient to the stimulatory task. How about saving the planet for livable habitation by putting millions to work on ecological retrofitting and clean energy? Tackling climate change and other environmental ills in a meaningful way means putting many millions of people to work at all skill levels to design, implement, coordinate, and construct the environmental retrofitting of economy and society—the ecological reconversion of production, transportation, office space, homes, agriculture, and public space. What kind of work? To start, hundreds of thousands of so-called green-collar jobs involved in weatherizing and energy-retrofitting every building in the United States. There will be plenty of work for college-educated environmental engineers and architects and planners but even more work for people without college degrees. Here's an excellent passage from the environmental activist Van Jones's best-selling 2007 book *The Green Collar Economy*:

> When you think about the ... green economy, don't think of George Jetson with a jet pack. Think of Joe Sixpack with a hard hat and a lunch bucket, sleeves rolled up, going off to fix America. Think of Rosie the Riveter, manufacturing parts for hybrid buses or wind turbines.... If we are going to beat global warming, we are going to have to weatherize millions of buildings. Install millions of solar panels, manufacture millions of wind turbine parts, plant and care for millions of trees, build millions of plug-in hybrid vehicles, and construct thousands of solar farms, wind farms, and wave farms. This will require ... millions of jobs.... We will also need [well-paid] workers in a range of green industries: materials reuse and recycling, water management, local and organic food production, mass transportation and more.[47]

Science fiction aside, there is a big jobs and stimulus dividend to be garnered from a serious and substantive approach to the environmental crisis, including the climate catastrophe that Krugman once said would be "the dominant political and policy concern" of "a rational world."[48] There's an added benefit: helping save humanity from environmental self-destruction.[49]

A positive historical analogy is staring us in the face. Consistent with both Jones's reference to "Rosie the Riveter" and Krugman's understanding of what ended the Great Depression, it is World War II, when the United States taxed its rich like never before, reconverted its economy, and put millions to socially useful work, producing what the country and the world needed at the time: weapons and other goods to defeat fascism. As Chomsky notes, "Surely the US manufacturing industries could be reconstructed *to produce what the country needs*, using its highly skilled work force—*and what the world needs*, and soon, if we are to have some hope of averting major catastrophe. *It has been done before, after all. During World War II*, industry was converted to wartime production and the semi-command economy ... ended the Depression."[50]

There is no mythical extraterrestrial menace required. "Spaceship Earth" presents its own urgent social and ecological justifications for massive public works programs and investments. And if science-fiction alien invasions are required, then a far better citation is *They Live*, where the space invaders are already here, changing the climate ("acclimatizing us to their atmosphere") in the name of free enterprise.

Those on the radical left who worry that pursuing a Green New Deal and leading with the environmental issue means giving up on the struggle against the 1% and for a democratically transformed "world turned upside down" can rest easy. The green transformation required for human survival will be bright rouge. With its inherent privileging of private profit and exchange value over the common good and social use value, its intrinsic insistence on private management, its inbuilt privileging of the short-term bottom line over the long-term fate of the earth and its many species, with its deep-sunk cost investment in endless quantitative growth and the carbon-addicted way of life and death, and with its attachment to the division of the world into competing nations and empires that are incapable of common action for the global good, capitalism is simply inconsistent with the deep environmental changes required for human survival. "Green capitalism" is an oxymoron.[51] It is naïve to think that the green transformation required for civilization's survival can take place without an epic confrontation with—and defeat of—the concentrated wealth and power enjoyed by the capitalist elite and its profits system.[52]

The Duty of Struggle

Short term, the Next Real Left (should one come into being) will fight for numerous measures to try to make the world safer, more decent, and more democratic under the existing system. Longer term, since it seems increasingly unlikely that we can expect a democratic or decent future past one more generation (at most) of state capitalism, it must advocate anticapitalist transformation—transcendence of the predatory and exterminist nightmare that is the profits system. The rub is that we are now in something of an ecological race against time when it comes to getting past that system. The long-term project of revolution seems like an ever more short-term necessity. "The hour," to quote Bob Dylan, "is getting late."

There are no guarantees of success, of course. But, picking up on the examples of Occupy and its many predecessors (socialist, populist, communist, anarchist, syndicalist, and laborite), we have to try. "We are moving right now," Mario Savio said in late 1994, nearly two years before his death, "in a direction which one could call creeping barbarism. We have to be prepared, on the basis of our moral insight, to struggle even if we do not know that we are going to win."[53] Perhaps we have only a 20 percent, or worse, a 1 percent chance of success, of creating a better and democratic nation and world that are no longer lethally occupied by John Carpenter's "They"—by the "unelected dictatorship of money." Failure to believe in the worthiness of collective struggle for a decent and democratic future beyond that plutocratic occupation takes our odds down to zero.

We lose nothing by believing. We *lose everything by not believing*—quite literally everything given current environmental projections, which suggest that "we are really facing the prospect of species destruction for the first time in human history."[54] As the great Hungarian Marxist philosopher Istvan Meszaros put things in 2001, "Many of the problems we have to confront—from chronic structural unemployment to major political/military conflicts … as well as the ever more widespread ecological destruction in evidence everywhere—require concerted action in the very near future…. We are running out of time…. The uncomfortable truth of the matter is that *if there is no future for a radical mass movement in our time, there can be no future for humanity itself.*"[55]

The stakes could hardly be higher. It's not about the crystal ball.

Epilogue

After this book was essentially complete, former US president Jimmy Carter said something that should have been a headline story and a top item on the evening and cable television news. "America does not at the moment have a functioning democracy," Carter said at an event in Atlanta, Georgia, sponsored by Atlantik Bruecke ("Atlantic Bridge"), a nonprofit association dedicated to ensuring smooth relations between the United States and Germany. Carter's remarks didn't appear in the US "mainstream" (corporate state) media. They were reported by the German newsmagazine *Der Spiegel*, whose Washington correspondent Gregor Peter Schmitz said on Twitter that he was present at the event. "The story," *International Business Times* reporter Alberto Riva notes, "did not appear on the English-language section of the *Spiegel* website. It was available only in German."

Carter's comment was a response to the heroic whistleblower Edward Snowden's revelations about the National Security Agency's spying on American and other global citizens. According to Riva, "Carter is so concerned about the NSA spying scandal that he thinks it has essentially resulted in a suspension of American democracy."[1]

But what functioning US democracy was it, exactly, that got "suspended" by the NSA? And when exactly has such a democracy existed? The fundamental underlying conflict between democratic popular governance and the oligarchic rule of the few is as old in American history as the original republic. A functioning popular democracy was the Founding Fathers' ultimate nightmare, a violation of their republican world view, according to which people without substantial property held no meaningful stake in society and could be expected to use democracy to "despotically" expropriate their propertied "betters." "The people who own the country ought to run the country," US founder John Jay said, expressing a common sentiment among the wellborn architects of the US Constitution. The young republic's political and governing systems were accordingly constructed to protect the interests of the wealthy few over and against those of the unworthy many.[2]

The objective was largely if somewhat unevenly[3] attained and preserved across the 1800s. The nineteenth century saw the growth of giant, tyrannical workplace and other massive marketplace-capitalist hierarchies that rendered the attainment of universal white manhood suffrage largely irrelevant. It also witnessed the translation of free market doctrine into common law, the development of dramatically increased new state-coercive powers to discipline workers and unions,[4] and a restructured party system (divided between Republicans and Democrats) wherein "business and financial entrepreneurs had achieved effective control."[5] This is how the great Kansas populist orator Mary Ellen Lease put things to an angry crowd at the height of the Gilded Age in 1890, one hundred twenty-one years before Occupy Wall Street launched its encampment in lower Manhattan and twenty-seven years after Abraham Lincoln proclaimed that the dead of Gettysburg had fallen so "*that government of the people, by the people, for the people* shall not perish from the earth": "Wall Street owns the country. It is ... a government of Wall Street, by Wall Street, and for Wall Street.... Our laws are the output of a system which clothes rascals in robes and honesty in rags.... There are thirty men in the United States whose aggregate wealth is over one and one-half billion dollars. And there are half a million looking for work.... The people are at bay, let the bloodhounds of money who have dogged us thus far beware."[6]

Another sterling populist orator of the time spoke in similar terms, adding a critique of the two dominant parties' shared subservience to the moneyed power. A passage from Ignatius Donnelly's speech to the People's Party national convention on July 4, 1892, sounds hauntingly familiar today, very much like a statement the Occupy Movement might have issued before it was crushed by a coordinated federal campaign of repression directed by the corporate neoliberal Obama administration:

> We meet in the midst of a nation brought to the verge of moral, political, and material ruin. Corruption dominates the ballot-box, the Legislatures, the Congress, and touches even the ermine of the bench. The people are demoralized.... The newspapers are largely subsidized or muzzled, public opinion silenced, business prostrated, homes covered with mortgages, labor impoverished, and the land concentrating in the hands of capitalists....
>
> The urban workmen are denied the right to organize for self-protection, imported pauperized labor beats down their wages, a hireling standing army, unrecognized by our laws, is established to shoot them down.... The fruits of the toil of millions are badly stolen to build up colossal fortunes for a few, unprecedented in the history of mankind; and the possessors of these, in turn, despise the Republic and endanger liberty....
>
> We have witnessed for more than a quarter of a century the struggles of the two great political parties for power and plunder, while grievous wrongs have been inflicted upon the suffering people. We charge that the controlling influences dominating both these parties have permitted the existing dreadful conditions to develop without serious effort to prevent or restrain them.... Neither do they now promise us any substantial reform.... They

propose to sacrifice our homes, lives, and children on the altar of mammon; to destroy the multitude in order to secure corruption funds from the millionaires.[7]

Twelve years later, writing in the wake of a failed national strike against the leading US meatpacking corporations Swift and Armour, the American socialist, novelist, and pamphleteer Upton Sinclair captured a broadly held sentiment when he wrote the following in the widely read socialist newspaper *Appeal to Reason*:

Rise up ... and look about you.
They own all the instruments and means of production.
They own the railroads and the telegraphs, the coal mines and the oil fields, the factories and the stores!
They own half the farms and have mortgages on the rest.
They own society. They own the government![8]

In 1906, Sinclair's best-selling novel *The Jungle*, set among the workers in Chicago's gigantic packinghouses, neared its conclusion with its battered proletarian protagonist standing transfixed before a mesmerizing radical orator who spoke of the shocking disparities that had emerged in early twentieth-century America. After detailing the rampant poverty and insecurity experienced by millions, the speaker asked his listeners to regard the luxuriant, parasitic lives and power of the wealthy few:

Turn over the page with me and gaze upon the other side of the picture. There are a thousand—ten thousand, maybe—who are the masters of these slaves, who own their toil.... They live in palaces, they riot in luxury and extravagance—such as no words can describe, as makes the imagination reel and stagger, makes the soul grow sick and faint. They spend hundreds of dollars for a pair of shoes, a handkerchief, a garter; they spend millions for horses and automobiles and yachts, for palaces and banquets, for shiny little stones with which to deck their bodies. Their life is a contest among themselves for supremacy in ostentation and recklessness, in the destroying of useful and necessary things, in the wasting of the labor and the lives of their fellow creatures, the toil and anguish of the nations, the sweat and tears of the human race!
It is all theirs ... all the wealth of society comes to them. The farmer tills the soil, the miner digs the earth, the weaver tends the loom, the mason carves the stone, the clever man invents, the shrewd man directs, the wise man studies, the inspired man sings—and all the results ... are gathered in one stupendous stream and poured into their laps! The whole of society is in their grip, the whole labor of the world lies at their mercy.... They own

not merely the labor of society, they have bought the governments; and everywhere they used their raped and stolen power to entrench themselves and their privileges, to dig deeper and wider the channels through which the rivers of profit flow to them![9]

In the original serialized version of *The Jungle*, Sinclair used a fictional representation of the socialist presidential candidate Eugene Debs to extend his observation that the wealthy "masters" owned "the whole of society" by having the candidate claim that "the *two* [dominant US] *political parties*"—the Democrats and the Republicans—were "*two wings of the same bird of prey.* The people [are] allowed to choose between their candidates, and both of them [are] controlled, and all their nominations [are] dictated by, the same [money] power."[10] This was hardly a negligible sentiment among Americans during the Progressive Age (1890–1917), a high-water mark for socialist electoral success in the United States and legislative action to address the system's most malignant abuses.[11]

Within ten years the great American philosopher John Dewey gave his previously quoted observation[12] that US politics were "the shadow cast on society by big business" and his prediction that things would stay that way as long as "business for private profit" controlled the nation's means of finance, production, and communication.

It *might* seem that Dewey spoke too soon. Between the 1930s and the 1970s, a significant reduction in overall economic inequality (though not of racial inequality) and an increase in the standard of living of millions of working-class Americans occurred in the United States. This "Great Compression" occurred thanks to the rise and expansion of the industrial workers' movement (sparked to no small extent by Communists and other radical left militants), the spread of collective bargaining, the rise of a relatively pro-union New Deal welfare state (on whose left margins Sinclair would push during the 1930s), and the democratic domestic pressures of World War II and subsequent powerful social movements. Still, core capitalist prerogatives and assets—Dewey's "private control" and "business for profit"—were never dislodged, consistent with New Deal champion Franklin Roosevelt's boast that he had "saved the profits system" from radical change. The gains enjoyed by ordinary working Americans were made possible to no small extent by the uniquely favored and powerful position of the United States economy (and empire) and the remarkable profit rates enjoyed by US corporations in the post-WWII world.

When that position and those profits were significantly challenged by resurgent Western European and Japanese economic competition in the 1970s and 1980s, the comparatively egalitarian trends of postwar America were reversed by the capitalist elites, who had never lost their critical command of the nation's core economic and political institutions.[13] Working-class Americans have paid the price ever since. For the past four decades, wealth and income have been sharply concentrated upward, returning to pre–Great Depression levels, marking a New or Second Gilded Age that is directly traceable to a number of regressive and plutocratic policies that have nothing to do with any shift right in the populace and in fact run contrary to majority progressive opinion.

Curiously enough, the decisive undemocratic shift right in the nation's economic policy started not under the Republican presidencies of Richard Nixon or Ronald Reagan but under the Democratic interregnum of Jimmy Carter. The neoliberal policies that have loosened financial regulation, undercut social protections, deepened economic inequality, and produced crisis have been a richly bipartisan affair going back to the Carter administration. As liberal political scientists Jacob Hacker and Paul Pierson have noted, in a critique of popular liberal historian Rick Perlstein's book *Nixonland,*

> If one wanted a book title to capture the great turning point [rightward] in modern American political history, it would be more accurate, if less catchy, to call it *Carterland*. 1977 and 1978 marked the rapid demise of the liberal era and the emergence of something radically different. Tax reform: defeated. A new consumer protection agency: defeated.... Health care reform: defeated. A proposal to tie the minimum wage to the average manufacturing wage to prevent its future erosion: defeated. An overhaul of outdated labor relations: successfully filibustered in the Senate despite the presence of sixty-one Democrats and a Republican minority containing some genuine supporters of organized labor, not to mention far, far more moderates than in the GOP we know today....
>
> By 1978, at a time of unified Democratic control of the House, Senate, and White House, the precursors of the Reagan revolution were already visible. Congress passed a tax bill whose signature was a deep cut in the capital gains tax—a change that would largely benefit the wealthy. This followed hard on the heels of a decision to sharply raise payroll taxes, the most regressive federal levy. These two initiatives—fully a decade removed from the supposed turning point of Nixon's rise—marked the beginning of [a] pronounced [regressive] reversal in federal tax policy.... At the same time, Congress and the president embarked on a major shift in economic policy, embracing the argument that excessive regulation had become a serious curb on growth ... [starting a] deregulatory stream [that soon] ... flooded over its narrow banks to become an ever-widening attack on the very idea of economic regulation ... the story begins in the 1970s, not the 1980s.[14]

If Jimmy Carter wanted to know why we have "no functioning democracy" in the United States he should have looked deeper than NSA phone spying. A serious inquiry into the question would include an honest examination of his own corporatist presidency, itself a fitting prelude to the neoliberal Democratic administrations of Bill Clinton and Barack Obama.

Of course, there's an intimate relationship between the surveillance activities that Carter deplores and the plutocracy he advanced as president, now drowning the democratic ideal in the icy waters of corporate and financial calculation. As Chris Hedges noted in a remarkable interview on the Real News Network in July 2013,

> We are being ... reconfigured into a kind of neo-feudal society, an oligarchic society where increasingly the bottom two-thirds of Americans are hanging on by their fingertips. You have a shrinking, diminishing middle class and an elite that is ... making obscene amounts of money at our expense.... They will push and push and push until there is a backlash.... What we're seeing with the security and surveillance state is a preparation for that backlash—the destruction of civil liberties, which has been brutal, the wholesale surveillance and monitoring of virtually every American citizen, which I think many of us suspected and Edward Snowden ... made ... palpably real.... They know what's coming. The NSA has run all sorts of scenarios on economic collapse, and especially climate change. And they're preparing.[15]

Harsh as Hedges sounds, this is the cold truth of contemporary and oxymoronic "really existing capitalist democracy" (RECD/"wrecked") in the United States. "Scenarios" of economic and ecological breakdown leading to popular unrest and militarized domestic repression are worked up and run through regularly across the nation's sprawling and ever more technologically potent security and surveillance state. The "homeland" repression of egalitarian dissenters is enacted with greater force under a Democratic administration than under its Republican predecessor. This is yet another chilling reminder of the richly bipartisan nature of the nation's unelected and interrelated dictatorships of money and empire and of the harsh limits of "change" under the reigning business-ruled two-party system, where the dominant political organizations function as "two wings of the same bird of prey."

Required now not just to rescue and reinvent democracy but also to save a livable planet and the prospects of a decent future, serious and substantive progressive change will have to come from outside the system and the bottom up, in ways that the Occupy Movement began to embody, garnering thereby an unleashing of the state's iron fist combined with an elite effort to co-opt its language. The spirit of that movement—and of the broader global struggle against inequality, austerity, neoliberal corporate globalization, and indeed capitalism (a struggle of which Occupy was/is just one part)—lives on, like that of the British Diggers, who arose to demand an equal, common, democratic, and participatory society in 1649, at the height of the first great bourgeois revolution, only to be pushed by soldiers off St. George's Hill, near London, where they proposed to cultivate the nation's wastelands in common. They insisted, in the words of the early socialist Gerrard Winstanley, "That the earth shall be made a common Treasury of livelihood to whole mankind, without respect of persons" and that "the earth must be set free from intanglements of Lords and Landlords ... it shall be a common treasury for all, as it was first made and given to the sonnes of man." True "freedome," Winstanley said, "lies in the community of spirit, and community in the earthly treasury" and "is the man that will turn the world upside down ... no wonder he hath enemies."

"Words and writings" were not enough, Winstanley felt, adding his belief that "for action is the life of all, and if thou dost not act, thou dost nothing."[16]

Notes

Epigraphs

1. Quoted on the website of Brandeis University at www.brandeis.edu/legacyfund /bio.html and in *Harvard Magazine* (March 2011) at http://harvardmagazine.com/2011/03 /quotable-harvard. The original source in the latter is *Labor*, October 14, 1941.
2. Herve Kempf, *How the Rich Are Destroying the Earth* (White River Junction, VT: Chelsea Green, 2007), xiii.

Introduction

1. Written prior to Occupy Wall Street's emergence, Charles Derber and Yale Magrass's book *The Surplus American: How the 1% Is Making Us Redundant* (Boulder, CO: Paradigm Publishers, 2012) is scripted in part around an imagined confrontation between the financial elite and protestors on Wall Street.
2. Mike Davis, *Be Realistic: Demand the Impossible* (Chicago: Haymarket Books, 2011), 1.
3. Anthony Dimaggio and Paul Street, "Occupy Wall Street, Mass Media, and Progressive Change in the Tea Party Era," *Economic and Political Weekly* (India), Vol. 46, No. 46 (November 19, 2011): 10–14.
4. To understand how and why OWS achieved this when it did, I have suggested, it is useful to look at another and much more famous and widely viewed piece of US cinematographic history: *The Wizard of Oz.* See Paul Street, "Dorothy and the Occupiers vs. the Wizard of Ozbama and the Power behind the Curtain," *ZNet*, November 5, 2011, www .zcommunications.org/dorothy-and-the-occupiers-vs-the-wizard-of-ozbama-and-the-power -behind-the-curtain-by-paul-street.
5. John Pilger, "The World War on Democracy," Johnpilger.com, January 19, 2012, at http://johnpilger.com/articles/the-world-war-on-democracy; emphasis added.
6. Sheldon Wolin, *Democracy Incorporated: Managed Democracy and the Specter of Inverted Totalitarianism* (Princeton, NJ: Princeton University Press, 2008). The quotation comes from the book's hardcover dust jacket.
7. See Alex Carey, "The Orwell Diversion," in Carey, *Taking the Risk Out of Democracy: Corporate Propaganda versus Freedom and Liberty* (Urbana: University of Illinois Press, 1997), 133–139.
8. Istvan Meszaros, *Socialism or Barbarism: From the "American Century" to the Crossroads* (New York: Monthly Review Press, 2001), 80; emphasis added.
9. Public Broadcasting System, *Frontline*, "The Choice," October 9, 2012, www.pbs .org/wgbh/pages/frontline/choice-2012/.

10. Quoted on the website of Brandeis University at www.brandeis.edu/legacyfund /bio.html and in *Harvard Magazine* (March 2011) at http://harvardmagazine.com/2011/03 /quotable-harvard. The original source in the latter is *Labor*, October 14, 1941.
11. Howard Zinn, "Election Madness," *Progressive*, March 2008.

Chapter 1

1. Dennis Bernstein, "What the Cops Really Did in Oakland," *Counterpunch*, November 2, 2011, www.counterpunch.org/2011/11/02/what-the-cops-really-did-in-oakland/.
2. CBS Evening News, "Goldman Sachs CEO: Entitlements Must Be Contained," November 19, 2012, www.cbsnews.com/8301-18563_162-57552173/goldman -sachs-ceo-entitlements-must-be-contained/.
3. Josh Richman, "Obama Collects $1 Million at San Francisco Fundraiser," *San Jose Mercury News*, October 26, 2011, www.mercurynews.com/bay-area-news/ci _19190085.
4. Richman, "Obama Collects $1 Million."
5. Andy Kroll, "Obama Has, on Average, Attended a Fundraiser Every 5 Days in 2011," *Mother Jones*, December 1, 2011, http://motherjones.com/mojo/2011/12 /barack-obama-fundraiser-every-five-days-2011.
6. F. Schouten, "Obama Tops Recent Presidents in Fundraising Attendance," *USA Today*, March 6, 2012, A1.
7. "This is an impressive crowd—the haves and the have mores," Bush said, adding, "Some people call you the elite. I call you my base." See "George Bush—the Elite My Base," speech to Al Smith Dinner, October 20, 2000, www.youtube.com/watch?v=mn4daYJzyls.
8. Ken Layne, "Four More Years: Obama Raises Money in San Francisco as Cops Gas Oakland Protesters," *Wonkette*, October 26, 2011, http://wonkette.com/455208/obama -raises-money-in-san-francisco-as-cops-gas-oakland-protesters; http://motherjones.com /mojo/2011/12/barack-obama-fundraiser-every-five-days-2011.
9. Bernstein, "What the Cops Really Did in Oakland."
10. Jonathan Weisman and Laura Meckler, "Democrats' Populist Puzzle," *Wall Street Journal*, October 7, 2011, A1.
11. Yves Smith, "Police State: #OWS, Other Crackdowns Part of National, Coordinated Effort," Naked Capitalism, November 15, 2011, www.nakedcapitalism.com/2011/11 /police-state-ows-other-crackdowns-part-of-national-coordinated-effort-bloomberg-defies -court-order-to-let-protestors-back-into-zuccotti-park.html.
12. Jeff Madrick, "The Fall and Rise of Occupy Wall Street," *Harper's Magazine*, March 2013, 9–10.
13. Marsha Coleman-Adebayo, "Obama Silent, Bloomberg Wrong on Constitutional Rights," *Black Agenda Report*, November 22, 2011, http://blackagendareport.com/content /obama-silent-bloomberg-wrong-constitutional-rights; emphasis added.
14. Josh Harkinson, "'They're Holding Us Hostage,'" *Mother Jones*, December 1, 2011, http:// motherjones.com/mojo/2011/11/occupy-wall-street-free-speech-zones-obama-protest-video.
15. "Spike Lee Hosts President Obama Fundraiser," *Huffington Post*, January 20, 2012, www.huffingtonpost.com/2012/01/20/spike-lee-hosts-president-obama -fundraiser_n_1218479.html; Alex Marin, "$38,500 a Head Spike Lee Dinner for Barack Obama," *policymic*, January 21, 2012, www.policymic.com/articles/3267/38-500-per-person -spike-lee-dinner-for-obama-contradicts-president-s-fundraising-claims.
16. Josh Vorhees, "Team Obama Calls Billion Dollar Campaign Rumors 'Bulls**t,'" *Slatest*, December 29, 2011, http://slatest.slate.com/posts/2011/12/29

/obama_2012_jim_messina_says_billion_dollar_ campaign_rumors_are_bullshit_.html; Marin, "$38,500 a Head Spike Lee Dinner."

17. Holly Bailey, "Occupy Protestor Hands President Obama a Note," *Yahoo News, The Ticket,* November 22, 2011, http://news.yahoo.com/blogs/ticket/occupy-protestor-hands -president-obama-note-201229558.html.

18. David Lindorff, "Police State Tactics Point to a Coordinated National Program to Try and Unoccupy Wall Street and Other Cities," *This Can't Be Happening,* November 15, 2011, http://thiscantbehappening.net/node/900; Andy Kroll, "Mayors and Cops Traded Strategies for Dealing with Occupy Protestors," *Mother Jones,* November 16, 2011, http://motherjones .com/mojo/2011/11/occupy-protest-coordinate-crackdown-wall-street; Nigel Duara, "Mayors, Police Chiefs Talk Strategy on Protests," Associated Press, November 15, 2011, www .boston.com/news/nation/articles/2011/11/15/mayors_police_chiefs_talk_strategy_on _protests/.

19. Partnership for Civil Justice Fund, *FBI Documents Reveal Secret Nationwide Occupy Monitoring,* December 22, 2012, www.justiceonline.org/commentary/fbi-files-ows .html; Naomi Wolf, "Revealed: How the FBI Coordinated the Crackdown on Occupy," *Guardian,* December 29, 2012, www.guardian.co.uk/commentisfree/2012/dec/29/fbi -coordinated-crackdown-occupy.

20. "The FBI vs. Occupy: Secret Docs Reveal 'Counterterrorism' Monitoring of OWS from Its Earliest Days," *Democracy Now!,* airdate December 27, 2012, www.democracynow .org/2012/12/27/the_fbi_vs_occupy_secret_docs.

21. Wolf, "Revealed."

22. Pam Martens, "Financial Giants Put New York City Cops on Their Payroll," *Counterpunch,* October 10, 2011, www.counterpunch.org/2011/10/10/financial-giants-put -new-york-city-cops-on-their-payroll/.

23. An especially useful reflection on the classist-racist demonization and its historical roots and cultural and political power is Steve Macek's book *Urban Nightmares: The Media, the Right, and the Moral Panic Over the City* (Minneapolis: University of Minnesota Press, 2006).

24. Elizabeth Kneebone et al., *The Re-Emergence of Concentrated Poverty: Metropolitan Trends,* Brookings Institution, November 4, 2011, 2, www.brookings.edu/~/media/Files/rc /papers/2011/1103_poverty_kneebone_nadeau_berube/1103_poverty_kneebone_nadeau _berube.pdf.

25. Kneebone et al., *Re-Emergence of Concentrated Poverty.*

26. Kneebone et al., *Re-Emergence of Concentrated Poverty,* appendix B, 24–26; Andrew Dalton and Christina Hoag, "Streets Re-Opened after Occupy Los Angeles Protest," *Bloomberg/BusinessWeek,* November 28, 2011, www.businessweek.com/ap /financialnews/D9R9Q4L80.htm; "Occupy Chicago Arrests: Nurses Picket Mayor Rahm Emmanuel's Office," *International Business Times,* October 24, 2011, www.ibtimes.com /articles/236640/20111024/occupy-chicago-arrests-nurses-protest-mayor-rahm-emanuel -office-grant-park.htm.

27. David McNally, *Global Slump: The Economics and Politics of Crisis and Resistance* (Oakland, CA: PM Press, 2011), 126, 218n271.

28. David Graeber, *The Democracy Project: A History, a Crisis, a Movement* (New York: Spiegel and Grau, 2012), xi–xii.

29. Chris Hedges, "America Is a Tinderbox," Real News Network, July 24, 2013, http://therealnews.com/t2/index.php?option=com_content&task=view&id=31&Itemid =74&jumival=10461.

30. Jonathan D. Salant, "Why the 2012 Election Will Cost $6 Billion," *Bloomberg News,* September 29, 2012, www.businessweek.com/magazine/why-the-2012-election-will-cost -6-billion-09292011.html.

31. Robert McChesney and John Nichols, "The Money and Media Election Complex," *Nation*, November 29, 2010, www.thenation.com/article/156391/money-media-election -complex; Robert McChesney and John Nichols, "The Bull Market: Political Advertising," *Monthly Review*, Vol. 63, No. 12 (April 2012).

32. Lewis H. Lapham, "Word Order: The Internet as the Toy with a Tin Ear," *Tomdispatch*, April 22, 2012, www.tomdispatch.com.

33. Sunlight Foundation, *The Political One Percent of One Percent*, December 13, 2011.

34. Kevin Drawbaugh, "Romney Draws More Wall Street Donations Than Obama," Reuters, *Christian Science Monitor*, February 2, 2012, www.csmonitor.com/USA/Elections /From-the-Wires/2012/0202/Mitt-Romney-draws-more-Wall-Street-donations-than -Obama.

35. John Pilger, "Obama and Empire," speech to the International Socialist Organization, San Francisco, July 4, 2009, http://louisporyect.workpress.com/2009/08/18 /john-pilger-obama-is-a-corporate-marketing-creation/; emphasis added.

36. Matthew Rothschild, "Rampant Xenophobia," *Progressive*, November 2009, http:// progressive.org/mr1110.html.

37. Edward S. Herman and David Peterson, "Riding the 'Green Wave' at the Campaign for Peace and Democracy and Beyond," *Electric Politics*, July 22, 2009, http:// mrzine.monthlyreview.org/2009/hp240709.html; Paul Street, "America's Unelected Dictatorship of Money," *ZNet*, April 14, 2011, www.zcommunications.org/america -s-unelected-dictatorship-of-money-by-paul-street.

38. Matt Taibbi, *Griftopia: A Story of Bankers, Politicians, and the Most Audacious Power Grab in American History* (New York: Spiegel and Grau, 2010), 28.

39. Paul Street, "Whose Black President? Getting Things Done for the Rich and Powerful," *Counterpunch*, July 30, 2012, www.counterpunch.org/2011/07/30whose-black-president/; Paul Street, *The Empire's New Clothes: Barack Obama in the Real World of Power* (Boulder, CO: Paradigm Publishers, 2010), 9–45, 109–127.

40. William Greider, "Obama Asked Us to Speak but Is He Listening?," *Washington Post*, March 22, 2009.

41. John Cassidy, "What Good Is Wall Street?," *New Yorker*, November 29, 2010, www .newyorker.com/reporting/2010/11/29/101129fa_fact_cassidy.

42. Chrystia Freeland, "Super-Rich Irony," *New Yorker*, October 8, 2012, www .newyorker.com/reporting/2012/10/08/121008fa_fact_freeland.

43. Chrystia Freeland, "Obama, the Super-Rich, and the Election," Reuters, November 9, 2012, http://blogs.reuters.com/chrystia-freeland/2012/11/09/obama-the-super-rich -and-the-election/.

44. Chrystia Freeland, *Plutocrats: The Rise of the New Global Super Rich and the Fall of Everyone Else* (New York: Penguin, 2012), x; emphasis added.

45. Quoted in Jacob Hacker and Paul Pierson, *Winner-Take-All Politics: How Washington Made the Rich Richer and Turned Its Back on the Middle Class* (New York: Simon and Schuster, 2010), 75.

46. Doug Henwood, "Would You Like Change with That?," *Left Business Observer*, No. 117 (March 2008), www.leftbusinessobserver.com/Obama.html.

47. Noam Chomsky, *Interventions* (San Francisco: City Lights Books, 2007), 97.

48. Paul Street, "Dorothy and the Occupiers vs. the Wizard of Ozbama and the Power behind the Curtain," *ZNet*, November 5, 2011, www.zcommunications.org/dorothy -and-the-occupiers-vs-the-wizard-of-ozbama-and-the-power-behind-the-curtain-by-paul -street.

49. Ryan Griffin, "Dick Durbin: Banks 'Frankly Own the Place,'" *Huffington Post*, May 30, 2009, www.huffingtonpost.com/2009/04/20/dick-durbin-banks-frankly_n_193010.html; emphasis added.

50. Jill Stein, "Obama Budget Throws American People Under the Bus," April 11, 2013, www.jillstein.org/obama_budget.

51. Noam Chomsky, "America in Decline," *New York Times Syndicate*, August 5, 2011, reprinted in Noam Chomsky, *Making the Future: Occupations, Interventions, Empire, and Resistance* (San Francisco: City Lights Books, 2012), 285–286.

52. George Packer, "The Broken Contract: Inequality and American Decline," *Foreign Affairs* (November–December 2011), www.foreignaffairs.com/articles/136402/george-packer /the-broken-contract; emphasis added.

53. Justin Hardy, "We Are the 99 Percent," December 22, 2011, http://wearethe99per-cent .tumblr.com/post/14640198372/im-just-as-tired-as-everyone-else-there-is-a; emphasis added.

54. Joseph E. Stiglitz, *The Price of Inequality* (New York: W. W. Norton, 2012), x, xix.

55. Stiglitz, *Price of Inequality*, 345n4.

56. Marjorie Connely, "Occupy Protestors Down on Obama, Survey Finds," *New York Times*, October 28, 2011.

57. Carl Franzen, "Occupy Wall Street Demographics Will Surprise You," Talking Points Memo, October 19, 2011, http://idealab.talkingpointsmemo.com/2011/10/occupy -wall-street-demographic-survey-results-will-surprise-you.php.

58. Anna Sale, "Unlike Tea Party, Wall Street Protests Ignore Electoral Politics," WNYC Radio, October 7, 2011, www.wnyc.org/articles/its-free-country/2011/oct/07/unlike-tea -party-wall-street-protests-ignore-electoral-politics/; emphases added.

59. Leo Gerard, "Party of Entitled Rich Threatens Economy," *Huffington Post*, November 19, 2012, www.huffingtonpost.com/leo-w-gerard/party-of-entitled-rich-th_b_2154693.html.

60. Barack Obama, "Remarks by the President on the Economy in Osawatomie, Kansas," December 6, 2011, www.whitehouse.gov/the-press-office/2011/12/06/remarks -president-economy-osawatomie-kansas.

61. Obama would repeat the basic populist-sounding "middle class" vs. the wealthy theme of the Osawatomie speech during a spate of addresses to middle American audiences in late July 2013. The speeches contained little if any policy muscle, amounting largely to an effort to soften up the populace for a new round of unpopular austerity coming in the fall of that year. See Jack Rasmus, "Obama's Speaking Tour: More 'Talk the Talk' Again," JackRasmus.com, July 23, 2013, http://jackrasmus.com/; and Paul Street, "The Obama Disgrace Deepens," *ZNet*, July 28, 2013, www.zcommunications.org/the-obama-disgrace-deepens-by-paul-street.

62. Tami Luhby, "Romney: 'I'm Not Concerned about the Very Poor,'" CNNMoney, February 1, 2012, http://money.cnn.com/2012/02/01/news/economy/romney_poor/index .htm.

63. Ezra Klein, "Romney's Theory of the 'Taker Class,' and Why It Matters," *Wonkblog, Washington Post*, September 17, 2012, www.washingtonpost.com/blogs/wonkblog/wp /2012/09/17/romneys-theory-of-the-taker-class-and-why-it-matters/; Maureen Dowd, "Let Them Eat Crab Cake," *New York Times*, September 19, 2012, A27; Frank Bruni, "Mitt's Mortification," *New York Times*, September 28, 2012.

64. Paul Street, "The Plutocrats Keep Their Shirts," *Z Magazine*, January 2013; Gerard, "Party of Entitled Rich"; Lynn Stuart Parramore, "The People Who Elected Obama Don't Want Cuts to Social Security and Medicare," *Alternet*, November 7, 2012, www.alternet.org /election-2012/people-who-elected-obama-dont-want-cuts-social-security-and-medicare; Democracy Corps/Campaign for America's Future, "The Real Mandate: CAF/Democracy Corps Election Poll 2012," November 8, 2012, www.ourfuture.org/report/2012114508 /cafdemocracy-corps-election-poll-2012.

65. Barack Obama, "Transcript of Barack Obama's Election Night Speech," *New York Times*, November 7, 2012, www.nytimes.com/2012/11/07/us/politics/transcript-of-president -obamas-election-night-speech.html?pagewanted=all; emphasis added.

66. Organization for Security and Cooperation in Europe, Office for Democratic Institutions and Human Rights, *United States of America: General Elections, November 6, 2012*, www.osce.org/odihr/elections/99573.

67. Paul Street, "Elections 2012 v. Issues That Matter: Reflections on the Latest Quadrennial Extravaganza," *Z Magazine*, December 2012, 5–6.

68. Freeland, "Obama, the Super-Rich, and the Election."

69. "The 2012 Money Race," *New York Times*, http://elections.nytimes.com/2012/campaign-finance, accessed April 11, 2013.

70. Toby Harnden, "Obama Has Held More Re-Election Fundraisers Than 5 Previous Presidents Combined," *Daily Mail* [UK], April 29, 2012, www.dailymail.co.uk/news/article-2136851/Obama-held-fundraisers-previous-Presidents-combined-visits-key-swing-states-permanent-campaign.html.

71. L. Gordon Crovitz, "Obama's 'Big Data' Victory," *Wall Street Journal*, November 19, 2012.

72. Street, "Elections 2012"; Bruce Dixon, "Closer Than You Think: Top 15 Things Romney and Obama Agree On," *Black Agenda Report*, August 29, 2012, http://blackagendareport.com/content/closer-you-think-top-15-things-romney-and-obama-agree.

73. Public Campaign, *Un-Shared Sacrifice: How "Fix the Debt" Companies Buy Washington Influence and Rig the Game*, November 2012, www.publicampaign.org/reports/unsharedsacrifice; emphasis added.

74. Paul Krugman, *End This Depression Now!* (New York: W. W. Norton, 2012), 130–149; Stiglitz, *Price of Inequality*, 208–211, 216–217.

75. CBS Evening News, "Goldman Sachs CEO: Entitlements Must Be Contained," November 19, 2012, www.cbsnews.com/8301-18563_162-57552173/goldman-sachs-ceo-entitlements-must-be-contained/.

76. For more details, sources, and commentary, see Paul Street, "Rising Above with Disdain: On Class Rule and 'the Fiscal Cliff,'" *ZNet*, December 8, 2012, www.zcommunications.org/rising-above-with-disdain-class-entitlement-and-the-fiscal-cliff-by-paul-street.

77. Roger Bybee, "CEOs Say Slash Safety Net at Bottom of Fiscal Cliff," *Progressive*, December 4, 2012, www.progressive.org/ceo-s-say-slash-safety-net-at-bottom-of-fiscal-cliff.

78. This is a more accurate term than "deficit hawks" when it comes to describing the powerful Washington lobbying and propaganda complex that purports to be obsessed with the federal deficit. The complex has never been serious about reducing the deficit, as is clear from its long-standing attachment to cutting government revenues by slashing taxes for the wealthy few. As Krugman observes, "recent events have … demonstrated what was already apparent to careful observers: the deficit-scold movement was never really about deficits. It was about using deficit fears to shred the social safety net." Paul Krugman, "Hawks and Hypocrites," *New York Times*, November 12, 2012, A29.

79. Christie Wilkins, "'Fix the Debt' CEOs Underfund Employee Retirement, Demand Cuts for Elderly," *Huffington Post*, November 27, 2012, www.huffingtonpost.com/2012/11/27/fix-the-debt-ceo-retirement-cuts-elderly_n_2195461.html.

80. Jack Rasmus, "The Three Faces of the Fiscal Cliff," *Z Magazine*, January 2013, 38–43.

81. Jill Stein, "Fig Leaf: The Real Obama Emerges, Again," *Z Magazine*, March 2013, 5.

82. Stein, "Fig Leaf," 5–6.

83. Stein, "Fig Leaf," 5; "Social Security Keeps Seniors Out of Poverty," *Face the Facts: A Project of George Washington University*, November 17, 2012, www.facethefactsusa.org/facts/all-that-stands-between-many-seniors-and-poverty/.

84. Katrina vanden Heuvel is quoted in "Already? Obama Tells Supporters to Expect Bitter Pills," *Common Dreams*, November 14, 2012, www.commondreams.org/headline /2012/11/14.

85. "Joseph Stiglitz: 'This Deficit Fetishism Is Killing Our Economy,'" Associated Press, August 9, 2012, www.huffingtonpost.com/2012/08/09/joseph-stiglitz-inequality_n_1760296 .html.

86. Stein, "Obama Budget."

87. Jack Rasmus, "Who Really Won the November 2012 Election?," *ZNet*, November 10, 2012, www.zcommunications.org/who-really-won-the-november-2012-election-by-jack-rasmus; emphasis added.

88. Joel Geier, "Capitalism's Long Crisis," *International Socialist Review* 88 (March–April 2013): 1–6; Paul Street, "Profits System 101," *ZNet*, April 19, 2013, www.zcommunications .org/profits-system-101-by-paul-street.

89. Donald L. Barlett and James B. Steele, *The Betrayal of the American Dream* (New York: Public Affairs, 2012), xiii; emphasis added.

90. Public Broadcasting System, *PBS NewsHour*, "Fundraising Rules Change for 2013 Presidential Inauguration Ceremonies," airdate January 14, 2013.

91. Peter Rugh, "Historic Rally Pushes Climate Change," *Z Magazine*, April 2013, 15.

92. Rugh, "Historic Rally," 15.

93. Paul Street, "Military Keynesianism Survives Sequestration," *Z Magazine*, May 2013, 20.

94. Stein, "Obama Budget"; "Top Ten Facts about Social Security," Center of Budget and Policy Priorities, November 6, 2012, www.cbpp.org/cms/?fa=view&id=3261.

95. Stein, "Obama Budget."

96. "The Kingfish [Huey Long] had a primal understanding of the essence of American politics. That essence, when distilled, consists of the manipulation of populism by elitism. That elite is most successful," Hitchens wrote in 1999, "which can claim the heartiest allegiance of the fickle crowd; can present itself as most 'in touch' with popular concerns; can anticipate the tides and pulses of public opinion; can, in short, be the least apparently 'elitist.' It's no great distance from Huey Long's robust cry of 'Every man a king' to the insipid 'inclusiveness' of [Bill Clinton's slogan] 'Putting People First,' but the smarter elite managers have learned in the interlude that solid, measurable pledges have to be distinguished by a 'reserve' tag that earmarks them for the bankrollers and backers." Christopher Hitchens, *No One Left to Lie To: The Values of the Worst Family* (New York: Verso, 2000), 17–18.

Chapter 2

1. Richard B. Freeman, *America Works: Critical Thoughts on the Exceptional US Labor Market* (New York: Russell Sage Foundation, 2007), 44.

2. For details and sources, see Paul Street, "Anti-Plutocracy Is as American as Apple Pie: A Short History of American Populist Anger," *ZNet*, May 3, 2013, www.zcommunications .org/anti-plutocracy-is-as-american-as-apple-pie-a-short-of-history-of-american-populist -anger-by-paul-street.

3. Jeffrey Williamson and Peter Lindert, *American Inequality: A Macroeconomic History* (New York: Academic Press, 1980), 33.

4. Kevin Phillips, *Wealth and Democracy: A Political History of the American Rich* (New York: Broadway, 2002), 43.

5. Edward N. Wolff, *Top Heavy: A Study of the Increasing Inequality of Wealth in America* (New York: The New Press, 2002), 83.

6. Phillips, *Wealth and Democracy*, 63.

7. Judith Stein, *Pivotal Decade: How the United States Traded Factories for Finance during the 1970s* (New Haven, CT: Yale University Press, 2010), 2.

8. "'One Third of a Nation': FDR's Second Inaugural Address," January 20, 1937. History Matters, http://historymatters.gmu.edu/d/5105.

9. Williamson and Lindert, *American Inequality*, 33.

10. Claudia Goldin and Robert Margo, "The Great Compression: The Wage Structure of the United States at Mid-Century," *Quarterly Journal of Economics*, Vol. 107, No. 1 (1992): 1–39; Stein, *Pivotal Decade*, xi.

11. Paul Krugman, *The Conscience of a Liberal* (New York: W. W. Norton, 2007), 40–43; Wolff, *Top Heavy*, 80; Goldin and Margo, "Great Compression."

12. Joseph E. Stiglitz, *The Price of Inequality* (New York: W. W. Norton, 2012), 4.

13. Howard Zinn, *Postwar America, 1945–1971* (Indianapolis, IN: Bobbs-Merrill, 1973), 90–94; Godfrey Hodgson, *America in Our Time: From World War II to Nixon: What Happened and Why* (New York: Vintage, 1976), 83–85; Gabriel Kolko, *Wealth and Power in America: An Analysis of Social Class and Income Distribution* (New York: Praeger, 1962); Herman Miller, *Rich Man, Poor Man* (New York: Signet, 1965); Richard Parker, *The Myth of the Middle Class* (New York: Liveright, 1972); Michael Harrington, *The Other America* (New York: Penguin, 1964).

14. Zinn, *Postwar America*, 92–93.

15. Zinn, *Postwar America*, 93.

16. Stein, *Pivotal Decade*, 14–15.

17. Stein, *Pivotal Decade*, 13.

18. Claudia Goldin and Lawrence Katz, "Long-Run Changes in the US Wage Structure: Narrowing, Widening, Polarizing," September 2007, www.economics.harvard.edu/faculty/katz/files/GoldinKarz_BNWP-1107.pdf.

19. Krugman, *The Conscience of a Liberal*, 38–39, 55; emphasis added.

20. Krugman, *The Conscience of a Liberal*, 44.

21. Krugman, *The Conscience of a Liberal*, 44.

22. Irving Kristol, *Wall Street Journal*, December 18, 1997, A22.

23. Krugman, *The Conscience of a Liberal*, 44.

24. Melvyn Dubofsky and Athan Theoharis, *Imperial Democracy: The United States since 1945* (Englewood Cliffs, NJ: Prentice-Hall, 1988), 72.

25. Williamson and Lindert, *American Inequality*, 33, 63.

26. Hedrick Smith, *Who Stole the American Dream?* (New York: Random House, 2012), 100.

27. Ron Suskind, *Confidence Men: Wall Street, Washington, and the Education of a President* (New York: HarperCollins, 2011), 62.

28. Wolff, *Top Heavy*, 8–9; CNNMoney, "American Dream Deferred," October 29, 2011, http://money.cnn.com/2011/10/20/news/economy/occupy_wall_street_income/index.htm.

29. Smith, *Who Stole the American Dream?*, xv, citing Emmanuel Saez, "Striking It Richer: The Evolution of Top Incomes in the United States (Updated with 2008 Estimates)," Working Paper (Berkeley: Institute for Research on Labor and Employment, University of California at Berkeley), July 17, 2010.

30. Roger Bybee, "The War on Wages," *Z Magazine*, December 2012, 26.

31. Stiglitz, *Price of Inequality*, 4; emphasis added.

32. Smith, *Who Stole the American Dream?*, 101.

33. Truth-O-Meter, "Michael Moore Says 400 Americans Have More Wealth Than Half of All Americans Combined," *Journal-Sentinel PolitiFact Wisconsin*, March 2011, www.politifact.com/wisconsin/statements/2011/mar/10/michael-moore/michael-moore-says-400-americans-have-more-wealth-.

34. Nicholas Kristof, "America's Primal Scream," *New York Times*, October 15, 2011, www.nytimes.com/2011/10/16/opinion/sunday/kristof-americas-primal-scream.html?_r=0.

35. Michael Norton and Dan Ariely, "Building a Better America One Wealth Quintile at a Time," *Perspectives on Psychological Science*, Vol. 6, No. 1 (January 2011): 9–12.

36. Sylvia Allegretto, "The Few, the Proud, the Very Rich," The Berkeley Blog, December 5, 2011, http://blogs.berkeley.edu/2011/12/05/the-few-the-proud-the-very-rich/.

37. *Tampa Bay Times*, "Bernie Sanders Says Walmart Heirs Own More Wealth Than Bottom 40 Percent of Americans," *PolitiFact.com*, July 31, 2012, www.politifact.com/truth-o-meter /statements/2012/jul/31/bernie-s/sanders-says-walmart-heirs-own-more-wealth-bottom-.

38. Robert Reich, Foreword, in Richard Wilkinson and Kate Pickett, *The Spirit Level: Why Greater Equality Makes Societies Stronger* (New York: Bloomsbury, 2010), x.

39. Robert Frank, *The High-Beta Rich* (New York: Crown, 2011), 9; emphasis added.

40. Chrystia Freeland, "The Rise of the New Global Elite," *Atlantic*, January/February 2011, www.theatlantic.com/magazine/archive/2011/01/the-rise-of-the-new-global-elite /308343/; emphasis added.

41. Robert Frank, *Richistan: A Journey through the American Wealth Boom and the Lives of the New Rich* (New York: Crown, 2007), 2–3; emphasis added.

42. Frank, *Richistan*, 3–4; emphasis added.

43. Frank, *Richistan*, 3–4.

44. Larry Samuel, *Rich: The Rise and Fall of American Wealth Culture* (New York: American Management Association, 2009), 229.

45. Samuel, *Rich*, 229–230.

46. Samuel, *Rich*, 229.

47. Samuel, *Rich*, 234.

48. Phillips, *Wealth and Democracy*, 359.

49. Bruce Nussbaum, "The Summer of Wretched Excess," *BusinessWeek*, August 2, 1998, www.businessweek.com/printer/articles/61950-commentary-the-summer-of-wretched -excess?type=old_article.

50. Jeff Madrick, "The Anti-Economist: Half Empty," *Harper's Magazine*, December 2012, 11; Robert Reich, *Beyond Outrage: What Has Gone Wrong with Our Economy and Our Democracy and How to Fix It* (New York: Vintage, 2012), xiii.

51. Pew Research Center, *Lost Decade of the Middle Class*, August 22, 2012, www .pewsocialtrends.org/2012/08/22/the-lost-decade-of-the-middle-class/.

52. Stiglitz, *Price of Inequality*, 14; Jacob S. Hacker and Paul Pierson, *Winner-Take-All Politics: How Washington Made the Rich Richer and Turned Its Back on the Middle Class* (New York: Simon and Schuster, 2010), 22.

53. Madrick, "The Anti-Economist," 11.

54. Stiglitz, *Price of Inequality*, 13; Hacker and Pierson, *Winner-Take-All Politics*, 30–31.

55. Madrick, "The Anti-Economist," 11.

56. Frank, *High-Beta Rich*, 156; Noam Chomsky, *Making the Future: Occupations, Interventions, Empire, and Resistance* (San Francisco: City Lights Books, 2012), 303–304.

57. Robert Frank, "U.S. Economy Is Increasingly Tied to the Rich," *Wall Street Journal*, August 5, 2010; Frank, *High-Beta Rich*, 157.

58. Smith, *Who Stole the American Dream?*, 104.

59. Stiglitz, *Price of Inequality*, 22.

60. Freeman, *America Works*, 44; emphasis added.

61. Uri Dadush and Kemal Dervis, "The Inequality Challenge," *Current History*, Vol. 112, No. 750 (January 2013): 14.

62. Nicholas D. Kristof, "Our Banana Republic," *New York Times*, November 6, 2010; Kristof, "A Hedge Fund Republic?," *New York Times*, December 17, 2010. The block quote comes from the later column.

63. Stiglitz, *Price of Inequality*, 23.

64. Josh Bivens, *Failure by Design: The Story of America's Broken Economy* (Ithaca, NY: Cornell University Press, 2011), 73.

65. Stiglitz, *Price of Inequality*, 16.

66. Stiglitz, *Price of Inequality*, 14.

67. Bivens, *Failure by Design*, 71, 73.

68. Among the EPI's many annual volumes, see Lawrence Mishel and Jared Bernstein, *The State of Working America, 1992–93* (New York: M. E. Sharpe, 1993), 439–443; Lawrence Mishel, Jared Bernstein, and Heather Boushey, *The State of Working America, 2002–03* (Ithaca, NY: Cornell University Press, 2003), 416–419; Lawrence Mishel, Jared Bernstein, and Heidi Schierhoz, *The State of Working America, 2008–09* (Ithaca, NY: Cornell University Press, 2009), 108–110.

69. Stiglitz, *Price of Inequality*, 17–18, 307–308.

70. Dadush and Dervis, "Inequality Challenge," 17.

71. Alan B. Kreuger, "The Rise and Consequences of Inequality in the United States," address delivered at the Center for American Progress, January 12, 2012; Dadush and Dervis, "Inequality Challenge," 17.

72. Stiglitz, *Price of Inequality*, 19.

73. Stiglitz, *Price of Inequality*, 18; Kreuger, "The Rise and Consequences."

74. Suskind, *Confidence Men*, 16; Bivens, *Failure by Design*, 65, 70.

75. Ha Joon Chang, *23 Things They Don't Tell You about Capitalism* (New York: Bloomsbury, 2010), 137–147.

76. Kristof, "America's Primal Scream."

77. Chang, *23 Things*, 146 and passim; Paul Street, "Capitalism: The Real Enemy," 9–22 in Francis Goldin, Debby Smith, Michael Steven Smith, and Steven Wishnia, eds., *Imagine: Living in a Socialist USA* (New York: HarperCollins, 2013).

78. For recent iterations in relation to the 2007–2009 Great Recession and the ongoing economic crisis, see John Bellamy Foster and Fred Magdoff, *The Great Financial Crisis: Causes and Consequences* (New York: Monthly Review Press, 2009); Fred Magdoff and Michael D. Yates, *The ABCs of the Economic Crisis* (New York: Monthly Review Press, 2009).

79. Magdoff and Yates, *The ABCs*, 60.

80. Magdoff and Yates, *The ABCs*, 55–104; Foster and Magdoff, *The Great Financial Crisis*, 27–109; David McNally, *Global Slump* (Oakland, CA: PM Press, 2011), 1–24, 121–127.

81. Hacker and Pierson, *Winner-Take-All-Politics*, 31–33.

82. Frank, *High-Beta Rich*, 11.

83. Stephanie Clifford, "Even Marked Up, Luxury Goods Fly Off Shelves," *New York Times*, August 3, 2011, www.nytimes.com/2011/08/04/business/sales-of-luxury-goods-are-recovering-strongly.html.

84. Elizabeth Kneebone et al., *The Re-Emergence of Concentrated Poverty: Metropolitan Trends*, Brookings Institution, November 4, 2011, 2, www.brookings.edu/~/media/Files/rc/papers/2011/1103_poverty_kneebone_nadeau_berube/1103_poverty_kneebone_nadeau_berube.pdf.

85. Jason DeParle et al., "Older, Suburban, and Struggling, 'Near Poor' Startle the Census," *New York Times*, November 18, 2011.

86. CBS News, "Census Data: Half of U.S. Poor or Low Income," December 15, 2011, www.cbsnews.com/8301-201_162-57343397/census-data-half-of-u.s-poor-or-low-income/.

87. Ashley Portero, "U.S. Poverty Data: 1 in 15 Live in Extreme Poverty—A Record," *International Business Times*, November 4, 2011, www.ibtimes.com/articles/243600/20111104/u-s-poverty-data-1-15-live.htm.

88. McNally, *Global Slump*, 125–126.

89. Rich Morin and Seth Motel, "A Third of Americans Now Say They Are in the Lower Classes," Pew Research Canter, September 10, 2012, www.pewsocialtrends.org/2012/09/10/a-third-of-americans-now-say-they-are-in-the-lower-classes/.

90. Jim Rutenberg and Jeff Zeleny, "Obama Mines for Voters with High-Tech Tools," *New York Times*, March 8, 2012, www.nytimes.com/2012/03/08/us/politics /obama-campaigns-vast-effort-to-re-enlist-08-supporters.html?pagewanted=all; emphasis added.

91. Tavis Smiley and Cornel West, *The Rich and the Rest of Us: A Poverty Manifesto* (New York: Smiley Publications, 2012), 13–14.

92. Amanda Censky, "How the Middle Class Became the Underclass," CNNMoney, February 16, 2011, http://money.cnn.com/2011/02/16/news/economy/middle_class, cited in Smiley and West, *The Rich and the Rest of Us*, 211.

93. Barbara Ehrenreich and John Ehrenreich, "The 1 Percent, Revealed," *Mother Jones*, December 15, 2011, www.motherjones.com/politics/2011/12/class-warfare-explained -superrich-one-percent?page=1.

94. Frank, *High-Beta Rich*, 11.

95. Joe Nocera, "Romney and the Forbes 400," *New York Times*, September 25, 2012, A21.

96. Samuel, *Rich*, 260–261.

97. Emmanuel Saez, "Striking It Richer: The Evolution of Top Incomes in the United States (Updated with 2009 and 2010 Estimates)," Working Paper (Berkeley: Institute for Research on Labor and Employment, University of California at Berkeley), March 2, 2012, elsa.berkeley.edu/~saez/saez-UStopincome-2010.pdf, cited in Smith, *Who Stole the American Dream?*, xv, 446.

98. Quoted in Sam Pizzigati, "Madison Avenue Declares 'Mass Affluence' Over," *Campaign for America's Future*, May 30, 2011, www.ourfuture.org/print/67690.

99. Pizzigati, "Madison Avenue Declares 'Mass Affluence' Over."

100. Pizzigati, "Madison Avenue Declares 'Mass Affluence' Over"; Paul Solman, "What Happens to a Dream Betrayed? Authors Blame Trade for Middle Class Demise," *PBS News-Hour*, October 16, 2012, www.pbs.org/newshour/bb/business/july-dec12/makingsense_10-16 .html.

101. Fareed Zakaria, GPS, October 24, 2011, http://globalpublicsquare.blogs.cnn .com/2011/10/24/irving-kristol-why-inequality-doesnt-matter/.

102. Chris Hedges, "America Is a Tinderbox," Real News Network, July 24, 2013, http://therealnews.com/t2/index.php?option=com_content&task=view&id=31&Itemid=74 &jumival=10461.

103. US Council on Foreign Relations, *Iraq: The Day After* (Washington, DC: CFR, 2003), 48, www.cfr.org/iraq/iraq-day-after/p6075.

104. Paul Street, "The United States as a Broken Society," *Z Magazine*, May 2012, 26–29.

105. Richard Wilkinson and Kate Pickett, *The Spirit Level: Why Greater Equality Makes Societies Stronger* (New York: Bloomsbury, 2010).

106. Wilkinson and Pickett, *Spirit Level*, 166.

107. Marc Mauer, *Race to Incarcerate* (New York: The New Press, 1999); Paul Street, *The Vicious Circle: Race, Prison, Jobs, and Community* (Chicago: Chicago Urban League, 2002); Paul Street, "Color Bind," 30–40 in Tara Herivel and Paul Wright, *Prison Nation: The Warehousing of America's Poor* (New York: Routledge, 2003); Michelle Alexander, *The New Jim Crow: Mass Incarceration in the Age of Colorblindness* (New York: The New Press, 2010).

108. Wilkinson and Pickett, *Spirit Level*, 173.

109. Wilkinson and Pickett, *Spirit Level*, 176–177.

110. Wilkinson and Pickett, *Spirit Level*, 371–372.

111. Massachusetts Institute of Technology (MIT), "Climate Change Odds Much Worse Than Thought: New Analysis Shows Warming Could Be Double Previous Estimates," *MIT News*, May 19, 2009, http://web.mit.edu/newsoffice/2009/roulette-0519.html#.

112. Common Dreams Staff, "Earth Facing Imminent Environmental Tipping Point: Report," *Common Dreams*, June 7, 2012, www.commondreams.org/headline/2012/06/07-3. On the current grave and deepening environmental crisis, see John Bellamy Foster, Brett Clark, and Richard York, *The Ecological Rift: Capitalism's War on the Planet* (New York: Monthly Review Press, 2010); MIT, "Climate Change Odds"; Bill McKibben, *Eaarth: Making Life on a Tough New Planet* (New York: Times Books, 2010); Mark Lynas, *Six Degrees: Our Future on a Hotter Planet* (London: Fourth Estate, 2007); Chris Williams, *Ecology and Socialism: Solutions to Capitalist Ecological Crisis* (Chicago: Haymarket, 2010); James Gustav Speth, *The Bridge at the End of the World: Capitalism, the Environment, and Crossing from Crisis to Sustainability* (New Haven, CT: Yale University Press, 2008); Herve Kempf, *How the Rich Are Destroying the Earth* (White River Junction, VT: Chelsea Green, 2007).

113. McKibben, *Eaarth*, 13–15.

114. John Bellamy Foster and Brett Clark, "The Planetary Emergency," *Monthly Review*, Vol. 54, Issue 7 (December 2012), http://monthlyreview.org/2012/12/01/the -planetary-emergency; Paul Street and Janet Razbadouski, "The Ecological Poverty of Liberal Economics," *ZNet*, August 12, 2012, www.zcommunications.org/the-ecological -poverty-of-liberal-economics-by-paul-street; Paul Street, "Less Than Zero: The 1% and the Fate of the Earth," *ZNet*, December 9, 2011, www.zcommunications.org/less -than-zero-the-1-percent-and-the-fate-of-the-earth-by-paul-street.

115. Kempf, *How the Rich Are Destroying the Earth*, 70, 73.

116. Wallich and Monbiot are quoted in William Greider, *Come Home America: The Rise and Fall (and Redeeming Promise) of Our Country* (New York: Rodale, 2009), 202.

117. Greider, *Come Home America*, 202.

118. Quoted in Kempf, *How the Rich Are Destroying the Earth*, 63–64.

119. Wilkinson and Pickett, *Spirit Level*, 230; Juliet Schor, *The Overspent American* (New York: Basic Books, 1998), 3–109.

120. Jeff Faux, *The Servant Economy: Where America's Elite Is Sending the Middle Class* (New York: John Wiley and Sons, 2012), 174.

121. The intimate connection between climate change and the short-term time frame of capitalism and US politics is at the heart of Charles Derber's important book *Greed to Green: Solving Climate Change and Remaking the Economy* (Boulder, CO: Paradigm Publishers, 2010).

122. McKibben, *Eaarth*, 81.

123. Ricardo Levins-Morales, "Revolution in the Time of Hamsters," *ZNet*, September 1, 2009, www.zcommunications.org/revolution-in-the-time-of-the-hamsters -by-ricardo-levins-morales.

124. Noam Chomsky, "Plutonomy and the Precariat," *Huffington Post*, May 8, 2012, www .huffingtonpost.com/noam-chomsky/plutonomy-and-the-precari_b_1499246.html.

Chapter 3

1. Josh Bivens, *Failure by Design: The Story of America's Broken Economy* (Ithaca, NY: Cornell University Press, 2011), 3–4.

2. Chrystia Freeland, "Super-Rich Irony," *New Yorker*, October 8, 2012, www .newyorker.com/reporting/2012/10/08/121008fa_fact_freeland; emphasis added.

3. A useful Web-linked compendium of the elite skills gap consensus is SitkaPacific investment adviser Mike Shedlock, "Obama to Close 'Skills Gap'; Where?," MISH's Global Economic Trend Analysis, November 27, 2012, http://globaleconomicanalysis.blogspot .com/2012/11/obama-to-close-skills-gap-where-how-why.html. Quote from Hedrick Smith, *Who Stole the American Dream?* (New York: Random House, 2012), 104.

4. "American Workers Better Off in 1979 Than Those Today," *Employment Spectator*, August 2012, www.employmentspectator.com/2012/08/american-workers-in-1979-were-better-off-than-those-today-where-have-the-jobs-disappeared/.

5. John Schmidt and Janelle Jones, *Where Have All the Good Jobs Gone?* (Washington, DC: Center for Economic and Policy Research, 2012), www.cepr.net/documents/publications/good-jobs-2012-07.pdf.

6. Ha Joon Chang, *23 Things They Don't Tell You about Capitalism* (New York: Bloomsbury, 2010), 178–179.

7. Jacob S. Hacker and Paul Pierson, *Winner-Take-All Politics: How Washington Made the Rich Richer and Turned Its Back on the Middle Class* (New York: Simon and Schuster, 2010), 35.

8. Judith Stein, *Pivotal Decade: How the United States Traded Factories for Finance during the 1970s* (New Haven, CT: Yale University Press, 2010), 280.

9. Stein, *Pivotal Decade*, 295; J. Michael Donnelly, Congressional Research Service, *Report for Congress: U.S.-World Merchandise Trade Data, 1948–2006* (Washington, DC: Congressional Research Service, February 23, 2007), CRS-5. The first US merchandise trade deficit ($1.4 billion) after World War II came in 1971. The deficit "skyrocketed" (Stein) in the 1990s and through the early 2000s.

10. Schmidt and Jones, *Where Have All the Good Jobs Gone?* The authors calculate that just less than a quarter (24.6 percent) of US employment positions counted as "good jobs" in 2010, down from 27.4 percent in 1979.

11. Hacker and Pierson, *Winner-Take-All Politics*, 35–36.

12. Smith, *Who Stole the American Dream?*, 105.

13. Stein, *Pivotal Decade*, 280.

14. Smith, *Who Stole the American Dream?*, 104–105. "After all," Judith Stein writes, "why didn't Europe experience growing income inequality despite its use of technology?" Stein, *Pivotal Decade*, 280.

15. Shedlock, "Obama to Close 'Skills Gap'"; Roger Bybee, "Elites Push the Skills Gap Myth," *Z Magazine*, April 2013, 23, 25.

16. Marc Levine, *The Skills Gap and Unemployment in Wisconsin: Separating Fact from Fiction*, University of Wisconsin at Milwaukee, Center for Economic Development, www4.uwm.edu/ced/publications/skillsgap_2013-2.pdf.

17. Bybee, "Elites Push Skills Gap," 22.

18. Transcript of Marc Rubio's speech at the RNC, August 30, 2012, www.foxnews.com/politics/2012/08/30/transcript-marco-rubio-speech-at-rnc/.

19. Bivens, *Failure by Design*, 70.

20. Quoted in David McNally, *Monsters of the Market: Zombies, Vampires, and Global Capitalism* (Leiden, Netherlands: Brill, 2011), 69.

21. Joseph E. Stiglitz, *The Price of Inequality* (New York: W. W. Norton, 2012), xx.

22. David Harvey, *The New Imperialism* (New York: Oxford University Press, 2003), 45, 67, 137–182; quotation from 182. On "robbery" and "the original accumulation," see Karl Marx, *Capital, Volume 1* (New York: Penguin Classics, 1990 [1867]), 873–904.

23. Stiglitz, *Price of Inequality*, 28–51.

24. Stiglitz, *Price of Inequality*, 49.

25. Stiglitz, *Price of Inequality*, 31–32.

26. Bivens, *Failure by Design*, 3–4, 51, 55–92; Stiglitz, *Price of Inequality*, 28–82; Hacker and Pierson, *Winner-Take-All Politics*, 11–72.

27. Stiglitz, *Price of Inequality*, 30.

28. Stiglitz, *Price of Inequality*, 72–73.

29. Stiglitz, *Price of Inequality*, 71.

30. Stiglitz, *Price of Inequality*, 34.

31. Paul Krugman, "Oligarchy, American-Style," *New York Times*, November 4, 2011; Stiglitz, *Price of Inequality*, 118–264; George Packer, "The Broken Contract: Inequality and American Decline," *Foreign Affairs* (November–December 2011), www.foreignaffairs.com /articles/136402/george-packer/the-broken-contract; Barack Obama, "Remarks by the President on the Economy in Osawatomie, Kansas," December 6, 2011, www.whitehouse.gov /the-press-office/2011/12/06/remarks-president-economy-osawatomie-kansas.

32. Karl Marx, *Capital, Volume 3: The Process of Capitalist Production as a Whole* (New York: International, 1967), 211–266; David McNally, *Global Slump* (Oakland, CA: PM Press, 2011), 61–84; Chris Hartman, *Zombie Capitalism: Global Crisis and the Relevance of Marx* (Chicago: Haymarket, 2009), 5–85; Makato Itoh, *Value and Crisis* (New York: Monthly Review Press, 1980); Richard Wolff, *Democracy at Work: A Cure for Capitalism* (Chicago: Haymarket, 2012), 19–52.

33. Bivens, *Failure by Design*, 13.

34. Bivens, *Failure by Design*, 7.

35. Bivens, *Failure by Design*, 97.

36. Pierre Bourdieu, *Acts of Resistance* (New York: Free Press, 1998), 2, 24–44; John Pilger, *The New Rulers of the World* (London: Verso, 2002), 5, 116; Paul Street, *Empire and Inequality: America and the World since 9/11* (Boulder, CO: Paradigm Publishers, 2004), xiii–xiv; Paul Street, "Military Keynesianism Survives Sequester," *Z Magazine*, May 2013.

37. Paul Krugman, *The Conscience of a Liberal* (New York: W. W. Norton, 2007), 46–48.

38. Krugman, *Conscience of a Liberal*, 48–51; Robert Zieger, *American Workers, American Unions: The Twentieth Century* (Baltimore, MD: Johns Hopkins University Press, 2002).

39. Ira Katznelson, *When Affirmative Action Was White: An Untold History of Racial Inequality in Twentieth-Century America* (New York: Norton, 2005), 113–114. The quote in the footnote is from p. 114.

40. Godfrey Hodgson, *America in Our Time: From World War II to Nixon: What Happened and Why* (New York: Vintage, 1976), 3–98, quotations from 51 and 52.

41. Krugman, *Conscience of a Liberal*, 44–53; Charles Maier, *Among Empires: American Ascendancy and Its Predecessors* (Cambridge, MA: Harvard University Press, 2006), 191–237; Eric Hobsbawm, *The Age of Extremes: A History of the World, 1914–1991* (New York: Pantheon, 1994), 258. "By 1913," Hobsbawm notes, "the US had already become the largest economy in the world, producing over one third of its industrial output—just under the combined total for Germany, Great Britain, and France. In 1929 it produced over 42 percent of the total world output, as against just under 28 percent for the three European industrial powers." Hobsbawm, *Age of Extremes*, 97.

42. Wolff, *Democracy at Work*, 95–96.

43. Wolff, *Democracy at Work*, 95–96. On the importance of union decline (a result of employer opposition) to the rightward shift of US politics and policy in the neoliberal era, see Jacob S. Hacker and Paul Pierson, *Off Center: The Republican Revolution and Erosion of American Democracy* (New Haven, CT: Yale University Press, 2007), 115, 194–200; Hacker and Pierson, *Winner-Take-All Politics*, 139–143.

44. Madeline Morgenstern, "'We Built It': The Rallying Cry of the RNC," *The Blaze*, August 30, 2012, www.theblaze.com/stories/2012/08/30/we-built-it-the -rallying-cry-of-the-rnc/.

45. Buffett and Simon are quoted in Peter Singer, "What Should a Billionaire Give—and What Should You?" *New York Times Magazine*, December 17, 2006, 61.

46. Paul Street, "Capitalism: The Real Enemy," 9–22 in Francis Goldin, Debby Smith, Michael Steven Smith, and Steven Wishnia, eds., *Imagine: Living in a Socialist USA* (New York: HarperCollins, 2013).

47. Stiglitz, *Price of Inequality*, 37, 314n13; Paul K. Piff et al., "Higher Social Class Predicts Increased Unethical Behavior," *Proceedings of the National Academy of Sciences*, February 27, 2012.

48. Psychological testing indicates that one in twenty-five Americans is objectively sociopathic, that is, fundamentally devoid of conscience and the capacity to care or empathize with others. See Martha Stout, *The Sociopath Next Door: The Ruthless versus the Rest of Us* (New York: Broadway, 2007), 9.

49. Stiglitz mentions the important case of Tim Berners-Lee. Berners-Lee invented the World Wide Web but has never appeared on the Forbes list. He "could have become a billionaire but chose not to—he made his idea available freely, which greatly speeded up the development of the Internet."

50. McNally, *Global Slump*, 73–74.

51. The maddening complexity and its authoritarian relevance are captured nicely (with no interest in Marxian analysis whatsoever) in Matt Taibbi, *Griftopia: A Story of Bankers, Politicians, and the Most Audacious Power Grab in American History* (New York: Spiegel and Grau, 2010). A useful attempt to explain the current financial complexity to everyday citizens is Les Leopold, *The Looting of America* (White River Junction, VT: Chelsea Green, 2009).

52. Sven Beckert, *The Monied Metropolis: New York City and the Consolidation of the American Bourgeoisie, 1850–1896* (New York: Cambridge University Press, 2001), 17–77, 151–154, 242–243; Sean Willentz, "The Rise of the American Working Class, 1776–1877," 83–151 in J. Carroll Moody and Alice Kessler-Harris, *Perspectives on American Labor History* (DeKalb: Northern Illinois University Press, 1989).

53. Barry Bluestone and Bennett Harrison, *The Deindustrialization of America* (New York: Basic Books, 1982); Stein, *Pivotal Decade*.

Chapter 4

1. Quoted in David Bensman and Roberta Lynch, *Rusted Dreams: Hard Times in a Steel Community* (New York: McGraw-Hill, 1987), 88.

2. John Cassidy, "What Good Is Wall Street?," *New Yorker*, November 2010.

3. Adam Smith quoted and paraphrased in Noam Chomsky, "Crisis and Hope: Theirs and Ours," *Boston Review* (September–October 2009), http://bostonreview.net/BR34.5/chomsky.php; Noam Chomsky, *World Orders Old and New* (New York: Columbia University Press, 1996), 5; Noam Chomsky, *Making the Future: Occupations, Interventions, Empire, and Resistance* (San Francisco: City Lights Books, 2012), 196, 236–237.

4. Quoted in Noam Chomsky, *Turning the Tide: US Intervention in Central America and the Struggle for Peace* (Boston: South End Press, 1985), 45.

5. The title of Stein's latest book, in fact, as cited above.

6. Chomsky, *Making the Future*, 302.

7. Noam Chomsky, "The Plutonomy and the Precariat: On the History of the US Economy in Decline," *Huffington Post*, May 8, 2012, www.tomdispatch.com/archive/175539/.

8. Chomsky, *Making the Future*, 289.

9. Judith Stein, *Pivotal Decade: How the United States Traded Factories for Finance during the 1970s* (New Haven, CT: Yale University Press, 2010), 296.

10. Maxwell Strachan, "Financial Sector Back to Accounting for Nearly One Third of US Profits," *Huffington Post*, March 30, 2011, updated May 30, 2011, www.huffingtonpost.com/2011/03/30/financial-profits-percentage_n_841716.html.

11. Cassidy, "What Good Is Wall Street?"

12. Paul Krugman, "The Competition Myth," *New York Times*, January 24, 2011.

13. Nelson D. Schwartz, "As Wall Street Soars in Tough Era, Company Size Is a Factor," *New York Times*, April 15, 2013, A1, B9.

14. Stein, *Pivotal Decade*, xii.

15. Stein, *Pivotal Decade*, 295.

16. Giovanni Arrighi, *Adam Smith in Beijing: Lineages of the 21st Century* (New York: Verso, 2007), 171–172.

17. Jeff Faux, *The Servant Economy: Where America's Elite Is Sending the Middle Class* (New York: John Wiley and Sons, 2012), 174–175; emphasis added.

18. Louis Uchitelle, "GM Seeks More Imports from Low-Wage Regions," *New York Times*, May 17, 2009; emphasis added.

19. A brilliant account is Ron Suskind, *Confidence Men: Wall Street, Washington, and the Education of a President* (New York: HarperCollins, 2011).

20. Joel Geier, "Capitalism's Long Crisis," *International Socialist Review*, Vol. 88 (March–April 2013), 6.

21. Faux, *Servant Economy*, 174.

22. Faux, *Servant Economy*, 175.

23. Faux, *Servant Economy*, 7.

24. Mike Davis, interviewed by Bill Moyers, Public Broadcasting System, *Bill Moyers' Journal*, May 20, 2009, www.pbs.org/moyers/journal/03202009/watch2.html.

25. Chomsky, "The Plutonomy and the Precariat."

26. Chomsky, *Making the Future*, 303.

27. Dylan Ratigan, *Greedy Bastards: How We Can Stop Corporate Communists, Banksters, and Other Vampires from Sucking Us Dry* (New York: Simon and Schuster, 2012), 36–37.

28. Stein, *Pivotal Decade*, 288.

29. Eric Lipton and Steven Labaton, "The Reckoning: Deregulator Looks Back, Unswayed," *New York Times*, November 16, 2008, www.nytimes.com/2008/11/17/business/economy/17gramm.html?pagewanted=all&_r=0.

30. Ratigan, *Greedy Bastards*, 32–39.

31. Joseph E. Stiglitz, *The Price of Inequality* (New York: W. W. Norton, 2012), 49.

32. Matt Taibbi, *Griftopia: A Story of Bankers, Politicians, and the Most Audacious Power Grab in American History* (New York: Spiegel and Grau, 2010), 21.

33. Ratigan, *Greedy Bastards*, 37.

34. Jacob S. Hacker and Paul Pierson, *Winner-Take-All Politics: How Washington Made the Rich Richer and Turned Its Back on the Middle Class* (New York: Simon and Schuster, 2010), 98–100.

35. Charles Ferguson, *Predator Nation: Corporate Criminals, Political Corruption, and the Hijacking of America* (New York: Crown, 2012), 11–12, 22, 119, 138, 143, 172–188, 207, 246–252, 281, 284; Glenn Greenwald, *With Liberty and Justice for Some* (New York: Metropolitan, 2011), 101–154.

36. Quoted in Ratigan, *Greedy Bastards*, 21.

37. Ron Suskind, *Confidence Men: Wall Street, Washington, and the Education of a President* (New York: HarperCollins, 2011), 231–232.

38. Suskind, *Confidence Men*, 234–235.

39. Suskind, *Confidence Men*, 242; emphasis added.

40. Suskind, *Confidence Men*, 241.

41. Hedrick Smith, *Who Stole the American Dream?* (New York: Random House, 2012), 148–151.

42. Richard Wolff, *Democracy at Work: A Cure for Capitalism* (Chicago: Haymarket, 2012), 75–76; Paul Street, "The Plutocracy Grinds On," *ZNet*, July 25, 2013, www.zcommunications.org/the-plutocracy-grinds-on-by-paul-street; Peter Eavis, "Big Banks, Flooded in Profits, Fear Flurry of New Safeguards," *New York Times*, July 18, 2013, A1, B8.

43. Cassidy, "What Good Is Wall Street?"

44. Les Leopold, *The Looting of America: How Wall Street's Game of Fantasy Finance Destroyed Our Jobs, Pensions, and Prosperity* (White River Junction, VT: Chelsea Green, 2008), 191.

45. Cassidy, "What Good Is Wall Street?"

46. Cassidy, "What Good Is Wall Street?"

47. Taibbi, *Griftopia*, 32.

48. Ratigan, *Greedy Bastards*, 7, 9.

49. Jeff Faux, *The Global Class War: How America's Bipartisan Elite Lost Our Future and What It Will Take to Win It Back* (New York: Wiley, 2006), 1.

50. Christopher Lasch, *The Revolt of the Elites and the Betrayal of Democracy* (New York: Scribner, 1995), 46, quoted in David Rothkopf, *Superclass: The Global Power Elite and the World They Are Making* (New York: Farrar, Straus and Giroux, 2008), 11.

51. Chrystia Freeland, *Plutocrats: The Rise of the New Global Super Rich and the Fall of Everybody Else* (New York: Penguin, 2012), 57–59.

52. Freeland, *Plutocrats*, xiv.

53. Freeland, *Plutocrats*, 58–59.

54. C. Wright Mills, *The Power Elite* (New York: Oxford University Press, 1956), 4.

55. Rothkopf, *Superclass*, 9.

56. Rothkopf, *Superclass*, 7–12.

57. Michael Powell, "Profits Are Booming, Why Aren't Jobs?," *New York Times*, January 8, 2011.

58. Powell, "Profits Are Booming."

59. Pallavi Gogoi, "Where Are the Jobs? For Many Companies, Overseas," Associated Press, December 28, 2010, http://news.yahoo.com/s/ap/20101228/ap_on_re_us/us_overseas _hiring, emphasis added; James R. Hagerty, "Caterpillar Loses Ground in China's Excavator Market," *Wall Street Journal*, July 20, 2011, http://online.wsj.com/article/SB1000142405270 2304567604576454201635431380.html11.

60. Gogoi, "Where Are the Jobs?"

61. Faux, *The Global Class War*, 168.

62. Robert Reich, interviewed by Jeffrey Brown, *PBS NewsHour*, airdate January 21, 2011, www.pbs.org/newshour/bb/business/jan-june11/obamabusiness_01-21.html.

63. For related and further reflections on the address and Obama's relationship to the US corporate and financial sectors, see Paul Street, "State (of) Capitalist Absurdity: Reflections Before and After Obama's State of the Union Address," *ZNet*, January 28, 2011, at www .zcommunications.org/state-of-capitalist-absurdity-reflections-before-and-after-obama-s -state-of-the-union-address-by-paul-street.

64. Donald L. Barlett and James B. Steele, *The Betrayal of the American Dream* (New York: Public Affairs, 2012), 8–9. See also "What Happens to a Dream 'Betrayed'? Authors Blame Trade for Middle Class Demise," *PBS NewsHour*, airdate October 16, 2012, www .pbs. org/newshour/bb/business/july-dec12/makingsense_10-16.html.

65. Chrystia Freeland, "The Rise of the New Global Elite," *Atlantic*, January/February 2011, www.theatlantic.com/magazine/archive/2011/01/the-rise-of-the-new-global-elite/308343/.

66. Freeland, "Rise of the New Global Elite."

67. Freeland, "Rise of the New Global Elite."

68. "A Measure of Justice," *USW@Work* (Winter 2012), 22–23.

69. "A Measure of Justice."

70. Frederick Balfour and Tim Culpan, "The Man Who Makes Your iPhone," *BusinessWeek*, September 9, 2010, www.businessweek.com/magazine/content/10_38 /b4195058423479.htm.

71. Balfour and Culpan, "The Man Who Makes Your iPhone."

72. Alex Kotlowitz, *The Other Side of the River: A Story of Two Towns, a Death, and America's Dilemma* (New York: Doubleday, 1998), 29–31.

73. Jesse Jackson, "Time for an Uprising in Benton Harbor," *Chicago Sun Times*, April 25, 2011, www.suntimes.com/news/jackson/5013203-452/time-for-an-uprisingin-benton -harbor.html; Paul Street, "No Justice, No Peace: A Police Killing and a Riot in Benton Harbor, Michigan," *ZNet*, June 30, 2003, www.zcommunications.org/no-justice-no-peace -a-police-killing-and -a-riot-in-benton-harbor-by-paul-street; Paul Street, "'For the Children': Class, Race, Place, and Late Capitalist Eco-Enclosure in Benton Harbor, Michigan," *ZNet*, September 23, 2007, www.zcommunications.org/for-the-children-class-race-place-and-late -capitalist-eco-enclosure-in-benton-harbor-by-paul-street.

74. Harriet Rowan, "Defying Michigan Voters, Gov. Rick Snyder Takes Over Detroit," *AlterNet*, March 28, 2013, www.alternet.org/news-amp-politics/defying-michigan-voters -gov-rick-snyder-takes-over-detroit; Ashley Woods and David Sands, "'Right to Work' Michigan: Gov. Rick Snyder Says New Legislation Gives Union Workers 'Freedom,'" *Huffington Post*, December 26, 2012, www.huffingtonpost.com/2012/12/06/right-to-work-michigan -snyder-unions_n_2250601.html; John Nichols, "GOP, Koch Brothers Sneak Attack Guts Labor Rights in Michigan," *Nation*, December 6, 2012, www.thenation.com/blog/171641/gop -koch-brothers-sneak-attack-guts-labor-rights-michigan#.

75. Michael Corkery and Matthew Dolan, "Detroit's Bankruptcy Sparks Pension Brawl," *Wall Street Journal*, July 19, 2013, A1, A4.

76. Paul Street, "The Plutocracy Grinds On," *ZNet*, July 25, 2013, www .zcommunications.org/the-plutocracy-grinds-on-by-paul-street.

77. Corkery and Dolan, "Detroit's Bankruptcy."

78. Jane Slaughter, "The Scourging of Detroit," *Counterpunch*, July 23, 2013, www .counterpunch.org/2013/07/23/the-scourging-of-detroit/.

79. Monica Davey and Mary Williams Walsh, "Billions in Debt, Detroit Tumbles into Insolvency," *New York Times*, July 19, 2013, A3; emphasis added.

80. Ratigan, *Greedy Bastards*, 12.

81. Taibbi, *Griftopia*, 114.

82. *Webster's New Twentieth Century Dictionary Unabridged, Second Edition* (New York: Simon and Schuster, 1979), 269.

83. Paul Street, "Capitalism: The Real Enemy," in Francis Goldin, Debby Smith, Michael Steven Smith, and Steven Wishnia, eds., *Imagine: Living in a Socialist USA* (New York: HarperCollins, 2013), 9–22.

84. Bensman and Lynch, *Rusted Dreams*, 88; David McNally, *Global Slump* (Oakland, CA: PM Press, 2011), 70.

85. Arrighi, *Adam Smith in Beijing*, 142–143.

86. Fernand Braudel, *Civilization and Capitalism, 15th–18th Century, Volume III: The Perspective of the World* (New York: Harper and Row, 1984), 604, quoted in Arrighi, *Adam Smith in Beijing*, 93.

87. Michael Harrington, *The Next America: The Decline and Rise of America* (New York: Holt, Rinehart, and Winston, 1981), 153–154; emphasis added.

88. Joel Bakan, *The Corporation: The Pathological Pursuit of Profit and Power* (New York: Free Press, 2004), 36–37. This is known as "'the best interests of the corporation' principle," whereby "corporate social responsibility is thus illegal—at least when it's genuine."

89. Stiglitz, *Price of Inequality*, 35.

90. Rana Foroohar and Bill Saporito, "Made in the USA," *Time*, April 22, 2013, 22–29.

91. Geier, "Capitalism's Long Crisis," 6.

92. Alan Nasser, "The Political Economy of Redistribution: Outsourcing Jobs, Off-shoring Markets," *Counterpunch*, December 2–4, 2011, www.counterpunch.org/2011/12/02/outsourcing-jobs-offshoring-markets/.

93. Geier, "Capitalism's Long Crisis," 6.

Chapter 5

1. Joseph E. Stiglitz, *The Price of Inequality* (New York: W. W. Norton, 2012), 137, 146. For some dark reflections on the betrayal of Lincoln's hopes in the Gettysburg Address, see Paul Street, "Gettysburg Reflections," *ZNet*, July 4, 2013, www.zcommunications.org/gettysburg-reflections-by-paul-street.

2. Larry Bartels, *Unequal Democracy: The Political Economy of the New Gilded Age* (Princeton, NJ: Princeton University Press, 2009), 130–131. For more survey data citations, see Michael Norton and Dan Ariely, "Building a Better America One Wealth Quintile at a Time," *Perspectives on Psychological Science*, Vol. 6, No. 1 (January 2011): 9–12; Katherine Adams and Charles Derber, *The New Feminized Majority* (Boulder, CO: Paradigm Publishers, 2008); Paul Street, "To Save the Capitalist System: Reflections on Orin Kramer's Understanding of Barack Obama's Duty to America," *Z Magazine*, December 2009, www.zcommunications.org/to-save-the-capitalist-system-by-paul-street.

3. John Bellamy Foster and Robert W. McChesney, "A New Deal under Obama?" *Monthly Review*, Vol. 66, Issue 9 (February 2009): 7.

4. John Dewey, *Democracy and Education* (New York: The New Press, 1916).

5. Noam Chomsky, "American Decline: Causes and Consequences," *Alakhbar English*, August 24, 2011.

6. Noam Chomsky, *Failed States: The Abuse of Power and the Assault on Democracy* (New York: Metropolitan, 2006), 225.

7. Noam Chomsky, "America in Decline," *New York Times Syndicate*, August 5, 2011, reproduced in Chomsky, *Making the Future: Occupations, Interventions, Empire, and Resistance* (San Francisco: City Lights, 2012), 287.

8. J. Mijin Cha, "Why Is Washington Reducing the Deficit Instead of Creating Jobs?" *Demos*, December 7, 2012, www.demos.org/publication/why-washington-reducing-deficit-instead-creating-jobs.

9. Cha, "Why Is Washington Reducing the Deficit?"

10. Lydia Saad, "Americans Back Obama's Proposals to Address Gun Violence," *Gallup Politics*, January 23, 2013, www.gallup.com/poll/160085/americans-back-obama-proposals-address-gun-violence.aspx; Frank Newport, "Americans Wanted Gun Background Checks to Pass Senate," *Gallup Politics*, April 29, 2013, www.gallup.com/poll/162083/americans-wanted-gun-background-checks-pass-senate.aspx; Sabrina Saddiqui, "Assault Weapons Ban, High Capacity Magazine Measures Fail in Senate," *Huffington Post*, April 17, 2013, www.huffingtonpost.com/2013/04/17/assault-weapons-ban_n_3103120.html.

11. Food Research and Action Center, "Americans Continue to Voice Strong Support for SNAP and Strong Opposition to Cuts," May 9, 2013, http://frac.org/americans-continue-to-voice-strong-support-for-snap-and-strong-opposition-to-cuts/.

12. Editors, *New York Times*, July 12, 2013; Paul Krugman, "Hunger Games, USA," *New York Times*, July 14, 2013.

13. Jamie Raskin and John Bonifaz, "The Constitutional Imperative and Practical Imperative of Democratically Financed Elections," *Columbia Law Review*, Vol. 94, No. 4 (1994): 1160–1203.

14. National Voting Rights Institute (NVRI), "'The Wealth Primary'—Legal Theory" (n.d.), www.nvri.org/about/wealth1.shtml. "In the middle decades of the twentieth century,"

NVRI explains, "the US Supreme Court heard a series of cases that addressed efforts by white communities in southern states to exclude African-Americans from the franchise. In the first of these cases, which have collectively become known as the 'white primary' cases, the Supreme Court struck down all-white Democratic Party primary elections that were authorized by statute (*Nixon v. Herndon*, 273 US 536 (1927)), reasoning that primaries were so critical a part of the electoral process that they should be subject to the anti-discrimination provisions of the 14th and 15th Amendments to the Constitution." The "wealth primary" refers to the discriminatory de facto barrier to full and equal democratic political participation faced by nonaffluent candidates and voters "who are left behind in the fundraising process because of their lack of money and access to money."

15. Perry Anderson, "Homeland," *New Left Review*, Issue 81 (May–June 2013), http://newleftreview.org/II/81/perry-anderson-homeland.

16. Ray Henry, "Jimmy Carter: Unchecked Political Contributions Are 'Legal Bribery,'" *Huffington Post*, July 17, 2013, www.huffingtonpost.com/2013/07/17/jimmy-carter-bribery_n_3611882.html.

17. Thomas Ferguson, "Best Buy Targets Are Stopping a Debt Deal," *Financial Times*, July 28, 2011, www.ft.com/cms/s/0/7ead8528-b7af-11e0-8523-00144feabdc0.html#axzz2Sjg4xKmB; emphasis added.

18. Roger Hodge, *The Mendacity of Hope: Barack Obama and the Betrayal of American Liberalism* (New York: Harper, 2010), 8.

19. Jamie Raskin, "'Citizens United' and the Corporate Court," September 13, 2012, *Nation* (October 8, 2012).

20. "Katrina vanden Heuvel and Jamie Raskin on the Pro-Corporate Supreme Court," Moyers and Company, September 14, 2012, http://billmoyers.com/segment/katrina-vanden-heuvel-and-jamie-raskin-on-the-pro-corporate-supreme-court/; emphasis added.

21. Noam Chomsky, *Power Systems: Conversations on Global Democratic Uprisings and the New Challenges to US Empire* (New York: Metropolitan Books, 2013), 174.

22. Joel Bakan, *The Corporation: The Pathological Pursuit of Profit and Power* (New York: Free Press, 2004), 56–57; emphasis in original.

23. William Greider, *Who Will Tell the People? The Betrayal of American Democracy* (New York: Touchstone, 1992), 26.

24. Gary Olson, *Empathy Imperiled: Capitalism, Culture, and the Brain* (New York: Springer, 2012), 25.

25. Paul Street and Anthony DiMaggio, *Crashing the Tea Party: Mass Media and the Campaign to Remake American Politics* (Boulder, CO: Paradigm Publishers, 2011).

26. A key example is top corporate communications consultant Anita Dunn's pivotal role in the Obama 2012 reelection effort, detailed in Eric Lichtblau and Eric Lipton, "Strategizing for the President, and Corporate Clients Too," *New York Times*, October 19, 2012, A1.

27. Quoted in Lance Selfa, "The Democrats in the Obama Era," *International Socialist Review*, Issue 85 (September–October 2012), 11.

28. Paul Street, *Barack Obama and the Future of American Politics* (Boulder, CO: Paradigm Publishers, 2008), xvii–58.

29. John C. Harrington, *The Challenge to Power* (White River Junction, VT: Chelsea Green, 2005), 27.

30. Public Broadcasting System, "United States of ALEC," Moyers and Company, September 1, 2012, http://billmoyers.com/episode/full-show-united-states-of-alec/#.

31. Paul Street, "Budget Slavery, Budget Freedom Past and Present," *Z Magazine*, November 2013.

32. Mark Leibovich, *This Town: Two Parties and a Funeral Plus Plenty of Valet Parking in America's Gilded Capital* (New York: Blue Rider Press, 2013).

33. Bill Moyers, "Mark Leibovich on Glitz and Greed in Washington," Moyers & Company, PBS, August 23, 2013, http://billmoyers.com/segment/mark-leibovich-on-glitz -and-greed-in-washington/.

34. Quoted in Amy Goodman and Dennis Moynihan, *The Silenced Majority* (Chicago: Haymarket, 2012), 225; emphasis added.

35. On the haunting contemporary relevance of Bradbury's dystopian vision, see Paul Street, "Ray Bradbury's Nightmare Vision," *ZNet*, July 11, 2012, www.zcommunications.org /ray-bradbury-s-nightmare-vision-by-paul-street.

36. David Harvey, quoted in Olson, *Empathy Imperiled*, 44. On the disposable humans in the United States, see Derber and Magrass, *The Surplus American*.

37. Olson, *Empathy Imperiled*, 44.

38. Henry A. Giroux, *The Abandoned Generation: Democracy beyond the Culture of Fear* (New York: Palgrave MacMillan, 2003), 1–70; Henry A. Giroux, *The Terror of Neoliberalism: Authoritarianism and the Eclipse of Democracy* (Boulder, CO: Paradigm Publishers, 2004), 1–53, emphasis added.

39. Olson, *Empathy Imperiled*, 45.

40. "Noam Chomsky on the US Economic Crisis," *Democracy Now!*, airdate September 13, 2011, www.democracynow.org/2011/9/13/noam_chomsky_on_the_us_economic; emphasis added.

41. Bakan, *The Corporation*, 135; emphasis added.

42. Adolph Reed Jr., "Undone by Neoliberalism: New Orleans Was Decimated by an Ideological Program, Not a Storm," *Nation*, September 18, 2006, 26–30.

43. Quoted in Olson, *Empathy Imperiled*, xx.

44. Susan George, "A Short History of Neoliberalism: Twenty Years of Elite Economics," Conference on Economic Sovereignty in a Globalising World and Emerging Opportunities for Structural Change (Bangkok, Thailand, March 24–26, 1999), www.globalexchange.org /resources/econ101/neoliberalismhist.

45. Noam Chomsky, *World Orders Old and New* (New York: Columbia University Press, 1994), 187.

46. Alfred Chandler, *The Visible Hand: The Managerial Revolution in American Business* (Cambridge, MA: Harvard University Press, 1976); Martin J. Sklar, *The Corporate Reconstruction of American Capitalism, 1890–1916: The Market, Law, and Politics* (New York: Cambridge University Press, 1986).

47. See Paul Street, *Empire and Inequality: America and the World since 9/11* (Boulder, CO: Paradigm Publishers, 2004), xiii–xiv; Pierre Bourdieu, *Acts of Resistance* (New York: Free Press, 1998), 2, 24–44; John Pilger, *The New Rulers of the World* (London: Verso, 2002), 5, 116.

48. David Nibert, *Hitting the Lottery Jackpot: Government and the Taxing of Dreams* (New York: Monthly Review Press, 2000), 187–205.

49. Readers interested in more extensive and detailed reflections on bourgeois/neoliberal ideology in corporate-crafted "popular culture" are invited to read two essays of mine: "Resistance Gap: On Media, Time, and the Curious Absence of Riots," *ZNet*, February 9, 2009, www.zcommunications.org/the-resistance-gap-on-media-time-and-the-curious-absence-of -riots-by-paul-street; Paul Street, "More Than Entertainment: Neal Gabler and the Illusions of Post-Ideological Society," *Monthly Review* (February 2000): 58–62.

50. Dr. Spencer Johnson, *Who Moved My Cheese? An Amazing Way to Deal with Change in Your Life* (New York: G. P. Putnam's Sons, 1998), 21–75.

51. Stephen Kinzer, "Libya and the Limits of Intervention," *Current History*, Vol. 111, No. 748 (November 2012): 307–308.

52. Faux, *Servant Economy*, 11; Barbara Ehrenreich, *Bright-Sided: How Positive Thinking Is Undermining America* (New York: Metropolitan Books, 2009).

53. Faux, *Servant Economy*, 8–13; Lymari Mortales, "Fewer Americans See US Divided into 'Haves,' 'Have Nots,'" Gallup.com, December 15, 2011, www.gallup.com/poll/151556 /Fewer-Americans-Divided-Haves-Nots.aspx.

54. Faux, *Servant Economy*, 8.

55. Richard O'Connor, *Undoing Depression* (New York: Little, Brown, 2010), 13–15.

56. Edward P. Morgan, *What Really Happened to the 1960s: How Mass Media Failed American Democracy* (Lawrence: University Press of Kansas, 2012), 165–167.

57. Morgan, *What Really Happened to the 1960s*, 167.

58. Elizabeth A. Fones-Wolf, *Selling Free Enterprise: The Business Assault on Labor and Liberalism, 1945–1960* (Urbana: University of Illinois Press, 1994), 288–289.

59. Alex Carey, *Taking the Risk Out of Democracy: Corporate Propaganda versus Freedom and Liberty* (Urbana: University of Illinois Press, 1997), 14.

60. Neil Postman, *Amusing Ourselves to Death: Public Discourse in the Age of Show Business* (New York: Penguin, 1985), 126–132.

61. "Obama Wins Ad Age's Marketer of the Year," *Advertising Age*, October 17, 2008, http://adage.com/print?article_id=131810.

62. "Barack Obama and the Audacity of Marketing," *Advertising Age*, November 10, 2008, http://adage.com/print?article_id=132351.

63. See Olson, *Empathy Imperiled*, 61–69: "Chapter 7: Neuromarketing 101: Branding Empathy"; Paul Street, "The Golden Rule: Theirs and Ours," *ZNet*, April 5, 2013, www .zcommunications.org/the-golden-rule-theirs-and-ours-by-paul-street.

64. Jamin B. Raskin, *Overruling Democracy: The Supreme Court vs. the American People* (New York: Routledge, 2004), 91.

65. Bartels, *Unequal Democracy*, 29–63.

66. Faux, *Servant Economy*, 247–248; emphasis added.

67. Anderson, "Homeland."

68. Anderson, "Homeland."

69. Ezra Klein, "Block Obama!," *New York Review of Books*, September 27, 2012, giving Obama "liberal" defense against the preposterous Republican charge that the president is a leftist.

70. This was also very much the case during the late nineteenth century and the first three decades of the twentieth century in the United States. See historian Richard Oestreicher's brilliant essay, "Urban Working Class Political Behavior and Theories of American Electoral Politics, 1870–1940," *Journal of American History*, Vol. 74 (March 1988).

71. Faux, *Servant Economy*, 254–255; Thomas Edsall, "The Future of the Obama Coalition," *New York Times*, November 27, 2011.

72. Sheldon Wolin, *Democracy Incorporated*, 59, 64, 140, 239, 284–286.

73. Chris Hedges, "America Is a Tinderbox," Real News Network, July 2013, http:// therealnews.com/t2/index.php?option=com_content&task=view&id=31&Itemid=74 &jumival=10461.

74. Chomsky, *Making the Future*, 64.

75. Chomsky, *Making the Future*, 63.

76. Paul Street, "Labor Day Reflections: Time as a Democracy Issue," *ZNet*, September 5, 2002, www.zcommunications.org/labor-day-reflections-time-as-a-democracy-issue-by-paul-street.

77. Nelson D. Schwartz and Eric Dash, "In Private, Wall St. Bankers Dismiss Protestors as Unsophisticated," *New York Times*, October 14, 2011.

78. As the radical Australian propaganda critic Alex Carey noted in his posthumously published collection *Taking the Risk out of Democracy: Corporate Propaganda versus Freedom and Liberty* (Urbana: University of Illinois Press, 1997), "The twentieth century has been characterized by three developments of great political importance: the growth of democracy, the growth of corporate power, and the growth of corporate propaganda as a means of protecting

corporate power against democracy" (18). The phrase "corporate-managed democracy" appears on page 139, at the end of Carey's chilling essay, "The Orwell Diversion," which argued that the greatest contemporary totalitarian threat came not from Stalinism and the "left" but from the corporate sector's powerful means and methods of thought control honed in the "liberal" and "democratic" West.

79. Juliet Schor, *The Overworked American: The Unexpected Decline of Leisure* (New York: Basic, 1992), 1–105.

80. Schor, *Overworked American*, 74–76.

81. Kotler is quoted in Morgan, *What Really Happened to the 1960s*, 30. Anup Shah, "Poverty Facts and Stats," *Global Issues*, January 7, 2013, www.globalissues.org/article/26 /poverty-facts-and-stats#src1.

82. For important reflections on that attachment and the significant amount of ecologically toxic obsolescence it builds into the very means and processes of capitalist production, see John Bellamy Foster and Brett Clark, "The Planetary Emergency," *Monthly Review* (December 2012): xxx.

83. Taibbi, *Griftopia*, 14.

84. Editors, "The Real Spending Problem," *New York Times*, March 16, 2013, www.nytimes .com/2013/03/17/opinion/sunday/the-real-spending-problem.html?ref=editorials&_r=0.

85. By my observation over the past decade, this is an almost nightly occurrence during the work week on *PBS NewsHour*.

86. Robert W. McChesney, *Corporate Media and the Threat to Democracy* (New York: Seven Stories, 1997), 5–6.

87. McChesney, *Corporate Media*; Robert W. McChesney, *Rich Media, Poor Democracy* (Urbana: University of Illinois Press, 1999).

88. Noam Chomsky, quoted in the movie *Manufacturing Consent: Noam Chomsky and the Media*, directed by Mark Achbar and Peter Wintonick (1992), www.imdb.com/title /tt0104810/ and www.youtube.com/watch?v=Ci_1Ghk0CIc.

89. McChesney, *Corporate Media*; McChesney, *Rich Media*.

90. Quoted in Olson, *Empathy Imperiled*, 25.

91. James Madison, letter to W. T. Barry, August 4, 1822. *The Writings of James Madison*, Vol. 9., ed. Gaillard Hunt (New York: G. P. Putnam's Sons, 1900), 103.

92. Michael Norton and Dan Ariely, "Building a Better America: One Quintile at a Time," *Perspectives on Psychological Science* Vol. 6, No. 9 (2011), http://pps.sagepub.com /content/6/19.

93. Stiglitz, *Price of Inequality*, 147.

94. A properly disturbing but overly victim-blaming account is Rick Shenkman, *Just How Stupid Are We? Facing the Truth about the American Voter* (New York: Basic Books, 2008).

95. Stiglitz, *Price of Inequality*, 147.

96. Paul Street, "Imagine a People's Media in Chicago," *ZNet*, May 24, 2012, www .zcommunications.org/imagine-a-people-s-media-in-chicago-by-paul-street.

97. Paul Street, "Eco-cidal *Times*," *ZNet*, February 22, 2013, www.zcommunications .org/ecocidal-times-by-paul-street.

98. Morgan, *What Really Happened to the 1960s*, 91–143; Street, "Imagine a People's Media."

99. Paul Street, *Segregated Schools: Educational Apartheid in the Post–Civil Rights Era* (New York: Routledge, 2005), 78–80, including annotated quotes from Kozol and Giroux.

100. Street, *Segregated Schools*, 190.

101. Chomsky, *World Orders Old and New*, 87.

102. Ehrenreich and Ehrenreich, "The 1 Percent, Revealed."

103. Schor, *Overworked American*, 66–68.

104. Barbara Ehrenreich, *Nickel and Dimed: On (Not) Getting By in America* (New York: Metropolitan, 2001), passim. Quotations are from 208 and 211.

105. Marc Mauer, *The Race to Incarcerate* (New York: The New Press, 1999); Paul Street, *The Vicious Circle: Race, Prison, Jobs, and Community* (Chicago: Chicago Urban League, 2002); Paul Street, "Color Bind," 30–40 in Tara Herivel and Paul Wright, *Prison Nation: The Warehousing of America's Poor* (New York: Routledge, 2003).

106. Street, *Vicious Circle*, 4–14.

107. Bruce Western and Katherine Beckett, "How Unregulated Is the US Labor Market?" *American Journal of Sociology* (January 1999): 1030–1060.

108. Street, "Color Bind"; Michelle Alexander, *The New Jim Crow: Mass Incarceration in the Age of Colorblindness* (New York: The New Press, 2010).

109. Greg Palast, *The Best Democracy Money Can Buy* (London: Pluto, 2002), chapter 1, 6–42.

110. "From Cold War to Cold Peace?" *BusinessWeek*, February 12, 1949, cited and quoted in Noam Chomsky, *Turning the Tide: US Intervention in Central America and the Struggle for Peace* (Boston: South End, 1985), 209–210.

111. Quoted in Joel Bleifuss, "INSHORT … Leader of the PAC," *In These Times*, December 16–23, 1986, 4; emphasis added.

112. Charles Riley, "Pentagon Budget 'Loaded with Fat,'" CNNMoney, July 1, 2011, http://money.cnn.com/2011/07/01/news/economy/pentagon_budget/index.htm; National Priorities Project, "Sequestration, the Pentagon, and the States: United States, Fiscal Year 2013," February 21, 2013, http://costofwar.com/publications/2013/sequestration-pentagon-and-states/.

113. Lawrence Korb, "How to Cut $1 Trillion from the Pentagon," CNNMoney, January 5, 2011, http://money.cnn.com/2011/01/05/news/economy/lawrence_korb_defense_spending/index.htm?iid=EAL.

114. Heidi Wood et al., "Early Thoughts on Obama and Defense," Morgan Stanley Research, Aerospace and Defense, November 5, 2008, www.washingtonpost.com/wp-srv/business/governmentinc/documents/ObamaDefense.pdf.

115. Nathan Hodge, "Defense Industry Fears More Budget Cuts," *Wall Street Journal*, July 14, 2011, A4.

116. As Edward S. Herman noted in June 2009, "The Pentagon has regular gigantic overruns in its payments for weapons systems and fraud and waste are endemic. But the Pentagon is never threatened with 'insolvency.' Its overruns and waste are simply passed on to taxpayers. The supine media, while occasionally chiding the Pentagon for, say, 'running almost $300 billion over estimates and averaging 22 months behind delivery,' never talk about any crisis in the funding of overkill, military boondoggles, and waste…. We know that in the real world the taxpayer funds the Pentagon on an open-ended basis without any trust funds or limits beyond what logrolling can produce. After all, it is protecting our 'national security,' using the phrase with its usual infinite elasticity to cover anything the Pentagon, its contractors, their lobbyists, and the congressional servants of the military-industrial complex want." E. S. Herman, "John Yoo, Social Security, and Korean Threat," *Z Magazine*, June 2009.

117. Jack Rasmus, "Budgets, Taxes, and Classes in America," *Z Magazine*, June 2011, 32–33.

118. Gen. Smedley D. Butler, *War Is a Racket* (New York: Round Table Press, 1935; Port Townsend, WA: Feral House, 2003).

119. Ralph Nader, *The Seventeen Solutions* (New York: Harper, 2012), 165–170; William Blum, *Rogue State: A Guide to the World's Only Superpower* (Monroe, ME: Common Courage, 2005).

120. National Priorities Project, "Sequestration, the Pentagon, and the States"; Paul Street, "Military Keynesianism Survives Sequestration," *Z Magazine*, May 2013, 19–22.

121. Quoted in Andrew Bacevich, *The New American Militarism* (New York: Oxford University Press, 2005), 7.

122. James Madison, "Political Reflections," February 23, 1799, quoted and cited in Paul Street, *Empire and Inequality: America and the World since 9/11* (Boulder, CO: Paradigm Publishers, 2004), 1.

123. Nader, *Seventeen Solutions*, 159–160.

124. Garry Wills, "At Ease, Mr. President," *New York Times*, January 27, 2007, www .nytimes.com/2007/01/27/opinion/27wills.html?_r=0.

125. Nader, *Seventeen Solutions*, 158.

126. Glenn Greenwald, "Who Is the Worst Civil Liberties President in US History?," *Guardian*, November 2, 2012, www.guardian.co.uk/commentisfree/2012/nov/02 /obama-civil-liberties-history; Jonathan Turley, "Obama: A Disaster for Civil Liberties," *Los Angeles Times*, September 29, 2011, http://articles.latimes.com/2011/sep/29/opinion/la -oe-turley-civil-liberties-20110929/2.

127. William Miller, "Liberties Lost since 9/11," *Op Ed News*, November 6, 2011, www .opednews.com/articles/2/Liberties-Lost-Since-9-11-by-WILLIAM-FISHER-111106-299 .html; Dana Priest and William Arkin, *Top Secret America: The Rise of the New American Security State* (New York: Little, Brown, 2011).

128. Chris Hedges, "The NDAA and the Death of the Democratic State," *Truthdig*, February 11, 2013, www.truthdig.com/report/item/the_ndaa_and_the_death_of_the _democratic_state_20130211/.

129. Stephen Graham, *Cities under Siege: The New Military Urbanism* (New York: Verso, 2010); Paul Street, "The New Urban Militarism in NATO-Occupied Chicago," *ZNet*, May 17, 2012, www.zcommunications.org/the-new-military-urbanism-in-nato-occupied-chicago -by-paul-street.

130. For details and sources, see Paul Street, "Despotism Watch: The Sonic Cannon, the Pain Ray, and the Fate of the American Revolution," *ZNet*, February 15, 2012, www .zcommunications.org/despotism-watch-the-sonic-cannon-the-pain-ray-and-the-irony-of -the-american-revolution-by-paul-street; Street, "New Urban Militarism"; Street, "Imagine a People's Media."

131. Street, "Despotism Watch."

132. James Haddadin, "Drones at Home?" *Foster's Daily Democrat*, February 19, 2012, www.fosters.com/apps/pbcs.dll/article?AID=/20120219/GJNEWS_01/702199914.

133. Glen Greenwald, "Domestic Drones and Their Unique Dangers," *Guardian*, March 20, 2013, www.guardian.com.uk/commentsfree/2013/mar/29/domestic-drones-unique -dangers.

134. Hedges, "Death of the Democratic State."

135. Chomsky, *Power Systems*, 70–71.

136. "ACLU Blasts Supreme Court Rejection of Challenge to Warrantless Spying," *Democracy Now!*, February 27, 2013, www.democracynow.org/2013/2/27/aclu_blasts_supreme _court_rejection_of#.US5CVk6M9HY; "This Modern World," *Little Village: Iowa City's News and Culture Magazine*, Issue 131 (April 17–May 1, 2013), 3.

137. "Amazing Speech by War Veteran," YouTube, www.youtube.com/watch?v =akm3nYN8aG8, with 1,345,971 views as of October 11, 2012; personal discussion with Mike Prysner in Oxford, Ohio, June 23, 2012; "Michael Prysner's Testimony at Winter Soldier," *US Labor against the War*, www.uslaboragainstwar.org/article.php?id=15523, accessed October 11, 2012, emphasis added.

138. Kevin Phillips, *Wealth and Democracy: A Political History of the American Rich* (New York: Broadway, 2002), 359.

139. Ehrenreich and Ehrenreich, "The 1 Percent, Revealed."

140. Chrystia Freeland, "Rise of a New Global Elite," *Atlantic*, January/February 2011, www.theatlantic.com/magazine/archive/2011/01/the-rise-of-the-new-global-elite/308343/.

141. Jeff Faux, *The Global Class War: How America's Bipartisan Elite Lost Our Future and What It Will Take to Win It Back* (New York: Wiley, 2006), 60.

142. John Kenneth Galbraith, *The Age of Uncertainty* (New York: Houghton Mifflin, 1977), 44.

143. Ted Rall, "The Invisible Majority," n.d., reproduced in Robert Perucci and Early Wysong, *The New Class Society* (Lanham, MD: Rowman and Littlefield, 2003), 18.

144. Ehrenreich and Ehrenreich, "The One Percent, Revealed."

145. Joe Bageant, *Deer Hunting with Jesus: Dispatches from America's Class War* (New York: Broadway, 2008), 259.

146. Kalle Lasn and Micah White, "Why Occupy Wall Street Will Keep Up the Fight," *Washington Post*, November 17, 2011.

147. Faux, *The Servant Economy*, 184; emphasis added.

148. "Blame the ruling class? The ruling class is too obvious, too easy. We all see them, even though they are unseeable." Bageant, *Deer Hunting with Jesus*, 259.

149. Larry Samuel, *Rich: The Rise and Fall of American Wealth Culture* (New York: American Management Association, 2009), 181.

150. Samuel, *Rich*, 191.

151. Phillips, *Wealth and Democracy*, 359.

152. Peter W. Bernstein and Annalynn Swan, *All the Money in the World: How the Forbes 400 Make—and Spend—Their Fortunes* (New York: Alfred A. Knopf, 2007), 229.

153. Phillips, *Wealth and Democracy*, 357–358.

154. For a description of the United States somewhat ironically as "the world's most celebrated democracy," see Michael Scherer, "Blue Truth, Red Truth," *Time*, October 15, 2012, 26.

155. Charles Murray, *Coming Apart: The State of White America* (New York: Crown Forum, 2012), 101.

156. Murray, *Coming Apart*, 115.

157. Murray, *Coming Apart*, 101; emphasis added.

158. Dylan Ratigan, *Greedy Bastards: How We Can Stop Corporate Communists, Banksters, and Other Vampires from Sucking Us Dry* (New York: Simon and Schuster, 2012), 5.

159. Cara Buckley, "Upper East Side Protest March Makes House Calls," *New York Times*, October 11, 2011, http://cityroom.blogs.nytimes.com/2011/10/11/upper-east-side-protest-march-makes-house-calls/.

Chapter 6

1. Stephen Kinzer, "Libya and the Limits of Intervention," *Current History*, Vol. 111, No. 748 (November 2012): 307–308.

2. Noam Chomsky, "Can Civilization Survive Really Existing Capitalism?" *International Socialist Review*, Issue 88 (March–April 2013): 50–51; emphasis added.

3. Chomsky, "Can Civilization Survive?," 50–52.

4. Aristotle, *Politics*, book 4, chapters 2, 11; book 5, chapter 8; book 6, chapter 5; book 7, chapter 10, Richard McKeon, ed., *The Basic Works of Aristotle* (New York: Random House, 1941).

5. Edward P. Morgan, *What Really Happened to the 1960s: How Mass Media Failed American Democracy* (Lawrence: University Press of Kansas, 2012), 20–62; Howard Zinn, *A People's History of the United States* (New York: HarperPerennial, 1999), 443–562.

6. Morgan, *What Really Happened to the 1960s*, 243–246.

7. Sheldon Wolin, *Democracy Incorporated: Managed Democracy and the Specter of Inverted Totalitarianism* (Princeton, NJ: Princeton University Press, 2008).

8. Chris Hedges, "The NDAA and the Death of the Democratic State," *Truthdig*, February 11, 2013, www.truthdig.com/report/item/the_ndaa_and_the_death_of_the _democratic_state_20130211/.

9. Sorkin is quoted in Jeff Madrick, "The Fall and Rise of Occupy Wall Street," *Harper's Magazine*, March 2013, 9–10.

10. Frank and Henwood are quoted in Madrick, "The Fall and Rise."

11. Noam Chomsky, *Failed States: The Abuse of Power and Assault on Democracy* (New York: Metropolitan, 2006), 262.

12. Mike Albert, "Seize the Time," *ZNet*, October 14, 2011, www.zcommunications .org/seize-the-time-by-michael-albert.

13. Yotam Maron, "We Are Winning—What Do We Want?" *ZNet*, October 13, 2011, www.zcommunications.org/we-are-winning-what-do-we-want-by-yotam-marom.

14. Richard Wilkinson and Kate Pickett, *The Spirit Level: Why Greater Equality Makes Societies Stronger* (New York: Bloomsbury, 2010), 271.

15. Dan Lazare, "Sovereignty and the Constitution," June 16, 2013, http://daniellazare .com/; emphasis added.

16. Akhil Reed Amar, "The Consent of the Governed: Constitutional Amendment Outside Article V" (1994), Yale University Law School, *Faculty Scholarship Series*, Paper 982, http://digitalcommons.law.yale.edu/fss_papers/982; Kelly Gerling, interview, October 5, 2013.

17. Wilkinson and Pickett, *Spirit Level*, 271.

18. Gar Alperovitz, "America beyond Capitalism," *Dollars and Sense*, November 4, 2004, www.dollarsandsense.org/archives/2004/1104alper.html.

19. Gar Alperovitz, "The Question of Socialism Is about to Open Up in These United States," *Truthout*, April 12, 2013, www.truth-out.org/news/item/15680-the-question-of -socialism-and-beyond-is-about-to-open-up-in-these-united-states; Rick Wolff, *Democracy at Work: A Cure for Capitalism* (Chicago: Haymarket, 2012); Mike Albert, *Parecon: Life after Capitalism* (New York: Verso, 2003). Many of the books mentioned in this paragraph are cited in Alperovitz's essay.

20. A. Phillip Randolph Institute, *A Freedom Budget for All Americans—A Summary* (New York: A. Phillip Randolph Institute, January 1967), read original online at www.prrac.org /pdf/FreedomBudget.pdf.

21. Paul Le Blanc and Michael Yates, *A Freedom Budget for All Americans: Recapturing the Promise of the Civil Rights Movement in the Struggle for Economic Justice Today* (New York: Monthly Review Press, 2013), 11–13.

22. Le Blanc and Yates, *A Freedom Budget*, 9–10, 93–95, 120–144, 181.

23. Le Blanc and Yates, *A Freedom Budget*, 10.

24. Le Blanc and Yates, *A Freedom Budget*, 145–146.

25. Paul Le Blanc, interviewed by Scott McLemee, "A Freedom Budget for All," *Inside Higher Ed*, August 21, 2013, www.insidehighered.com.

26. Le Blanc, "A Freedom Budget for All."

27. Martin Luther King Jr., "Beyond Vietnam—A Time to Break the Silence," April 4, 1967, www.youtube.com/watch?v=3Qf6x9_MLD0.

28. Le Blanc and Yates, *A Freedom Budget*, 145. On King's suspicions regarding capitalism, see Michael Eric Dyson, *I May Not Get There with You: The True Martin Luther King Jr.* (New York: Touchstone, 2001), 78–100; Paul Street, "The Pale Reflection: Barack Obama, MLK, and the Meaning of the Black Revolution," *Black Agenda Report* (March 20, 2007), www .blackagendareport.com/content/pale-reflection-barack-obama-mlk-and-meaning-black

-revolution; Paul Street, "Martin Luther King Jr., Democratic Socialist," *Black Commentator*, Issue 169 (February 2, 2006), www.blackcommentator.com/169/169_street_mlk_democratic _socialist.html.

29. http://nationalpriorities.org/.

30. Le Blanc, "A Freedom Budget for All."

31. Paul Street, "Budget Slavery, Budget Freedom—Past and Present," *Z Magazine*, November 2013.

32. Wilkinson and Pickett, *Spirit Level*, xv.

33. Wilkinson and Pickett, *Spirit Level*, 252.

34. Richard Hofstader, *The American Political Tradition and the Men Who Made It* (New York: Vintage, 1948), 6–7; emphasis added.

35. Noam Chomsky, *Power Systems: Conversations on Global Democratic Uprisings and the New Challenges to US Empire* (New York: Metropolitan Books, 2013), 43.

36. Brian Stelter, "Camps Are Cleared, But '99%' Still Occupies the Lexicon," *New York Times*, November 20, 2011, www.nytimes.com/2011/12/01/us/we-are-the-99-percent-joins -the-cultural-and-political-lexicon.html?_r=0.

37. Robert Reich, *Beyond Outrage: What Has Gone Wrong with Our Economy and Our Democracy and How to Fix It* (New York: Vintage, 2012), 5.

38. Madrick, "Fall and Rise," 10.

39. Chomsky, *Power Systems*, 65.

40. Madrick, "Fall and Rise," 10.

41. Chomsky, *Power Systems*, 32.

42. Chomsky, *Power Systems*, 23–24, 29–30.

43. Alperovitz, "The Question of Socialism."

44. The Pew Research Center for the People and the Press, *A Political Rhetoric Test*, December 28, 2011, www.people-press.org/files/legacy-pdf/12-28-11%20Words%20release .pdf; Alperovitz, "The Question of Socialism."

45. Alperovitz, "The Question of Socialism."

46. Greg Rosalsky, "Paul Krugman: Prepare for Alien Invasion," *Huffington Post*, June 19, 2012, www.huffingtonpost.com/2012/06/19/paul-krugman-alien-invasion_n_1609805 .html.

47. Van Jones, *The Green Collar Economy: How One Solution Can Fix Our Two Biggest Problems* (New York: Harper, 2009), 10–11.

48. Paul Krugman, "Cassandras of Climate," *New York Times*, September 27, 2009.

49. Chomsky's warning—that everything else progressives are talking about (including the reduction of poverty and inequality) won't matter if the accelerating drift into anthropogenic ecocide isn't halted—seemed totally unheard in Krugman's 2012 book *End This Depression Now*. The environmental crisis and the role that addressing it might play in economic policy and recovery was absent from his reflections in that volume. The climate problem does not even merit an index entry. Sadly, Krugman is not the only widely read and esteemed liberal economist who seems oddly indifferent to the combined stimulus and Earth-saving potential of a green jobs and infrastructure program. See Paul Street, "Some Big Things Ha Joon Chang Doesn't Tell You about Capitalism," *Dissident Voice*, June 14, 2011, http://dissidentvoice.org/2011/06/some-big-things-ha-joon-chang -doesn%E2%80%99t-tell-you-about-capitalism/; Paul Street and Janet Razbadouski, "The Ecological Poverty of Liberal Economics," *ZNet*, August 12, 2012, www.zcommunications .org/the-ecological-poverty-of-liberal-economics-by-paul-street.

50. Noam Chomsky, *Hopes and Prospects* (Chicago: Haymarket, 2010), 96. It is clear that Chomsky does not wish to see the replication of the ecologically toxic form of growth that emerged after World War II. Chomsky, *Hopes and Prospects*, 95–97; emphasis added.

51. For useful viewpoints from a Marxist red-green perspective, see John Bellamy Foster, Brett Clark, and Richard York, *The Ecological Rift: Capitalism's War on the Planet* (New York: Monthly Review Press, 2010); Chris Williams, *Ecology and Socialism: Solutions to Capitalist Ecological Crisis* (Chicago: Haymarket, 2010).

52. Paul Street, "Our Pass-Fail Moment: Livable Ecology, Capitalism, Occupy, and What Is to Be Done?," *Critical Education*, Vol. 3, No. 10 (2012).

53. Seth Rosenfeld, *Subversives: The FBI's War on Student Radicals* (New York: Farrar, Straus and Giroux, 2012), 502.

54. Chomsky, *Power Systems*, 43.

55. Istvan Meszaros, *Socialism or Barbarism: From the "American Century" to the Crossroads* (New York: Monthly Review Press, 2001), 80; emphasis added.

Epilogue

1. Alberto Riva, "NSA Controversy: Carter Says 'US Has No Functioning Democracy,'" *International Business Times*, July 18, 2013, www.ibtimes.com/nsa-controversy-jimmy -carter-says-us-has-no-functioning-democracy-1351389.

2. For sources and details, see Paul Street, "By All Means, Study the Founders," *Review of Education, Pedagogy, and Cultural Studies*, Vol. 25, No. 4 (October–December 2003): 281–301.

3. Jeffrey Williamson and Peter Lindert, *American Inequality: A Macroeconomic History* (New York: Academic Press, 1980).

4. See David Montgomery, *Citizen Worker: The Experience of Workers in the United States with Democracy and the Free Market in the Nineteenth Century* (New York: Cambridge University Press, 1995).

5. Larry Goodwyn, *The Populist Moment: A Short History of the Agrarian Revolt in America* (New York: Oxford University Press, 1981), 7.

6. Howard Zinn, *A People's History of the United States* (New York: Harper and Row, 1980), 282.

7. Goodwyn, *Populist Moment*, 167–168.

8. Upton Sinclair, "You Have Lost the Strike! And Now What Are You Going to Do about It?" *The Appeal to Reason*, September 17, 1904.

9. Upton Sinclair, *The Jungle* (New York: Vintage, 1985 [1906]), 363–364.

10. *The Appeal to Reason*, No. 459, September 17, 1904, 1, reproduced in Gene DeGruson, ed., *The Lost First Edition of Sinclair's "The Jungle"* (Atlanta: Peachtree Press, 1988), illustration L.

11. Zinn, *A People's History*, 314–349.

12. See above, p. 123.

13. Richard Wolff, *Democracy at Work: A Cure for Capitalism* (Chicago: Haymarket, 2012), 3–6, 10, 31–46, 96, 113, 152, 175.

14. Jacob S. Hacker and Paul Pierson, *Winner-Take-All Politics: How Washington Made the Rich Richer and Turned Its Back on the Middle Class* (New York: Simon and Schuster, 2010), 99–100.

15. Chris Hedges, "America Is a Tinderbox," Real News Network, July 2013, http:// therealnews.com/t2/index.php?option=com_content&task=view&id=31&Itemid=74 &jumival=10461. Hedges's "neo-feudal society" is of course militantly capitalist.

16. Gerrard Winstanley, "To the City of London, Freedome and Peace Desired" (August 26, 1649), reprinted in Charles H. George, *Revolution: European Radicals from Hus to Lenin* (Glenview, IL: Scott, Foresman, and Company, 1962, 1971), 100–102.

Index

Program on International Policy Attitudes, 149
Protest, marginalization of, 156–157
Prysner, Mike, 170–171
Public health, 14, 17–19, 66–73
Public opinion, 99, 154–155, 183; irrelevance of, 25, 37, 122–126, 149, 179, 200; manipulation of, 129, 144–145, 212n96; progressive, 25, 77, 122–125, 146

Quam, Jean, 11

Racial division and discrimination, 2, 21, 83, 85, 115, 136, 147–148, 162, 167, 202
Rall, Ted, 173
Raskin, Jamin, 126–128, 146
Rasmussen Reports, 194
Ratigan, Dylan, 100, 101, 106, 107, 117, 177
Rattner, Steve, 97–98
Real estate market (bubble), 52, 59, 79
Real Housewives of New Jersey, 173
"Really existing capitalist democracy" (RECD) (Chomsky), 178–179, 204
The Re-Emergence of Concentrated Poverty (Brookings), 18
Reich, Robert, 111, 191
Republican National Convention (2012), 77
Republicans/Republican Party, 12, 19, 21, 24, 25, 34, 37, 77, 115, 116, 123, 125, 126, 131, 132, 133, 147–148, 169, 192, 200, 202, 203, 204
"Reserve army of labor" (Marx), 90, 110, 118, 151
Retirement benefits, system, 22, 32, 33, 39, 51, 76, 82, 84, 85, 106, 113, 115, 116, 117, 136–137, 151, 160
The Revolt of the Elites (Lasch), 108
"Richistan," 47–49, 60–64, 171–178
"Right to Work" legislation (Michigan), 115
Rockefeller, John D., 46
Roderick, David, 93, 118
Romney, Mitt, 8, 21, 24, 28, 29, 31, 77, 126, 148, 181
Roosevelt, Franklin Delano, 40, 42, 66, 84, 103, 187, 202
Roosevelt, Theodore, 29
Rothkopf, David, 109, 172

Rubio, Mark, 77–78
Ruling class, as invisible to most Americans, 170–177

Salinas, Carlos, 108
Samuel, Larry, 48–49, 64, 175
Sanders, Bernie, 44, 45, 102
Savio, Mario, 66, 197
Schor, Juliet, 150
Scott, Robert, 111
Sequestration, 37, 166
"Skills gap" theory, 74–77, 156
The Servant Economy (Faux), 97
"Shared sacrifice," 31, 33, 211n71
"A Short History of Neoliberalism" (George), 50, 137–138
Simon, Herbert, 88–89
Sinclair, Upton, 201–202
Single-payer health insurance, 124, 183
"Skill and grill" testing, 158
Slaughter, Jane, 116–117
Smiley, Tavis, 63
Smith, Adam, 93
Smith, Hedrick, 44, 53, 76, 103
Snyder, Rick, 115
Social health, 66–68
Socialism, 7, 21, 50n, 77, 123, 186, 194–195
Social Security, 22, 25, 28, 29, 31, 32, 33, 34, 37, 50, 85, 136–137, 147, 152, 165, 194
Social wage, 33, 120, 159–160
Sociopathology (psychopathy): and corporations, 128–130; and the rich, 89–90
Soft power v. hard power, 180–181
Sonic cannon. *See* Long Range Acoustic Device (LRAD).
Sorkin, Andrew Ross, 181
Soros, George, 171
Soviet Union, 84, 102, 138, 164, 166, 190, 195
The Spirit Level (Wilkinson and Pickett), 66–68, 72–73, 183
"Square Deal," 29
Standardized tests, 158
Starcevic, Elizabeth, 27–28
Steele, James B., 35, 112
Stein, Jill, 25, 34, 37, 38
Stein, Judith, 40, 41, 75, 94, 95, 100, 191

About the Author

Paul Street is an independent journalist, activist, and author. Formerly, he was Vice President for Research and Planning at the Chicago Urban League. Among his recent books are *Crashing the Tea Party* (Paradigm, 2011), *The Empire's New Clothes: Barack Obama in the Real World of Power* (Paradigm, 2010), *Barack Obama and the Future of American Politics* (Paradigm, 2008), *Racial Oppression in the Global Metropolis: A Living Black Chicago History* (Rowman and Littlefield, 2007), and *Segregated Schools: Educational Apartheid in Post–Civil Rights America* (Routledge, 2005). His many articles have appeared in the *Chicago Tribune, Truthout, Counterpunch, In These Times, Dissent, Z Magazine, Black Commentator, Black Agenda Report, Al-Alkhbar* (Beirut, Lebanon), *Z Net, Monthly Review, Journal of American Ethnic History, Critical Sociology, Critical Education, Economic and Political Weekly* (Mumbai, India), *Tinabantu* (Cape Town, South Africa), *Opportunity, Dollars and Sense, Journal of Social History, New Left Project* (UK), and numerous other outlets. Street has a doctorate in US History from Binghamton University and has taught at numerous colleges and universities. He has been featured in more than 100 radio and television interviews and broadcasts, and on the popular book salon at "Firedog Lake."

CPSIA information can be obtained at www.ICGtesting.com
Printed in the USA
BVOW06s0528110615

404124BV00003B/13/P